Mary Ellen Hannibal

Good Parenting through Your Divorce

**THE ESSENTIAL
GUIDEBOOK TO HELPING
YOUR CHILDREN ADJUST
AND THRIVE—BASED ON
THE LEADING NATIONAL
PROGRAM**

Second Edition, Revised and Updated

Da Capo
LIFE
LONG

A Member of the Perseus Books Group

Copyright © 2002, 2007 by Mary Ellen Hannibal
Foreword copyright © 2007 by Ina Gyemant
Preface to the Second Edition copyright © 2007 by Jeff Cookston, PhD
Grateful Acknowledgment is made to Isolina Ricci, PhD, for the use of her "Business Relationship" concept, which appears on page 201.

Designed by Pauline Neuwirth, Neuwirth & Associates, Inc.

Cataloging-in-Publication data for this book is available from the Library of Congress.

ISBN: 978-1-56924-257-5

Published by Da Capo Press
A Member of the Perseus Books Group
www.dacapopress.com

Note: The information in this book is true and complete to the best of our knowledge. This book is intended only as an informative guide for those wishing to know more about health issues. In no way is this book intended to replace, countermand, or conflict with the advice given to you by your own physician. The ultimate decision concerning care should be made between you and your doctor. We strongly recommend you follow his or her advice. Information in this book is general and is offered with no guarantees on the part of the authors or Da Capo Press. The authors and publisher disclaim all liability in connection with the use of this book. The names and identifying details of people associated with events described in this book have been changed. Any similarity to actual persons is coincidental.

Da Capo Press books are available at special discounts for bulk purchases in the U.S. by corporations, institutions, and other organizations. For more information, please contact the Special Markets Department at the Perseus Books Group, 2300 Chestnut Street, Suite 200, Philadelphia, PA, 19103, or call (800) 810-4145, ext. 5000, or e-mail special.markets@perseusbooks.com.

10 9 8 7 6 5 4 3

To Jeanne Ames and Ann Van Balen, catchers in the rye

Contents

Foreword

By Judge Ina Gyemant

CHILDREN INEVITABLY SUFFER the most in a divorce. I know, because as the divorce court judge for many years in San Francisco, California, I often witnessed the pain and heartache firsthand. Though a divorce causes enormous, gut-wrenching changes in the lives of a husband and wife, one or both ultimately want the divorce, and as adults they have many places to go for the psychological and emotional support needed to deal with this cataclysmic event. They speak to family and friends about their feelings and frustrations, they confide in their attorneys and, at least in California, they go through mandate court-sponsored mediation to help them resolve custody disputes. But, I often wondered, what about the children? Where do they go? To whom do they talk?

Children face a lot of issues. In many cases the family home is sold, children move, change schools, and lose friends. Importantly, the children lose a parent from their home on a part-time basis, at least—usually their father. At the same time, there is frequently a high level of animosity between the parents and heated conflict about the children and child-rearing decisions. Children caught in this turmoil have an unmet need to express their feelings and have their topsy-turvy world explained to them. And so, the idea for Kids' Turn was born. Kids' Turn would be a safe place for children to go to learn about the changes that are taking place in their lives. A place to learn how to remove themselves from the conflict between their parents and to understand that they are not responsible for their parents' break up.

Foreword

The book you are about to read, *Good Parenting through Your Divorce*, is based on the extensive experience of those who created and shaped the Kids' Turn program over the years. It is also grounded in the valuable lessons that the facilitators and educators have gleaned from years of working exclusively with children and parents of divorce. If you are going through a divorce, this book will help you understand that while your family will never again be the way it was, it is still a family, it is your family, and with the help of this book you can make it the best it can be . . . for your children's sake, because now it's your kids' turn.

Judge Ina Levin Gyemant
August 18, 2002

JUDGE INA LEVIN GYEMANT recently retired after serving twenty years as a San Francisco Superior Court Judge for the State of California. While Presiding Judge of the Family Court, she cofounded "Kids' Turn" an educational program for children whose parents are separating or divorcing as well as the "Rally Project," which provides a safe place for pick up and drop off of kids whose parents are in high conflict. As Presiding Judge of Juvenile Court she spearheaded the creation of the drug court team that formulated the Youth Treatment and Education Court "YTEC", where despite her retirement, she continues to preside. She was a member of the California Commission of Judicial Performance (1989-1995); served on the Ethics Committee and on the Executive Board of the California Judges Association. Judge Gyemant has been active in judicial education in California since 1982 and was Chair of the Continuing Judicial Studies Program in 1988.

Preface to Second Edition

By Jeff Cookston

We're getting a divorce.

According to current estimates for the United States, about a million children each year are told something similar by their own parents. Most of these children know other children from single-parent or divorced homes. Children of a certain age have probably seen portrayals of divorce on television, have seen it on film, and hear about it on the radio. Without a doubt, divorce is an undeniable aspect of contemporary life in the United States.

If divorce is so common, then why is it so hard?

Divorce offers the promise of new hope. Divorce, as an event, evokes images of the moment the divorce becomes final, but anyone who's been through it knows it's more complicated and offers less finality than a single trip to the family court. Divorce is the race, not the finish line. It may involve months (possibly years) of unhappiness, of trust regained and lost again, of self-doubt and worry. You're probably reading this book because you are a parent who's divorcing or because you know or work with parents who are divorcing. You're worried about your children and how they're going to be impacted by this transition. You want to do something to make sure they not only cope with the change, but thrive. However, just as divorce is not a single definitive event, there's no single thing that protects children or places them at risk. Instead, there are a lot of little things that happen along the way. There are three general themes in how families experience divorce.

1. *The year before and the year after the separation/divorce are difficult.* This two—possibly three—year window represents a sensitive period in a family's history. In the year prior to the separation unhappiness, distraction, and an inability to be fully present are all common. Conflict between partners may become a common aspect of daily routines and rituals. Rarely is the decision to separate or divorce caused by a single event but is rather a product of cumulative stress between partners within the home. After either a short or long period, one parent moves out. In the year after the separation, the partners grapple with the legal, emotional, and procedural aspects of the decision. Boxes are packed and unpacked. Visitation is arranged and rearranged. New romantic opportunities may be considered and explored. Financial stress and support become daily concerns. Over time, usually within a year or two of the separation, different routines and patterns emerge and life assumes a degree of normalcy.

2. *The nature of this sensitive period of divorce has long-reaching implications for children and parents.* During the transition from being one of two parents to being either with or without the children marks a stark transition for many parents. Some struggle to adapt to being the primary care provider when they are with their children. Many experience debilitating depression, anxiety, and anger. All struggle to balance schedules, meals, professional demands, personal needs, and family time. During this transition period, parents and children are working out new ways to accomplish familiar routines. Preparing dinner occurs frantically; the dishes are cleaned less quickly. The kids get to watch more TV and spend more time unsupervised. Family rules that are typically enforced are either accomplished with greater conflict or abandoned altogether. Evidence from a number of research studies that have followed divorcing families suggests that there are a number of factors that influence the impact of this period for children.

There are four aspects of family life that are particularly important for children in the transition to divorce. First, exposure to conflict between parents is distressing, and the more frequent and intense the conflict, the worse it is for the children. Second, the inconsistent application of previously established rules is confusing and creates opportunities for further erosion in the established expectations between parent and child. Third, when it is appropriate, children need to be provided opportunities and encouragement to visit the parent who lives outside of the home. Finally, when parents are depressed and distracted, it impacts whether they fight with their ex, whether they have the resolve to remain consistent in parenting, and may lead to a lack of support for the child's relationship with the other parent. Although this seems a dour list, there is some good news.

3. *You have the ability to control how you respond to this crisis during this sensitive period.* Because divorce is so prevalent in the United States, there has been considerable research attention paid to the topic. Divorce researchers have developed and tested programs capable of teaching parents the skills that are effective in reducing the likelihood that a child from a divorced family will later develop a mental health disorder. Family courts also have responded to the needs of divorcing families by developing programs to serve families within their communities.

Good Parenting through Your Divorce draws heavily from Kids' Turn, a San Francisco-based program that's been providing divorcing parent education services since 1988. The program arose when Judge Ina Levin Gyemant noted the need for psychosocial education for children during divorce. Working with attorneys, social work specialists, the community, and families, the Kids' Turn program has been continually updated and improved in accord with current research evidence and the knowledge that comes from having served thousands of parents and children over the years. This book conveys the details of the program in a manner that gives voice to the experience of newly divorced parents, explains the effects of divorce for children in a manner that is consistent with research, emphasizes how children's experiences of divorced are affected by their age, and provides grounded down-to-earth advice on how to change your behaviors with your children and your child's other parent. As you work through the chapters, try to actively think about how the suggestions and activities might work in your own home. Some activities won't match your parenting style and others won't fit your child's personality, but each offers a perspective on how families cope with the divorce experience. Of course, don't expect overnight change. Just as it takes months to develop bad habits, it takes time find more appropriate ones. You may find it frustrating to actively work to de-escalate conflict with your child's other parent without the other parent also making an effort; however, over time such dedication should yield results and conflict should lessen. (At the least, you'll be happier with your role in the conflict.) In short, you need to evaluate your own family situation and ask what more you can do you help your child. Could you more faithfully apply the suggestions for shared parenting with your child's other parent? Might individual therapy for yourself or your child be more beneficial? As a parent, you have a better sense of whether your child is doing okay than anyone else. Your perception that your child needs help is one of the best predictors of whether the child ever gets that help. Remember, regularly asking your children if they are feeling okay, regardless of whether they provide an answer, is a good way to let them know you're available when they need help.

Good Parenting through Your Divorce offers an important contribution to the reading list of divorcing families (and comes recommended by family court specialists who interact with such families on a daily basis). Although I recommend you read it from cover to cover, you can also dip in to find particular tools to help you think about a familiar family problem in a new light. New to this second edition is a subject index that will facilitate your ability to access information quickly. Also included in this edition is more information on managing conflict with your child's other parent. Finally, you will also find new information on issues relevant to ethnic minority families during their transition to divorce. Although the title of this book emphasizes good parenting through your divorce, the skills and methods outlined have the potential to not only benefit in this time of drastic change, but to endure long after the transition is over.

Jeffrey Cookston, PhD, is an Assistant Professor in the Department of Psychology at San Francisco State University. Dr. Cookston's research focuses on the factors that protect children from stress during the divorce transition with special emphasis on the role of parent behavior and father involvement. Before moving to San Francisco, Dr. Cookston was a post-doctoral fellow at the Arizona State University Prevention Research Center where he worked with Sanford Braver and William Griffin, PhDs, to evaluate an intervention for divorced fathers called Dads for Life. It is the only program designed to change the conflict levels of parents after divorce. Dr. Cookston is presently evaluating the theory of the Kids' Turn program with data from families who have participated in the program compared with families who have not completed the sessions. Dr. Cookston lives in San Francisco with his wife and daughter.

Introduction

EVERY YEAR FOR the past twenty, one million American children have experienced the divorce of their parents. To take the statistics from another angle, currently only 20 percent of children under age eighteen live with two biological parents. In addition to divorce, many never-married people who have children together are faced with the challenges of co-parenting. The blended, reorganized family is a way of life in America today. There are many never-married people raising children together, parents who are separated but not divorced, and single parents trying hard to give their kids the upbringing they need.

When a family is changing, kids need special attention. Yet divorce is quite often a crisis for the adults involved, and parents may feel they are spending 100 percent of their energies just making it through the day. There is an undeniable reality to this—but the kids suffer when their needs aren't addressed. The intention of this book is to provide clear tools for helping your kids (and yourself) navigate the often-difficult waters of divorce. Having the right intentions and some solid factual information will help you connect and stay connected with your children, which is key to their healthy adjustment.

Family Values for Real Families

The prevalent views on divorce and its effect on kids has changed as divorce has become an ever more entrenched part of our lives. The conventional wisdom has been that children of divorce feel its negative effects for many years—including depression, trouble forming emotional relationships, and general underachievement. That there is a potential for children to suffer as a result of divorce has prompted many concerned professionals to bring their attention to the subject. It has been noted that children are woefully underrepresented in the divorce process. Most social and legal interventions related to divorce focus exclusively on the well-being of the parents at the time of divorce. There has been little official recognition in the courts of the fact that parenting children is a long-haul proposition. Children of divorce don't get a say in how their needs ought to be met now that their whole world is changing. Custody arrangements are made to suit the schedules and the understanding level of children as if they will never grow older, as if their needs will not change with time. Children are not seen and not heard.

As it becomes more clear that it is not just the divorce but the way it is handled that affects children, many legal professionals are much more sensitive to these issues. Parents need to be aware of them also, to advocate for their kids even while they undergo a major life change. It is the purpose of this book to codify what children generally experience during a separation and divorce, and to give you tools for helping them. It is also the intention of this book to be useful and positive. Will children feel the effects of divorce their whole lives? Yes, but that can be handled productively. A child may adapt very well at age eight when her parents divorce, but when she reaches puberty she will have to reconsider what her parents' divorce means to her in terms of sexuality and gender roles. If she decides to get married fifteen years after that, her parents' divorce will again be part of her decision-making process. It goes for all of us—major life experiences are going to remain touchstones on every part of the journey. If you can support her at age eight and at age thirteen, you will help your child internalize a positive way to accept and grow from even painful events.

Because some children do better than others through divorce, and many children do as well as their peers from intact families, it begs the question of what, exactly, puts children at risk in divorce. For example, for many years it was routine for judges to award sole custody of very small children to their mothers—the thinking being that infants and toddlers need their primary attachment figure above all else and should not be shuttled around. Is it possible that these children have actually been deprived of their fathers?

That negative developmental fallout from divorce, such as trouble forming healthy relationships later in life, might actually be due not to the breakup of the family per se, but to the loss of the father? There is movement afoot to educate the courts about the variable temperaments of small children, to suggest that some infants and toddlers not only can tolerate moving between two homes, but benefit by such an arrangement.

The Kids' Turn Program Behind the Book

The information in this book comes primarily from the Kids' Turn workshop program begun almost fifteen years ago in San Francisco. The Kids' Turn program was started by a family law judge, the Honorable Ina Gyemant, two attorneys, Ann Van Balen and Jennifer Jackson, who worked with the legal aspects, a prominent child psychiatrist, Dr. John Sikorski, and the mediator who is widely credited with helping change divorce legislation in California, Jeanne Ames. They saw that while adults have friends, therapists, lawyers, and mediators, children are virtually alone for the duration of an experience that is shaping their very lives.

Kids' Turn is made up of professionals from three disciplines—mental health, education, and law—working together to provide a framework for identifying common problems for kids and how to respond to them. The late Dr. Dorothy Huntington was a very early proponent of making a special effort on the behalf of very young children and infants during the divorce process. Many others, too numerous to name, have contributed to Kids' Turn over the years—including an active board and staff—but notable among these are Claire Barnes and Susanna Marshland.

It is hard to convey the magnitude of the good intentions and top-notch expertise these people have brought to bear on a program that has at its very heart the advocacy of children. Kids' Turn is a nonprofit organization and many of the professionals who have devoted hundreds of hours of their time to it have done so gratis. For those moments in life when all seems bleak and human nature a terrible mistake, think of these wonderful people who are truly compassionate about children and selfless in their dedication to them.

The writing of this book has not been possible without the support and encouragement of Dr. John Sikorski and Jeanne Ames. These two have been instrumental in honing the curriculum from the program's inception. They are each deeply knowledgeable about divorce research and literature—and it is worth mentioning that Dr. Joan B. Kelly's work on divorce has influenced them both. More than any research, however, the Kids' Turn curriculum has been shaped in response to the people who have completed the program, both children and adults. Participant feedback has been solicited and incorporated all along, to get at the heart of what really works for people.

The workshop is six weeks long, and it is rare among divorce programs in that both parents and children attend. Separated and divorced parents each join a group session while their children attend groups organized by age. The thinking behind this is that when the children go to their respective homes, their parents are equipped to follow through on key concepts addressed in the workshops. The groups are led by teachers and mental health professionals. They teach the kids at an age-appropriate level what some of the major divorce concepts mean, they get kids talking about divorce, and they get them expressing their feelings through artwork and imaginative play. They are also helped in problem-solving difficult or high-conflict situations. The parents are taught what different age kids are going through developmentally and how the divorce is likely to affect them. They are given tools for better co-parenting, including dealing with the children's other parent as a business partner, learning to use "I" statements to avoid escalating conflict, and practical guidance for sharing custody. This book contains all of this information, and more on the child's expressive self, solid parenting strategies, and the emotional trajectory of divorce.

Kids' Turn is not therapy, but in the language of public health it is a "primary prevention model," aimed at promoting health "before the organism suffers any ill effects." In this regard it is similar to the Head Start program. Primary prevention addresses a problem before it manifests and is the most effective in staving off what are the predictable consequences of divorce. The program has been studied by researchers looking for ways to mitigate the effects of divorce on children. One study quantified reduced anxiety in children and increased awareness in parents who have undergone the program. Another qualitative analysis concluded that after undergoing Kids' Turn, parents understand better what their children are going through by learning: "1) What reactions to expect of children at different developmental stages; 2) communication and negotiating skills between parents and parent/child; 3) setting limits, natural consequences, and consistency in parenting behaviors . . ." Additionally, Kids' Turn reiterates "the importance of the child having supportive parents [and reminds them] that this support can be offered to their child regardless of the level of cooperation from the child's other parent."

In June 2000, researchers from the California School of Professional Psychology completed a program evaluation, based on participant data from nearly 5,500 people, half children and half adults, gathered from 1993–1998. The data suggested "that parents overwhelmingly found the experience beneficial in some way. Further, this was true across the four ethnic groups studied—African American, Asian American, Hispanic, and White parents." The results showed that:

1. Most parents indicated that the six-week intervention affected how they see themselves, their child, and their child's other parent.
2. The program helped parents communicate more openly and effectively with their children.
3. The program helped parents understand their children's reaction to separation or divorce.
4. The parents felt the program helped their children.
5. The parents reported that their children displayed less anger, sadness, irritability, and crying after the program.
6. The children reported a reduction in feelings of discouragement, guilt, sadness, fear, hurt, confusion, loneliness, worry, and feeling pulled apart.
7. The children reported feeling more excitement, happiness, and calm.
8. The children were able to identify important coping strategies for adjusting to divorce.
9. One third of the parents were less likely to wind up in court over child custody issues.
10. More than half the parents reported improved co-parenting with the child's other parent.

Almost 100 percent of participants who have undergone Kids' Turn would recommend it to their friends. Kids' Turn is nationally recognized, widely credited as the best of its kind, and has received national media coverage: ABC's John Stossel did a *20/20* segment on the program, and NPR has also featured what one happy graduate called "divorce school."

This Book

Over and over again, at the end of the workshops parents said: more, more, we want more! *Good Parenting through Your Divorce* contains the distilled wisdom and experience of the Kids' Turn program. In writing it, I have been guided by the curriculum but have gone far beyond it into the primary literature on children and divorce, as well as basic mental health literature and parenting information. The book doesn't replace a workshop or a support group—and these are highly recommended, because during a divorce you need to be heard—but it consolidates the information you need to help your kids. While it is a good idea to read the whole thing through, to get a grasp of the entire issue of the divorce for your kids, what's involved, and how to handle it, the material is also organized so that when you come upon a problem, for example with discipline, you can refer back to that specific part of the book for help.

As much as I've read and researched to give this book the gravity the subject deserves, most of what you'll find in here is based on the real stories of real people. I attended numerous Kids' Turn workshops to observe exactly where kids are at when confronted by divorce and to really hear the struggles and concerns of their parents. I conducted in-depth interviews of adult workshop participants over the course of four years, and interviewed other people who hadn't gone through the program but who had much to tell about their divorces. While this is no scientific sample (those are amply represented in the studies, which also inform this book, included in the bibliography), more than any other source these people have shaped how this material is presented. The real stories of real people are interspersed in these pages to illustrate specific points. While the stories are extremely individual and particular, they yet illuminate very common and highly applicable situations faced by almost everyone going through a divorce. At the end of each chapter, there is a longer story—divorce can be an isolating experience, and it can help to be reminded that you are not alone in struggling with some of its issues. I have disguised the identities of the people herein to protect their privacy.

In interviews, many people told me that divorce books make them feel bad—drumming in the negative effects on children. Most parents really are trying their best for their kids, even if what we see from the outside looks like a woeful effort. With this in mind, I've tried to not exactly be positive about divorce, but to acknowledge that for many people divorce is a step they take in order to get a better life. I've tried to avoid doom and gloom language, but sometimes a heavily weighted warning has snuck in. This is because certain tenets really deserve your full attention; for example, it has been shown again and again that kids whose parents don't fight in front of them do better than their peers who are subject to high-conflict situations. Yet sometimes adults get so engaged in the conflict that they disregard what is best for their children—and when the time has come in this narrative to warn about that, I've done it strongly.

So, is divorce terrible for your kids? The answer is that it doesn't have to be. The most current research shows that the way divorce is handled is much more important to the child's health than the fact of the divorce itself. It has become clear that with careful, attentive parenting, children need not suffer the lowered school achievement, depression, aggression, anxiety, and so forth shown in earlier research. But it is not so easy to parent well when divorce is on the table. Adult problems come first when a divorce is hot—children are put on hold. Additionally, the divorce hardly puts an end to marital conflict; in many cases the divorce institutionalizes it as part of a family's general weather. People get stuck in divorce and live in constant reference to a failed past relationship. The children never quite come to the center again in these cases. And this is where the children really suffer. The adults are so preoccupied, so unhappy, they lose the ability to connect with their kids. The children get stuck at developmental moments they are meant to pass through. Maybe they learn to escape. One thing they don't learn is how to confront a situation and move on from it—and this has an impact on their ability to succeed in school, work, and other relationships.

The first chapter of the book addresses what to do first when you are getting a divorce. Many people neglect to tell their children about the divorce at all. It's not easy information to impart, it elicits disappointment and anger, and yet it is very necessary to face the issue head-on with your kids. Some parents claim their children won't even notice if their mother or father moves out of the house, but this is absolutely not the case, and when your child realizes what is going on, how much better it is to have a sympathetic, safe setting for the tears than to be confronted with this undeniable loss all alone.

The next chapter deals with how kids feel about divorce. Remarkably, almost all kids from all socioeconomic backgrounds have very similar responses to their parents' divorce. It's not always easy to recognize these reactions, because to the adult mind some of them seem irrational. Kids' Turn has documented these responses of kids over and over again, as have many other divorce researchers. Even if you don't see these responses in your kids, you can bet they are having them on some level to some degree.

All kids act out, but divorce poses special challenges both to how your child expresses himself and how to deal with it. There is so much going on and so much changing, people are quite often ensnarled in the issues of every day. In the workshops, the information parents most often request is about how to discipline their children, how to understand their kids' behavior and manage it so everyone can breathe a little easier. The chapter on discipline explains times-out and logical consequences, and brings attention to some of the underlying influences on how kids behave, including parenting style. So if you are looking for an answer or a strategy, you can go straight to that chapter and remind yourself of ways to deal with your kids when they act out.

A major tenet of the Kids' Turn program is that children experience divorce differently at different ages. So I've included a chapter on child development to help you understand your children during different phases in their lives. I hope this chapter will help you deal with multiple children of different ages, and help you look ahead to the sort of emotional terrain your growing child is heading into. The chapter on development emphasizes addressing your child's burgeoning self—the person they are becoming, as their life unfolds, and how this process is intimately connected with your child's relationship with both parents. Keeping the larger picture in mind can take the heat off the moment's crisis and provide a framework for understanding the developmental imperatives of certain kinds of behavior, which otherwise can be puzzling.

The chapter on communication has a twofold purpose—to help you communicate better with your children and with your co-parent. Staying connected with your child emotionally is of the utmost importance in helping them through your divorce; indeed, in helping them through life. Many, many of our troubles have to do with missed communication or lack of it altogether—this is a fundamental building block to a good relationship with your kids.

At the same time, lots of divorcing spouses have a difficult to impossible time interacting with each other in any way short of screaming and issuing subpoenas. This chapter should give you some concrete ways to present your needs in such a way that you don't stoke the fires of discord, but rather, help smooth your own way toward moving on from this chapter in your life. Even if you can't influence the way your co-parent communicates with you, you can help mitigate the situation mightily.

One art therapy teacher told me that you could easily see which children in high-conflict situations would "make it" and which were likely to have more and more trouble down the road. The kids who could express themselves through art, poetry, role-playing and other expressive modes were much more likely to survive tough times. Expressive play is a great aid to your child in relieving the pressures of living with conflict, discord, and change. The chapter on expression seeks to provide some guidance to this important element in your child's life and how to encourage it.

Divorce can feel like the end of the world, but in fact it is a process. There is a beginning, a middle, and an end to divorce, and it can help when you are in a difficult stage of it to know that where you are is natural, and that it will pass. It's common to feel hopeless and despairing when you're getting divorced. Others can feel empowered and excited about the change, but it is highly likely that if you are feeling good about the divorce, your co-parent is not. I've included a chapter on the emotional trajectory of divorce to present the experience as a framework. The chapter is part of this book about parenting because, after all, being a parent is not separate from being a person. When you are struggling with yourself or with understanding the behavior of your former partner, it can help to refresh your idea of divorce as an experience with fairly predictable milestones. Placing your own feelings within this context can help relieve the pressure of them and help keep you on the path toward the other end of this transition.

Along with discipline issues, divorcing parents have the most trouble with forging a new relationship with their former husband or wife. This is a critical part of healthy parenting. Your relationship with your child's other parent vastly influences your child's relationship with each of you. Kids' Turn promotes modeling your new relationship with your former spouse on a business model, and teaches you how to look at this person as a perhaps difficult but very important client. Separating your marriage from your parenting is not easy, yet it is a key component to helping your kids. Other goals pointed to in this chapter include a "normalized" divorce experience, so you and your kids don't feel so much like strangers in a world that sometimes still seems made of two-parent households, and a renewed sense that you and your kids do in fact form a "whole" family.

Your Child's Health and Success Are in Your Hands

If there is one thing that hurts kids the most when their parents divorce, it is that they can be more or less forgotten in the process. This may sound absurd—if all you seem to be doing is fighting over custody, that's about the kids, right? Yes and no. Your kids are experiencing the divorce even harder than you are. They have feelings that need to be expressed and heard. It is very hard to keep a healthy focus on what your kids need when the family is radically changing. This book is designed to help you help your kids. There is a bonus prize to this also. By keeping your focus on parenting issues, you will give yourself a road map for making it through the morass often presented when two people decide to sever their legal ties.

It is my sincere wish, and that of the many generous people who have contributed to Kids' Turn over the years, to help kids through their parents' divorce. The pain and distress this event causes for kids is very clear, as is the pain it causes adults. Yet it is equally clear that when children are given a forum for their feelings—when their expressive needs are met—they are inoculated against the risk factors of divorce. Children need stability, security, predictability, and both their parents (if safety is not an issue).

The goals of this book are to:

- normalize the divorce experience;
- address the whole family;

- give concrete tools to kids and their parents that enable them to move through difficulties;
- help parents learn to free kids up to feel OK about themselves and to just be kids;
- give support and permission to parents to help their kids and move on.

While I have never been divorced myself, the experience of being a working mother with two children sensitizes me utterly to the incredible demands on our time and attention of daily life. My husband's parents divorced when he was twelve, and our lives are still affected by that. My brother is divorced with two children, and perhaps Carly and Tyler are my true motivation here—I see how hard the change in their lives is on them, and this is my attempt to help.

How do you give everybody in a family what they need? Everybody needs some time each day, even you. Your kids need you to focus on them, to address them directly. Before bed, in the car on the way to school. You need time, so when you're with your kids, you aren't pulling away to get space for yourself, but you are ready to give them what they need, to respond to them. Yet finding these precious and critical moments on many days is impossible, even without a crisis like a divorce going on.

The good news is that children respond to good intentions. The quest of parenthood is not about protecting children from hard emotional truths, but about helping them confront their feelings and move through them. Kids' Turn has codified the most important touchstones for helping parents and their kids. By keeping these in mind, even on those impossible days when life feels like a traffic jam, you can do your best for your kids, and they will know that and feel its goodness. Emotional growth becomes the goal, and your kids will understand on some level that moving through difficulty is a very important part of growing up. Indeed, emotional growth is a goal to be shared with your children, through experiences of all kinds.

1

So You're Getting a Divorce

"It took me almost a year to understand that my husband really wanted to leave me; my oldest child seemed to get it before I did. I had trouble reassuring her when I was so scared myself."

—SUSAN BUCKLEY

YOU MAY BE sitting on the freeway or wheeling a grocery cart down an aisle when it strikes you: this is not going to work out. Whenever it is, whatever the situation has devolved to, whether you are both still under one roof or not, the moment you fully recognize that you are headed toward divorce is the time to connect with your kids about it.

"My husband had moved out about a month before I realized, hey, this is over." Susan Buckley is a deceptively soft-spoken woman—an officer at a large brokerage house, her job takes up sixty to seventy hours of her week. She has enormous fiduciary responsibility, yet the idea of being without her husband petrified her, and clouded her judgment. "Both of my kids had migrated to my bedroom—I let them sleep with me the very first night he was gone. We needed each other. The four-year-old was in bed with me and the seven-year-old dragged a sleeping bag onto the couch in the bedroom. She asked me once, 'Is Daddy coming back?' and at the time I said 'Yes, he is.'"

When Susan was able to focus on what was really happening, she had a talk with her daughter. "I told her that it turned out her father wasn't going to live with us anymore, but she would see him on the weekends. She didn't say anything. I couldn't figure out what to do for the four-year-old. All of it jelled when my husband got an apartment and could take them there. It wasn't anything anybody said, really, but I could see both the kids were relieved, and they were somehow ready to move on with it." She gave the kids a few more months to get back to sleeping in their own beds.

Susan Buckley is in plentiful company. Every day the tabloids report a celebrity divorce, but it is certainly not only the rarified few who decide to break the legal ties that bind them. According to the National Bureau of the Census, there were over one million divorces in the U.S. in 2001. For some people, divorce is a mutual decision arrived at after many long hours of discussion. For others, the idea that a spouse wants out is an utter shock. The separation process can be a relief or a torment. The moment of divorce is hardly one gonged by the town crier—and for some people, marital difficulties can go on for years before finding any resolution, legal or otherwise.

Kids feel it when things aren't working out between their parents. Yet people who are getting separated often don't tell their children about the event at all, even when it occurs. "My kids are not going to be affected by this," one woman said, as if the sudden absence of her husband in their household wasn't going to be noticed by her children. Sure, their father got up early to go to work and wasn't home until late—and with the marriage disintegrating, they had spent less and less time together around the house. But the fact is, a broken-up marriage is a life-changing event for kids and they need to be told about it. Otherwise, they internalize the feelings they are picking up on and often distort them.

What to Do First

OK, you're in new territory now, and it can be pretty confusing. Your very life is changing and that can be utterly preoccupying—many people have to find a place to live, get a new job, tell friends what's going on. One thing to do is to focus on your children. The following list of five checkpoints will help you cover the necessary bases for getting off to a healthy start, even if you are coming to this somewhere down the road into your divorce.

- *Tell your kids about the divorce.* If possible, do it with your former or estranged partner. Rehearse what you are going to say beforehand, so that any potential disagreements are worked out before you speak to the kids.
- *Define an action plan for the immediate future.* Include in this where the parent leaving the house plans to live for the short-term. Make a temporary schedule for keeping contact with the kids for each parent. For kids aged three and up, set up a time when they can speak to the parent moving out on the phone, if there's going to be more than a few days between when they can see each other.
- *Accept the divorce, and don't fight.* Research shows that children from divorced families are about two and a half times more likely to have psychological problems than kids from intact families. The good news is that you can help your kids. Two primary factors make the difference, and both are within your control. These are: accept the divorce, and don't fight. Parents who accept the divorce and adjust to a new life have children who are able to do the same. Even if you feel you are being ill-used by your former husband or wife, and even if the divorce was not your idea, since it is actually happening you help your kids by accepting that. Inter-parental hostility is the other factor that influences children for better or worse.
- *Keep your child's life consistent*, as much as you possibly can. If they regularly have play dates with friends, keep that up. If they take ballet lessons or do soccer practice, make sure they get to them. The structure of your child's life will help everyone as you negotiate new emotional terrain.

- *Tell others about the divorce, and don't be afraid to ask for help.* Speak to your child's teacher about the separation. It is very likely that the teacher will notice behavior changes in your child and it will help immeasurably if he or she has this frame of reference. Your child's teacher may have some valuable insight into what your child may particularly need through this time.

Tell Your Kids about the Divorce

Ella Stangle was struggling over whether to tell her bright five-year-old girl that her parents were separating. "Mike says she's too young to understand," Ella said. "When we fight, we do it behind closed doors. But Lucy knows something is going on." One day, about to pack up from the playground where Ella and a friend had taken their kids, Lucy suddenly refused to leave. "I kept saying, what's the matter, honey? And Lucy just kept crying, holding on to the gate at the front of the playground. Finally she told me she didn't want her friend to go back to our house with us. When I asked why not, she said, 'she'll know I don't have a daddy anymore.' I was flabbergasted. Mike hadn't moved out yet, but Lucy felt it, felt everything that was going on."

Without reassurance and explanation from her parents, Lucy extrapolated a stressful situation into one of total loss. Children do not have the cognitive ability to process events the same way adults do. While there is no doubt that the experience of having her father move out of the house was not an easy one, it did not mean she was losing him altogether. It's also interesting to notice the sense of shame she expressed—it's almost as if she could bear the loss herself, but couldn't stand her friend knowing about it. And these are five-year-olds!

"When we did get home I sat down with Lucy and told her Mike and I still loved her, but couldn't live together anymore. I told her it wasn't her fault. I told her she'll always have two parents who love her, even if we don't live together. She was so relieved, I could tell by the look on her face. We had thought that telling her would burden her beyond her years, but the concrete information seemed to relieve her of the burden she was already carrying."

It's interesting that so many adults assume their children don't need to be "in on" the fact of the separation. In a sense this attitude is a throwback to the days (and many of us grew up in households like this) when kids weren't really considered full human beings. They were valued, yes, but in the sense that they would become people in the future, when they became adults. The fact is, your kids are full-fledged people. Your family, whatever its shape, is their whole world. And they are paying attention to it, whether they seem to or not.

Define an Action Plan for the Immediate Future

Don't those words, "define," "action," and "plan" sound good, like you could really get things under some good control just by having the right intentions? Ha, ha, ha.

Here's an outline of a best-case scenario:

1. You and your parenting partner make the decision that it is best you don't live together anymore. Having worked on the issues between you with a counselor, you give yourselves time to reconsider the decision. Finally, there is an agreement between you that you should separate.

2. Both of you are able to sit down and rehearse how you're going to tell the kids. In order to make the transition as seamless as possible for them, when alternate living arrangements are made for the parent who will move out you also make arrangements for how the kids will visit that parent. Both of you acknowledge together that your kids are going to be disappointed, angry, confused. It bears mentioning that acknowledging this is pretty hard and can activate the desire to blame one another for the divorce. At this point you may just want to notice that and put the feeling aside to look at later. It is absolutely optimal during this time to not get stuck in your own feelings, but to remember together that your kids need space to have their feelings. Separately and together you will want to give them plenty of reassurance that, although you don't know the future, you are both completely committed to their well-being.

3. In order to tell the kids formally, it would be a good idea to set up a family meeting, say on a Saturday evening, when everyone's likely to be home. Even if there's been stress and upset in the house, even if you believe your decision to separate will come as a relief to your kids, they will be disappointed or scared at the actual event. Dinner will likely be ruined by the announcement—and you want to make sure your kids aren't too tired, like after school, when you sit them down. So, be sensitive to the fact that this is a major big deal for your kids and decide that the event of telling them about it will be about them, and not about you.

4. It will help your children if you are able to present a united front. It will implicitly demonstrate to the kids that this is an adult decision. You are showing them that the mature, responsible part of you that takes care of them and upon which they depend, is still intact. It shows them that although this will change their lives, the decision to separate is something you both are behind and can handle. By telling them outright, you help dispel the fantasy almost all kids have about their parents getting back together.

Accept the Divorce and Don't Fight

Although deliberately planned and carried-out divorces do exist, divorce is often a messy business. Many couples are splitting up because of another person, which complicates matters for everyone. Many splitting couples are not in agreement that this is what should happen. Suddenly, it seems, someone moves out. "I couldn't point to the moment we decided to call it quits," said one man. "It had been over for some time, but then it was really over."

The breakup of such a major relationship is a trauma, and when you're living it, it's hard to remember that your kids are living it too. It's common to feel horribly guilty about what's going on, to want to deny that your children could be interested, because deep down you know how disappointed they will be and possibly already are. Maybe you have a strongly held belief that children shouldn't have to grow up in a divorced household. Maybe your co-parent is having an affair, and you think the situation will blow over.

Mediate—Don't Litigate

SOME PEOPLE MANAGE to get divorced from each other without the aid of any professionals—they consult a how-to book and they get it done. Not too many separating spouses are in enough accord with each other to avoid the system around divorce altogether. It is likely that at some point you will at least consult a family law attorney. However, when it comes to resolving the disputes that almost invariably arise during a split, you will do your kids an enormous favor if you keep the conflict out of the courts. Mediators are equipped to handle not only the nuts and bolts of financial arrangements and custody but are also geared toward the peaceable resolution of emotional strife—something your average litigator is not professionally interested in.

You may be very angry with your co-parent and feel you are getting a dangerously short end of the proverbial stick. You may feel like firing back at this person with all the might you can muster, but do your kids a favor, and call a mediator to the table. You can locate a mediator by asking your attorney or by calling your family-court office.

There are reasons beyond the large expense to avoid litigation. In a custody battle, the court will evaluate the children—the evaluators are looking to assign assets and deficits to each parent. Evaluations can polarize a family, and put everyone on the defensive. Communication is shut down as a result, and so is growth. When you litigate over custody, fear is ruling the day. Fear that you will lose out on your children in terms of time and influence. That fear will be expressed as anger. You will not be able to contain your fear and anger, and your children will feel its reverberations. This is simply one of the worst types of conflict to subject your children to.

At some point of course, you will have to go through the legal system on the way to a divorce. While the system doesn't fit everyone and deals with a very broad spectrum of situation, if you work with the system, most family judges will work with you. A spirit of cooperation and flexibility will do wonders. Keep in mind that in all but cases of neglect and abuse, your children need exposure to both you and your co-parent. If you spend months vilifying this other person in the court system, you will make your own road much harder to travel as you chart the future.

Facts about Private Mediation
(courtesy of Jeanne Ames)

1. It is confidential.
2. Its goal is to develop a Parenting Plan that serves the children's best interests now and over time.
3. The Parenting Plan, when completed, can be made into a court order.
4. The mediator helps facilitate communication and the development of options.
5. The mediator does not make decisions but tries to help the parents come to the best possible resolution for the children's best interests.
6. Even if all issues are not resolved in mediation, reaching and retaining partial agreements can narrow the issues that may require court evaluation or court decision.
7. Mediation is solution-oriented even though there is an opportunity within the confidential context to air differences with the goal of finding mutually acceptable resolution.
8. All written correspondence submitted to the mediator by either parent must be simultaneously copied to the other parent.

Coming to grips that your marriage isn't working out is one of the best things you can do to help your children. If you are in the position of wanting your partner to return to you, try to keep your desire out of your dealings with your children. When one woman's husband rekindled a relationship with a college sweetheart, "I kept waiting for him to snap out of it. First he told me he was in love with this person, and then he moved out. Eventually he had this woman relocate to the town I live in—he moved in with her and came to our house to see the kids. It was all a sort of boundary-less mess. I was waiting for him to get over it, to send this woman back where she came from."

Two years went by, and that didn't happen. This is a good real-life case because it is so indistinct and messy—if that's your sort of situation, you are not alone. It would have been impossible for this woman to make an "action" plan—but her action was essentially, no-action. "Of course I should have gone straight into therapy," she says. "But I didn't want to hear it. I wanted the whole thing to go away."

Melissa's kids were three and six when her husband moved out. "The six-year-old knew something was up, but she didn't ask me about it," Melissa said. "She took my cue and tried to pretend it wasn't happening." But this little girl had some regressive episodes—bed-wetting and night terrors. "Of course I didn't say anything to her teacher," Melissa says. "I didn't say anything to anyone. But then her teacher phoned me and said my daughter was crying uncontrollably several times a week. She is a tactful person, so she never asked me what was going on, but when she was about to hang up the phone with me she said, 'Putting fears into words helps kids. Your daughter won't tell me what's on her mind, but maybe she'll tell you.'" Still, it took Melissa several more months to face her situation. "I knew I was hurting my kids, but I didn't know what else to do—I kept thinking it's him, he's the one hurting the kids. But one night in bed it came to me that I could actually help them by helping myself."

Did she harm her kids irreparably by not acknowledging the end of her marriage? No, of course not. "When I finally got real, the first thing I did was tell my husband he couldn't just come to the house anymore—it was now my house. He was shocked, because I had been letting him walk all over me. But he understood—on some level he was relieved that I was making the whole thing more real."

But the very indistinctness of the situation caused its own fallout. "We get along pretty well," says Melissa. "We never fight in front of the kids and there was never any question about his continued support, or the fact that we would split custody. But about a year after he moved out, I realized my daughter was just waiting for us to get back together. It was final for us, but not for her."

When Melissa did come to the "aha" moment, she was able to think more logically about how she interacted with her co-parent. "We sat down and worked out a visitation schedule. He had rented an apartment, which he took the kids to sometimes. We made that a regular thing, and set them up with permanent pajamas, toothbrushes, clothes, etc.

"We basically defined our own custody agreement before we even went to a lawyer." The kids seemed less afraid and more relaxed once they could place their father in a physical location that they could visit, that they could make their home, too.

Sometimes Melissa's negotiations and communications went smoothly with her co-parent, and sometimes they did not. "Of course when we actually got down to the divorce itself, a lot of very hard feelings came to the surface. I wanted to get half the assets and get on with my life. He was perfectly willing to kind of pretend we were still married, while he lived with someone else in an apartment on the other side of town, paying the credit card bill and giving me money every month for expenses. He felt really guilty and was very generous, until I wanted to be left alone!"

As discussed more fully in chapter 8, "The Emotionally Healthy Divorce," ambivalence is something almost everybody has at one point or another along the way. While it took Melissa a year to face the fact that her husband had left her, when she finally faced the truth, he made a turnaround and acted like he didn't really want it to happen.

They didn't really plan it this way, but because they set up a schedule for the kids before they started disagreeing over money, they ended up doing their children a huge favor. "The kids have never heard us fighting about this," she says. "I've been very careful about that." If you can take care of your children's needs before you dig deep into the heavy feelings of divorce, you will do your kids a similar favor.

Realistically, though, even people who did not have high conflict in their marriage find themselves at loggerheads during the divorce. Otherwise magnificently rational adults can turn a little bit crazy when they are separating. Chapter 8 is designed to give some background about why this is so. But the point to remember is: your fighting hurts your kids.

Children exposed to inter-parental conflict are stuck between a rock and a hard place. First of all, they can be frightened by the hostility, and this can cause them to retreat emotionally or to act out with commensurate violence. Even if you don't see a reaction to your fighting, your kids are having one and it will come out sooner or later. Conflict essentially stops kids in their tracks—they are less free to go about the business of being a kid, meeting the developmental tasks that are essential to forming a healthy self. This is right at the crux of where kids are in danger of depression and anxiety—both of which hamper their future progress. It can sometimes feel irresistible to shout back at a recalcitrant co-parent. Check the urge, for the sake of your kids. Above all, get yourself some help if you are feeling anger. There's an army of professionals out there very able to give you support.

Keep Your Child's Life Consistent

This sounds like a very straightforward directive—keep your child's life the same as it ever was. Consistency is a great comfort to all of us, any shards of it, particularly when big change is afoot. Children's lives feel topsy-turvy during their parents' divorce—fundamentally, everything will now be different. This event is a "before and after" for them (and for you). The more you can keep the same, the better. Particularly during a time when big changes are happening, small things mean a lot.

But this can often be a very hard intention to fulfill. If one person has moved out, and the kids go to visit this parent half the week, their life is different already. But let's say the kids live with their father during the week and easily follow their accustomed schedules—they're in aftercare at school and he picks them up at six, just like he always did. But now they spend the weekends at another location, with their mother. And one of the kids has soccer games every Saturday morning that are hard for her to get to. Birthday party invitations go to the dad's house and he forgets to give them to the mom, who is the one to take them to the parties on the weekend. It sounds small, but the kids start missing out on important routines and even their relationships with other kids can be weakened.

When kids are allowed to keep to their routines, these provide spaces where they can forget about the divorce for a while and just be themselves. If your daughter has taken ballet class at the same studio for several years, she will feel a level of consolation when she goes to ballet, dances with the same old mirrors around her, gets changed in the same old dressing room. Having this familiar container will help her process the other changes she's experiencing.

New situations demand a much greater output of energy be spent on just negotiating the terrain. There's nothing wrong with making adjustments and entering new situations—this can aid healthy growth—but now is not the time.

It's important to make the effort to fulfill your child's usual schedule because it will help lessen the feeling that everything is falling apart. When you arrange soccer practices and ballet lessons, you are telling your children that what they do matters to you, that you care about their lives. Let's say the dad in this case used to take the kids to soccer—but now because they're with the mom, he doesn't do that anymore. The kids lose out on soccer and on dad. It was an important thing they did together. Kids can feel like the divorce is more important than they are.

It's common for people to want to move out of their community once a divorce is happening—to get away from a bad memory, to move on and start over. Throughout this book there is one very strong continuous thread—your kids need both of you. It is not always possible, or even desirable in the case of adults who are violent or who abuse substances, but in most cases one real key to your child's ultimate success in getting through the divorce is keeping regular contact with both parents. It's worth the difficulty this sometimes entails.

One man is waiting until his kids graduate from high school to move out of state. "I'd go yesterday," he says. "But I do believe they need to see me. Their mother has custody so they live in the same house they always have and they'll go to the local high school. I wouldn't mind seeing them just on vacations and over the summer, but I can't have them learn everything about life from their mother."

In a divorce kids lose their family of origin. Moving them becomes another loss—loss of school, friends, the familiar. When at all possible, let your kids absorb, respond to, and move through one major transition at a time. If you must move them, try to wait two years after the divorce.

Keeping your child's life consistent will also help you keep a handle on your own. The routines we all feel enslaved by also help keep us grounded. Divorce is a big change for everyone. Things can feel dizzying and confused. Getting your kids to soccer practice can be a welcome focus for you when you are discombobulated.

Tell Others about the Divorce and Don't Be Afraid to Ask for Help

One of the first things for you to do for your kids is to tell their teachers about the separation or divorce. In fact, it would even help to tell major figures in your child's life that you are having marital difficulties, period. A teacher who knows this is going on will have a frame of reference for dealing with your child's behavior. Because your child will show some sort of behavioral adjustment—it may not be obstreperous, break-the-rules behavior, but your child is going through an emotional experience, and that comes out one way or another. When children have more than one teacher, or a principal who is active in the school's daily rounds, tell them also. Soccer coaches, ballet teachers—it will help you to tell them what's going on. Divorce can create some sticky scheduling problems, in addition to behavioral issues, and it will help your children if the adults in their life know what they're going through.

One preschool girl always dressed in ribbons and skirts and always behaved very, very well, and when her father moved in with another woman, this girl's behavior didn't change. Or didn't seem to change. Her teacher said, "She's always so good it's easy to forget about her. She never causes problems and always does what you ask her to. But then I began to realize— I'm forgetting about her too much. She isn't showing me new drawings or asking any questions. She's disappearing." The preschool teacher was able to talk to both parents about the girl.

"I was very happy she did," says the dad. "It was hard for me to face the fact that what was happening between Janet and me was affecting our daughter in a negative way. Since she is always so easy, I could fool myself." Sometimes teachers can see things about our kids we don't.

Then, of course, there are kids whose behavior gets out of hand, and this kind of thing can create real trouble at school. "I had another student who started hitting people and throwing things and crying all the time, and it always takes me a minute to say, 'Hey, what's going on with this child?' and not to just get angry at him," this teacher remarks. "Once I gave him a time-out, and he just collapsed in sobs in the hallway. I was angry at him because he had just destroyed another child's work, and I needed a time-out from him myself. But then I thought, 'Why is this time-out so hard for him?' I figured something else was going on." She led him back to the classroom and later called his mother.

"I'm always discreet, I don't want to put people on the spot," the teacher says. "But I told the mother, if there's something going on in this kid's life I need to know about it, because otherwise I can't help him. I was seriously thinking of asking her to remove him from my classroom—he was so disruptive to everyone else." When the boy's mother told her that she and her husband had split and everything at home was topsy-turvy, the teacher took a deep breath. "I decided to give the kid a chance. I kept the limits very firm, because I really have to. But if possible, I knew I could provide him with a piece of continuity while his family went through this hard time."

Knowing what was going on enabled the teacher to put the childrens' behavior within a framework, to look for openings where she could connect productively with them. Even children who have close relationships with their parents become estranged in one degree or another from both parents during a divorce. The child has allegiances to both parents and can't be 100 percent open about his feelings with either one of them, since now they are poised against each other. A teacher is a neutral person who isn't more loyal to either parent. As a consistent authority figure, he or she is more important to the child now than ever before.

You are lucky if your kids have sensitive, aware teachers. They can be great allies during this time. Even if you don't feel that great about certain teachers, it is wise to tell them about the divorce. It is better for you to call attention to your child in this way than for your child to do it first, through problematic behavior.

Many school districts and communities have support programs for kids whose parents are getting a divorce. Even if you feel your child is adjusting well, these programs are highly beneficial to kids. First of all, they provide a safe place for understanding the terminology of divorce, which they may hear all the time without fully comprehending. Second, they provide a safe place to let some of their feelings about the divorce come out. Third, they provide a peer group of other children who are experiencing the same thing. Divorce makes kids feel very alone, like outsiders, in their own home and everywhere. The divorce support group can show them that they have a new ground of connection with others, that they are not alone. Through the evidence of their peers, they will see that being part of a divorced family need have no special stigma.

By the same token, you may feel totally stressed for time, or perhaps think you are doing pretty well yourself, but a divorce support group is a really good idea for you, too. The Kids' Turn divorce program that informs this book is a wonderful example—it provides workshops to children and their parents and empowers the whole family with a common language. The parent workshops explain what the children are learning about, so that when everybody goes home, parents can follow through on key concepts.

Most divorce workshops or support groups are offered just to kids or just to adults, and if that's what is available, by all means join up. A program that has components for both parents and their kids offers something more, which is a framework for getting along although you are now two families instead of one.

A Note on Language

IN THIS BOOK former spouses are referred to as "co-parents." Co-parent may not describe your former partner very well right now, but in time you can develop a new relationship with this person, one that focuses on your children. Co-parent describes something positive and ongoing. Even "former spouse" or "ex-partner," while seemingly neutral, have a bit of negativity to them—the words describe something in the past, something discarded or left behind. While you want to leave your marriage behind, you don't want to leave your kids behind. It will help both you and your kids to use positive language.

In the same vein, this book repeatedly refers to your child's two homes. "Home" is not meant to describe a television version of a family domicile, and it is not assumed that both you and your co-parent live in such surroundings. Rather, "home" describes the two physical spaces your children share with each of their parents. The word is used, again, to be positive and holistic for your children. Whenever your children are spending regular time under the same roof with one of their parents, that is one of their homes. Thinking of it that way can help you treat the space in a way that nurtures your children's sense of continuity, safety, privacy, and shelter. Ideally, you want your children to feel they belong in both spaces provided by you and your co-parent.

Divorce Cheat Sheet

Important touchstones from this book are compressed into the following list. Each of the elements below will be discussed more fully in other parts of the text. Use this list to touch base with what's important—to remind yourself of first things first.

- *Keep the divorce low-conflict.* If you possibly can, mediate rather than litigate.
- *Come to terms with your divorce.* You may not be able to completely accept the fact that you are divorcing, but since it is happening, try to accept it. Your children will adjust much better if they feel you have.
- *Keep the kids out of the conflict.* That means don't fight in front of them, and don't ask them to serve as a go-between.
- *Communicate with your kids*: hear them. Connect with them.
- *Treat your ex-partner as a new business partner.* Kids mean you will have to work together on some level for quite a long time. View the relationship from a business perspective.
- *Provide regular contact for your children with both parents.* Anger and frustration can make it easy to decide that because contact with your former partner is difficult and negative for you, the same maintains for your kids. The truth is that excepting cases of abuse, children benefit enormously from maintaining contact with both parents. Children experience mother and father or their equivalents as fundamental parts of themselves.
- *Establish two homes for your children.* The emotional climate of each home is important. They should not be treated like weekend guests. They should not be treated like mini adults.
- *Keep focusing on your kids.* They need it, even when they don't seem to. Focusing on kids helps keep you rational about the outcomes you truly desire. Your kids are your future, just as you are their future.
- *Get help.* Support groups can help you work out the day to day exigencies of a new life and help keep your priorities in focus. Therapy can help address some of the larger conflicts unearthed by the divorce. Having safe sounding boards means you won't need to vent at your ex.

What's in Your Way

Divorce is a unique juncture in your life because it is about both an ending, of your marriage, and a beginning, of your new life. For your kids, it is very important to give them the space to grieve the loss of their family of origin. You will need time to do this yourself. Change is never easy—there's ambivalence around all leave-takings, no matter how clear it is that it must be done. There is no formula for how much time or what kind of expression your children will need to experience the negative aspect of the divorce. Like the rearing horse of history—said to go one step forward, several steps back—your child's emotions may progress one day and regress the next. The same goes for yours.

Within about six months of a separation or divorce, however, you do need to start focusing on the future, on how you want to live. This time, in which feelings about the divorce are still very hot, and emotions are not fully processed, is a time when people are very likely to get stuck in negative patterns. And now—here comes some of the strong language I warned about in the introduction—you really must examine yourself and how you are acting. Ask yourself if your behavior is helping your children or hurting them.

Another way of saying this is that even if you have the best of intentions for helping your children through your divorce, you may be hindering them. By not letting go of powerful negative responses to your co-parent. By engaging in high-conflict confrontations. By putting up barriers between your co-parent and your children. This is a time when your feelings are raw, and you are on the defensive, and it can be extremely painful to really examine your own behavior. You want to feel righteous, that your co-parent is the source of all evil. And even if your co-parent is having a true meltdown and is impossible to deal with, you may be contributing to the situation.

Most of what's in the way between you and helping your kids is how caught up you remain in the fact of the divorce and in fighting or struggling with your co-parent. One leader of parenting workshops for divorcing adults said that in a group of twelve, she expects only about seven people to really hear the information being given them. "The others aren't listening, because they're thinking about the divorce itself, which they haven't really dealt with. They want someone to pay attention to them, to hear their stories." Separation and divorce can be a huge trauma that causes you to completely fear for, challenge, and question your whole way of life. It often touches the heart of who you feel you are. It is hard for people to focus on their children, who are dependent on them, when they are so uncertain about themselves, the home base.

Even if you feel you are accepting the divorce pretty well, even if you've processed the effects of the experience in a group or with a therapist, there are still going to be times when something happens that sets you off. Divorce has long shock waves. In a sense it is more far-reaching than death, which is a definitive end. Divorce, when kids are involved, goes on and on and on. Children's needs change over time and the arrangements of their lives change as well. You will be dealing with your co-parent for many years to come. When your children have children, your divorce could still have reverberations. One girl whose father's parents had been divorced for over twenty years burst into tears because for grandparents' day at her school, she had only made two flowerpots, for two grandmothers—she worried that her grandfather's second wife would feel left out! Of course the teacher addressed the situation easily, but see, even a grandchild can feel caught in the middle when there's been a divorce.

Your Child's Point of View

You may feel you are handling everything just fine, and at the moment, everybody seems to be functioning pretty well. One reason to take the time and really do some formal divorce work with a therapist is that you may have put some coping mechanisms in place that work for you but not for your children. It's virtually impossible for any of us to have full knowledge of ourselves—everybody has blind spots.

One highly successful man went through his second divorce. He had one child from his first marriage, and this girl divided her time between her mother's house and his house. With his second wife, he had two more children. This woman developed a substance-abuse problem, which instigated the divorce; she joined a twelve-step program and this man was satisfied that she was competent to care for his kids. He makes a lot of money, but dividing his assets (this is California) felt like a big financial blow, which he compensated for by working harder.

"To her credit, she still takes good care of the kids," he says of his former second wife. For several years after the divorce, everything seemed fine. His kids were picked up from school half the week by their respective mothers, and during the portion of the week when he had custody, a nanny picked them up—the same woman who'd been working for him since his first child was an infant. The kids seemed to do fine—their lives weren't changed so very much by the divorce, since he had always worked long, hard hours, and his co-parents had always been the primary care providers.

As a result of working harder, he became even more successful. "I felt very powerful in my work," he says, "although like a complete personal failure." He developed a passion for bike racing, and pursuing this activity often took him away for weekends. He usually vacationed on a bike tour of some sort or another, without the kids. "I was used to not seeing the kids, and they were used to not seeing me. I missed them, I ached for them, but I had to go. I had to feel free and like there was some pleasure in my life, and I could afford it." The chickens came home to roost several years after the divorce, when his oldest child started to show signs of depression. Formerly a straight-A student, she began to get B minuses. "She was headed into adolescence, and I quaked at what was next."

The girl complained that when she was at home with his first wife, her mother, everything was fine. "The problem seemed to be with the nanny. Clara was turning thirteen, and although Ramona was devoted to her, she was hardly in a position to parent the girl. Clara said she wanted to go live full-time with her mother. At first, this man was ready to let her go. "But my other two kids were aghast. They both seemed to sink into depressions at the thought of Clara leaving. I was so clueless. It was my second wife who suggested family therapy. None of us really understood what the therapist put his finger on immediately, which was that Clara had become mother to her half-siblings in my absence, and was beginning to really feel the strain. Not only did she not have a mother half the week, she essentially never had a father."

"Oh the pain of what I heard!" he wailed, talking about the hard truths of therapy. "The kids felt completely abandoned by me. Like I didn't love them. I know that sounds obvious, but I had been working so hard for them, them, them. Or so I thought. Of course I had to stop traveling. And now I have to feel the pain that I haven't let myself feel for three years. And it hurts. Let me tell you, there's a reason for avoiding pain!" At home on the weekends, slugging it out in the daily rounds with his kids, not distracted by obsessive competition, he has to go through the awful feelings at the bottom of his divorces. To his eternal credit, he's doing it.

"People don't understand how perceptive kids are," observes the parenting workshop leader. "Kids always see the lie, and they always bear the brunt of it." When you don't deal with your pain, your kids have to deal with it double-time.

On the other hand, children really respond when they know you are trying. Even if your attempts are bumbling and seem awkward to you, if your heart is in the right place, your kids will get that. They know it if you are trying to educate yourself about how to be a more effective parent. They feel your good intentions. But they have to be honest good intentions. Many adults say, "I did it for the kids," when in fact, they did not do "it" for the kids. They found a handy excuse in the kids. Children are soulful. You may fool everyone else in the world but you won't fool them.

Things to Do

JOIN A DIVORCE group or go to a therapist. Find a container for your own confusion about the divorce and how it is changing your life. When you contain your own feelings and address them directly, it will keep your children free from them so they can focus on their own feelings and have their own experience of the divorce.

Connect with your kids. Educate yourself about how children respond to divorce at different ages, hear them out; give them the space to make their own adjustments, stay tuned—all of this helps head problems off at the pass. Concentrate on the organic, internal pieces of connection you can make with your child and less on the external stuff. Sure, if your child is doing badly in school, that needs to be addressed. Let her teachers do their part. Your part is to help build your child's sense of self. Your child knows instinctively how to develop herself, if she is: safe, secure, feels loved, has some freedom, has some boundaries. She should not be involved in your divorce—she should not be a mediator or a go-between. Remember to have a relationship with your child that is just about you and her. Share yourself with your child. Show her your interests, and let her participate in them if she wants to.

Stories

Delayed Reactions ॐ

MARIA AND PETER didn't tell their daughter, Sofie, that they were getting a divorce. "Not telling her was a bad decision—I didn't realize it then. My husband would not deal with what was happening, he kept wanting to deny it. I wanted him out of the picture, so I let it slide with Sofie."

A vibrant Russian immigrant in her mid-thirties, Maria has been in the States for all of Sofie's seven years. In that time, she's mastered English well enough to serve her in a demanding job as office manager of a large San Francisco consulting firm. "I love my work," she says. "I make good money. I'm around smart people. Things are happening. But nothing was happening for my husband. He wanted to sit around all the time and watch television. It was not going to be my life."

Tall, handsome Peter does well in the heating supply business, running his own small operation with several employees. "I make plenty of money!" he says, defending himself against Maria's charge that he lacks ambition. But his ideas about home and family are much more traditional than hers. "It's not right," he says. "She's the wife and mother. She should stay home and tend to things. I want my daughter to have a mother at home after school. I want her to have that safety, the world we had growing up...."

When, at Maria's insistence, Peter moved out of their apartment, he simply left with half of his belongings. The next weekend he came back for the rest. Sofie said, "What are you doing, Daddy?" But both parents put her off. "She sat down on the couch and watched him take his blasted television," laughs Maria. "I had to tell her we would get another one." The television seemed to symbolize what was going on for Sofie and the day her father walked out with it, she cried and cried. "You'll see him soon," Maria told her. But when her daughter asked exactly when she would see him again, there was no answer. "We just weren't speaking. We weren't on good terms. I didn't want to ask him."

Like many young girls, Sofie is good at adapting—outwardly good at it. At first she seemed to just accept the new situation. Furious with his wife, Peter left for Russia for several months, not specifying when he would return. "Of course I was coming back!" he says. "I wanted to see, what could I bring back that would be good for my daughter. Enough money for a big house? I want us to be together." During this period, Maria said nothing to her daughter about where her father was. He had told Sofie he would see her in two months—but she wanted to know how many times she had to go to sleep and wake up before she would see him again. "Forever or two months doesn't make any sense to children, I see that now," Peter says.

Maria's parents live close by and picked Sofie up every day from the day school she attends. But soon, her teachers began to share concerns about her. "She wasn't paying attention in class," Maria says. "She would keep talking and keep talking when the teachers asked her to stop." Always a good student, her work in school fell off. "I'm so glad this happened in first grade," says Maria. "Because we could pay attention to it before the grades really start to matter." On advice from the school, Sofie went to a counselor. Maria shakes her head. "Of course, she was upset about the divorce. She thought she'd never see her father again."

Eventually, Peter rented an apartment close to Maria's, and he alternates with her parents in picking Sofie up from school. "It's not the best situation," Peter says. "Because we should be a family under one roof. But I see my daughter half the week. She has her own room in my apartment. And we watch the television together!"

2

How Kids Feel
about Divorce and
How to Help Them

EVEN THE MOST stress-free, mutually agreed upon separation is a
loss for your child. Dismay, confusion, and feelings of sadness are
inevitable at some point during the time when a child's parents
decide they can no longer live together. It can be very hard for parents to face
their children's sad feelings—we try so hard to do the right thing for them, to
make them happy and give them the tools they need, it can be unbearable to
think that something we feel we must do is hurting them. But it's important
to face your child's disappointment and grief.

Many parents report that their children feel fine about the divorce, are taking it well, or even welcome it. "My daughter knows this marriage has been horrible for me," one woman said. "She's so happy I can get on with my life, a better
life for both of us." There may indeed be elements of your marriage that your

child does not like and is happy to see the end of. But even in a fairly hostile marriage, on a deep level your child wants you to stay together. Your child may say she understands that the relationship isn't good for you, but she doesn't understand this concept in the way you do. It is likely that she's telling you what you want to hear. Perhaps to be pleasing, but also because she doesn't have the language to say what she really feels. Adults who are wrapped up in how their marriages are affecting them don't usually have the distance to really evaluate what the situation means for their child.

It is in this gray area that a very crucial connection with your child can be lost. The good news is that this area also provides a venue for really meeting your children's needs. When kids' feelings are not acknowledged, or parental feelings are projected onto the children, children are in danger of disconnecting from their own true impulses and needs. The depression, anxiety, and acting out that are all associated with kids from divorced families begin right here—if a child is not able to acknowledge his own true feelings, he loses touch with what his true feelings are. When he's out of touch with his true feelings, he doesn't have a reliable rudder for navigating the waters of his experience. In addition, children are developing constantly. Divorce happens on an adult time clock, but it affects the developmental time clock of the child—there can be a stopgap in certain developmental attainments. With some understanding and attention, these stopgaps can be redressed, and the child can move on.

Children's response to divorce is very well documented. Almost all children will have the following feelings at one time or another. You may look at this list and recognize only one or two of the reactions, and indeed, maybe your child hasn't had all of them yet. It will highly benefit your kids if you keep all of these responses in mind, however. Some of them represent concepts that younger children can't formulate into words—but that doesn't mean they aren't feeling them. Some of the fears are so deep that to say them out loud feels threatening, like a nightmare a child doesn't want to repeat for fear of reactivating it. Some of these reactions can be easily addressed—children hate it when their parents fight, and you have a great deal of control over that. The desire kids have for their parents to get back together, and their fear of abandonment, are often more underground feelings that you can address best through constant reassurance.

This list is put together not only from much research into kids and divorce, but through the words of the children themselves in the Kids' Turn program. At a certain point in the workshop, the kids put together a newsletter for their parents—they tell their parents what they would like them to know. The newsletter is done as a group (by age) and presented anonymously—so if a child says, "I wish Fluffy could live with me and Dad instead of at Mom's house," that sentiment is changed to something like, "We wish we could have our pets with us more often." This anonymity allows kids to speak more freely about what they feel than if they were to be held individually accountable to their specific parents for their sentiments. The remarkable thing is that in nearly fifteen years of workshops, literally hundreds upon hundreds of newsletters from kids to parents have said the same things. These are expressed by all the children across all age groups. You can be sure that your child would like to express the following sentiments:

1. Kids fear abandonment and loss and wonder who will take care of them.
2. Kids want their parents to get back together and have a hard time accepting the fact that this won't happen.
3. Kids blame themselves for the divorce. They feel if they were better, it wouldn't have happened.
4. Children are frustrated at not being heard.
5. Kids fear parental anger focused on the other parent.
6. Their parents' divorce causes tremendous loyalty issues in kids. They feel very uncomfortable about acting as a go-between.
7. Related to loyalty issues, kids will sacrifice themselves to please you or to try to help you with your emotional struggles.
8. At some point or another over the years, kids feel frustrated at having to move between two homes.
9. Even very young children who would seem not to be aware of status issues feel shame or a sense of not belonging among peers from intact families.

Children who express these feelings and have them addressed are able to move beyond them to focus on the developmentally appropriate tasks that form the road to successful adulthood. It should be noted that although kids are disappointed, fearful, and frustrated, these are normal emotions all of us feel through the course of life. The point is not to avoid having these feelings. The point is to approach them honestly, with openness, and to address them. Not only are the specific feelings ameliorated this way, but kids are also given tools for coping that will help them through all the situations their lives will present. It bears repeating that it is not the fact of the divorce, but the way that it is handled, that matters the most in making the divorce transition a healthy one. These points are all discussed in more detail below, along with other guidelines for helping your kids.

Kids Fear Abandonment and Loss and Wonder Who Will Take Care of Them

There is this undeniable truth that occurs during separation and divorce: somebody moves out. The reality of this action is perhaps the strongest blow the child receives from the fact of your divorce, and your kid does not view this as husband leaving wife or wife leaving husband. Your child experiences this as: Mom leaving me; Dad leaving me. It opens up a can of worms. If one parent could leave, so could the other. And then what happens?

All kids fear losing their parents' love. On a very instinctive level, kids understand that they are dependent. They feel their parents' commitment to them as love. They know that they need this love in order to survive. Love is like the glue, the savings account, the part you can count on, and its foil is anxiety. As kids grow and develop, they experience natural anxieties, and they use the love they feel to cope with it. The tasks kids have to face include physical development, from the toddler learning to toilet train, to the adolescent going through puberty; these tasks include social challenges related to friendships and other relationships; and they include the expectations increasingly placed on them by the outside world, particularly in school. When kids are anxious that they may not be supported through love, they are compromised in their ability to bring more energy to these physical and social demands.

Children, even those from affluent families, also worry about losing it all, about becoming indigent and homeless. Not every child expresses this fully—but all of them understand this dimension of their dependence. In our world, they often see people who don't have homes, and in school and in church they learn about people who are less fortunate than they are. Their awareness that this is a possibility becomes a fear. The family structure has represented a kind of safe haven, and when the very fabric of that feels diminished, the child wonders what will happen next. This is another reason it is important to keep your money struggles out of your child's realm—children are powerless concerning money, and their worries won't do them any good.

Let's say you have been left, by your co-parent, and feel abandoned. This is a pretty difficult feeling to face, and you may not be able to take it on all at once. Your own survival issues may be activated. In fact, you may have to take some pretty strong actions to insure your own survival. Even if that is the case, it is best to not share your concerns on this level with your child. Instead, reassure your child that you will take care of him, that no matter what, he won't be lost or forgotten. You may need some serious help on this front, and it is there for you in your community, through schools and churches and other social services.

If this discussion seems not to touch you, and you are lucky enough to not have survival concerns, yet be apprised that your children are going to have these worries anyway. If at all possible, facilitate your children's time spent with your co-parent. Your commitment to your children may feel totally certain, but the connection with the other parent is just as important to your child.

The solution to fears of abandonment is constant reassurance. If both parents can reassure the child of their continued love, so much the better. Even if your child is not expressing this issue, don't assume it isn't there— it may be striking him on a level he can't articulate, or he may be too afraid by the feeling to let it show. It's important for you to assume your child is worried about losing both parents. Tell him all the time that you love him and are committed to caring for him.

If the parent who moves out does not seem capable of contact with the child, or doesn't respond to anyone's suggestion (or court order) that he or she keep up contact with the child, there's not much you can do. But your child will need help with this sometime down the road. You may not feel like you can handle it now, but keep the idea of therapy for your child in the back of your mind (if not the front).

An example of how the repercussions of divorce persist into adult life is given by one woman whose father left her mother when she was two. She didn't see her father again until she was in her twenties. "Because my mother remarried and my life resembled everyone else's, nobody thought about what it meant to me that my father left." She was faced with a pretty terrible romantic track record when she went into therapy and traced the source of her essential self-rejection to this early loss. This story is illustrative of the kinds of shadows divorce can leave behind, which may not feel threatening or dangerous to emotional health in the moment, but which nevertheless continue to interfere with growth as a person matures. The story shows exactly why acknowledging the pain of divorce for a child and addressing the emotions it incites is such a good idea from the get-go.

Money and Security

MONEY IS A real hot spot in divorce. Although the traditional division of labor between men and women is changing and is more fluid than ever, it is usually the father who has the money, and the mother who is in the position of needing it from him. If you are the breadwinner, and you are angry with your former partner, try very hard not to use money as a weapon. Money issues are hand-in-glove with survival issues. You may deeply feel that your co-parent needs to get a job, or a better job, and to stop spending your money; you may feel taken advantage of and exploited; you may feel enraged that after working so hard to get to a certain level of financial security, your divorce ratchets you down several notches. These are hard feelings to have and often they are warranted. If your former partner is truly irresponsible or in a dream world about your financial situation, the best thing for you to do is have a mediator go over the finances with both of you and make a plan that works. Having a mediator do it means that your parenting partner will find it easier to accept the results, since they won't be freighted by the bad blood between you.

The important thing is to keep your own feelings out of the money issue, for the simple reason that if it is in the air, your kids will pick up on it. Kids will fear indigence. They will fear losing it all—home, car, the ability to go to school. They will experience themselves as a financial burden on you and they will feel shaken in their self-esteem—they will feel you would rather be rid of them. You may want your co-parent to get a healthy dose of fear to stop the spending, but you don't want the fear to spread to your kids. Money is the place for you to take the high road.

If your children weather the first several years of your divorce without worrying about money, you will have done them a huge favor. There is nothing kids can do about money, so it is much better to leave them out of any discussion about it. On the other hand, most people suffer financially as a result of divorce, and the child understands the correlation.

If you have to move because of money, or to make part of your house into an apartment to get more income, find another way of framing the situation. If you do mention money, put it in a positive framework. "Well, your mother doesn't live here anymore so we have some extra room. We can become landlords!" Does this sound like Pollyanna? Maybe it is. But to protect your kids, you may have to put a more positive face on things than you think the situation calls for. But when you do put the situation positively, you will also do yourself a favor. It will help you get through hard times to view it all more benignly.

Kids Want Their Parents to Get Back Together and Have a Hard Time Accepting That This Won't Happen

One of the biggest boulders in the way of kids getting over their parents' divorce is the fact that they hold on to the fantasy that all will be reinstated one day and the family will live happily ever after. The original love that brought the child's parents together and from which he was created will rise again. Even kids whose parents remarry have a secret wish that the original nuclear family that created them will be reconstituted.

The reason for this is that kids so deeply internalize their moms and dads as components of themselves, that they have a hard time conceptualizing themselves outside the paradigm. If you think about it, one of the major tasks of developing a self, from childhood through adolescence and into adulthood, is to separate from the parents, to be a free-standing person, yet endowed with strength and preparation from the original parental unit. A kid whose parents are divorced has to conceptualize himself as separate before he is developmentally wired to make this leap. Even adolescents, who are most actively going through the separation process, have a hard time with divorce because the concept of separation is being imposed from outside rather than prompted from within.

This is, therefore, a very persistent fantasy related to the child's sense of himself. The best thing you can do for it is to very firmly and gently insist that no, you won't be getting back together again. On the other hand, since the child really does need both parental figures in the ongoing process of developing a self, it is important to create a system of relationship among all of you that is not a single family. Later on in the book, we'll discuss forming a business relationship with your co-parent. You can think of this business as the manufacturing plant for your child's healthy self. And to run at its best, the plant needs both parents functioning well on behalf of the child, in relationship with the child.

If you haven't accepted the divorce yourself, this really gets in your child's way. This is basically the reason why parental acceptance of divorce figures so prominently in whether kids make a healthy adjustment or not.

When one parent hasn't accepted the divorce, that person's emotional life takes on a distorted shape. Everything becomes about what could have been, what should have been, how I was done so wrong. Some people pin their whole self-concept on a relationship, and when that relationship falls apart, they have no ground to stand on. This is a serious state of affairs in a person's life, a crisis. If it is not approached and dealt with, it can be seriously damaging to their kids.

When one parent continues to live in reference to a relationship that no longer exists, the child is frozen in time also. The child can't move on if his mother or his father can't move on. Sometimes kids in this situation will take on a preternatural maturity. As they get older, into the teenage years, they will even say, "yes, my father is still stuck in the past," or "my mother never really got over it." That impairment in the parent's development directly becomes an impairment in the child's development—because on an important level, that parent is not available to the child. Parents cannot help their children grow up and face the stresses and hurdles of life when they haven't done it for themselves. The child who cognitively recognizes this has been deprived of an important emotional space. That is the emotional space to be a child.

If you feel uncomfortably like you fit into the category of those who haven't gotten over the divorce, you may need more time, you may need more help. At a certain point, even if you were desperately wronged, it is important to let it go and move on. You may not be able to imagine future happiness for yourself, but it is there for you, if you meet it halfway.

One woman with teenage sons was divorced from their father over ten years ago. Periodically, she moves in with her former husband or he moves in with her. "I think we may get it together this time," she says. "I'm hoping." When her former husband decides it isn't working out for him, which he does regularly, there are no fights, no harsh words. He takes the blame for the failure of the relationship on himself totally. "He's the nicest guy," she says.

What about her sons? "Oh, they're sick of it, but I think my youngest would really like us to get back together again." This woman has her sons in on her fantasy that some day this will all work out—if one of her sons figures out the truth, that it never will work out, he's going to be facing it on his own. Not only will he bear his own disappointment, but his mother's implicit disappointment, which she will not face, as well. If neither son becomes clear about the situation, they are going to repeat some version of it in their own romantic lives, in some other aspect of their lives, or in many different areas of their lives.

The hard task of really confronting yourself may not seem worth it, for you. You may have underlying feelings of unworthiness—like this woman, who feels the only man for her is one who leaves her every six to nine months. Look at it another way—facing your most horrible weakness is something you do to strengthen your kids, to free them to live better lives. You may not feel you are worth it, but you know your kids are definitely worth it. Let yourself get some help in order to help them.

Basically, if the parents cope with the divorce, the children can let it go. Kids can allow the issue to be a grown-up one. If the parents are struggling, or one of them is, the child will take it on. Not only is the child emotionally unprepared to do that, but there's nothing a child can do to resolve adult problems, period. They will sense themselves as a failure, because they haven't been able to do what is impossible anyway. Many kids can feel this giant sense of unresolve—and it can get in the way of their pursuit of their own lives.

Kids Blame Themselves for the Divorce:
They Feel If They Were Better, It Wouldn't Have Happened

One little girl asked her mother, "Do you hate the part of me that's Daddy?" In a sense, her question says it all. She identifies with both parents; she sees her parents not getting along; she projects the disapproval they have for each other directly onto herself. Even parents who don't fight have to watch out for and address these feelings in their kids when there's a divorce. These feelings are part of why children blame themselves for the divorce. They don't see it as outside themselves at all.

Developmentally, kids are more or less self-centered—that changes as they get older. It isn't that they are egotistical in a negative way. They simply can't conceptualize the world except through the lens that is "I." We are all like this to a certain extent, but getting older, we understand other people's points of view. Adolescents are pretty good at being able to see that your marriage isn't working for you and that's about you. Still, even adolescents are going to have a little voice inside that says, "If I were better, they would be happy."

When one person leaves, the implicit message is rejection. No matter what you say, you are leaving. No matter what you say, the child is clearly not compelling enough to make you stay. And if one parent leaves, so can the other. What goes with the feeling of being abandoned is that on some level the child must deserve it. So a horrible sense of unworthiness, of not being lovable, threatens the child from deep within his psyche.

This is a bitter pill. One person is leaving. If you are the one leaving, the best thing you can do is to establish a very regular means of communicating with your kids, preferably on a daily basis. After things quiet down and everyone gets used to the situation, daily contact isn't necessary, especially with older children.

Again, this area is one in which it is very important for there to be parental acceptance of the divorce. If you are calm about the separation, and reassure your child that it is an adult piece of business that is between you and your co-parent, your child will be in a better position to let go of the nagging feeling that he caused the divorce. As with every area of divorce, it is important here to keep promises to kids, to keep them in mind, to let them know that you are thinking about them. Kids need to know you value them. They need to hear about that a lot. If they feel you don't value them, they will internalize a sense of not being worthy, of being "wrong," of causing the divorce.

It's important to understand that the divorce is felt by your child as a blow to his self-esteem. All the normal, everyday things you do to support your child's self-esteem are even more important now.

Children are Frustrated at Not Being Heard

One teenage girl was fed up with her father. "He was drinking too much. He fell apart after the divorce. He cried and moaned and said he wanted to see us, but when we were at his house he spent time with his girlfriend. It was making me crazy." This girl maintained a fairly close, healthy relationship with her mother, who tried to help her deal with her father. "Finally, I said, 'Dad, if you don't shape up I'm not coming over here anymore.'" To his credit, he heard her. He went into a twelve-step program and things got a lot better.

This story is a bit double-edged. On the one hand this girl was old enough and mature enough to articulate how awful it was for her that her father couldn't cope. He said he wanted to see his kids, but he didn't help that happen. He was a wreck for many months around the divorce and that's not uncommon. He's lucky to have such an incredible daughter, who clearly had some very vital support. At the same time, it's a bit heartbreaking when a child, which a teenager still is, has to be the mature one. She simply can't cope with her disappointment in him and her fear that part of her, the part that he contributed, is something of a wreck. These are feelings that will surface later in her life. On the other hand, she displayed really fine coping skills. She established some firm boundaries and followed through on them. When she does hit a snag in her life (and who doesn't?), she is very likely equipped to deal productively with it.

Smaller kids or children who don't have the benefit of one supportive parent are not in such a good position. Many people don't even tell their kids about the divorce—as if the kids were not people with responses of their own. Such an attitude discounts children's feelings, and every step of the way, every custody decision you make, every fight you have over money, your child is going to have feelings about it.

Listening to kids is a relatively new idea. Even the generation growing up in the '70s didn't really experience children as respected. What children needed, wanted, and feared had been considered the province of adult discretion. The trouble is that adult conjecture about how children feel, what they need, and what they want is fueled by adult projections of their own needs, feelings, and beliefs.

Listening to your kids will empower them in small ways, which will go far toward ameliorating their frustration over not having any influence over the divorce itself. Ask them what their preferences are in terms of pajamas, toothbrushes, what to bring to their other parent's house. Ask them what is difficult for them and problem-solve. It is very common for kids to be uncomfortable with the way they are picked up and dropped off between parental houses. If you allow them some control over how this is done, it will help them feel a vital part of what is occurring, that they have serious agency in this situation that indeed does centrally concern them. It will help them not feel they are being shuttled around at will.

Part of what kids are expressing here is their frustration at being left out of the divorce process. Nobody asked *them*. And they are the ones whose lives are most affected. This is an area where you have to apply some judgment. You do want to ask your kids how they feel about what is going on and how they would like things to be changed. And you want to accommodate their wishes whenever possible—they won't feel so powerless if you can do this. On the other hand, it is important that kids understand that in fact, they don't have a say about the divorce. It may feel empowering in the moment for them to have an opinion, but if they truly were orchestrating events, it would undermine their sense of security in the world. Part of their security is based on trusting that adult affairs are taken care of well by adults. And that they don't have to worry about things over which they have no control. You want to respect your kids, but you don't want to give them inappropriate power. It will hurt them in the long run. All of us forget to ask our kids how they feel. Kids may have the sense that they are not being heard, and we have completely misread their attempts at being heard. Direct communication is best.

DIVORCE WORDS

DEPENDING ON THEIR individual maturity, kids can benefit from learning the terms the outside world uses to define divorce. It helps orient them to their own experience. You can use the following list to go over the nuts and bolts of divorce with your child, sensitive of course to his cognitive ability to understand. Older kids will definitely understand—and it's a good idea to go over this stuff with them before they hit the adolescent's stand of rebellion. Ideally, you should give your child an opening to ask questions about any of these terms, if you can provide neutral, supportive answers. In other words, don't define a stepparent as one who steals a spouse, or custody as something to fight over.

Divorce or Dissolution	A legal judgment ending a marriage.
Counselor	An adult who listens and helps people understand their problems.
Half Brother or Half Sister	A boy or girl born to your parent and your stepparent.
Judge	An adult who hears disputes in a court of justice and decides how they should be resolved.
Lawyer	An adult trained to help parents proceed with getting a divorce.
Separation Agreement	A written agreement between both parents describing the terms by which they agree to end their marriage and the rules they will observe after their divorce.
Child Custody	A plan that describes who children will live with, who will take care of them, and how the major decisions will be made.
Child Support	How much money each parent will pay to help take care of their children.
Visiting Rights	Certain times set aside for children to spend with the parent they do not live with.
Alimony or Spousal Support	Money one parent pays to the other after they have separated.

Stepparent	Someone who marries your mother or father.
Stepsister or Stepbrother	A girl or boy born to your stepparent and his or her former spouse.
Joint Custody	When both parents have responsibility for their children.
Mediation	When parents meet with a third person who helps them discuss and make agreements (settle arguments) about their children.
Parenting Plan	A written agreement between parents about how they will care for and be responsible for their children.

Kids Fear Parental Anger Focused on the Other Parent

Along with parental acceptance of the divorce, the level of fighting between you is the other major factor in your child's healthy adjustment to your divorce. In addition, your fighting is an utter agony to your children. In a way, the level of fighting is intimately related to the level of acceptance of the divorce. You may really despise your co-parent, and you may be so happy you are divorced, but you can't help it, you get into screaming fits whenever you two talk. Are you really over it?

When parents fight, it makes kids wonder and worry. They wonder what's going to happen next. They worry about one or both of you being hurt, or that in the midst of the rage they are witnessing, they will be hurt. Remember, children's boundaries of self include parent figures, so they interject themselves into the midst of the fighting. They may block their eyes and ears and run away when you fight—they are trying to escape your fighting, and they can't really do that. You have to stop fighting.

When children are worried, they are more vulnerable to all their fears. They become more focused on survival, on holding tight, and become less willing to venture forth and try. They may seem to be bold in some ways, but are they internally, emotionally? They will need to feel strong on the inside as well as on the outside to make it through the world productively. Children who invest less in expanding themselves are spending too much energy on emotional survival.

We all know how debilitating anxiety is, how distorting it can be. When a child has his hands over his ears, it's not just your fighting he's blocking out. He's stopping himself, she's stopped in time. That mean's he's interrupting himself in mastering the developmental tasks appropriate for his age. Conflict takes up a lot of space in the room, and that's oxygen your child should be nourished with, not deprived of.

Handling It

THE WAY A child experiences the separation is in the way it is handled. If his parents are fighting and screaming, he will feel immense distress but have no tools for dealing with the violence he is internalizing.

It helps your kids to say:

"Your mother and I can't speak without arguing, so I'm going to pick you up from school instead of having her drop you off." You have owned the problem, so it's not your child's problem. You have dealt with it and found a way to work things out.

It hurts your kids to say:

"Your mother is a raving lunatic who screams at me every time I see her." This may be a truth for you, but it has no use for your kids and compromises their relationship not only with their mother, but also with you.

Divorce Causes Tremendous Loyalty Issues in Kids;
They Feel Very Uncomfortable About Acting as a Go-Between

Their parents' divorce causes tremendous loyalty issues in kids. They feel very uncomfortable about acting as a go-between

When you fight you put your child in an impossible position. If Dad says Mom is bad, the kid feels he is bad too—because Mom is part of him. Kids also champion the underdog, and can be very compassionate. If one parent is lonely, they will suffer on his or her behalf. When you say something incendiary, your kids suffers both for you and the perceived harm done you, and on behalf of the person you are flaming. To put it simply, you and your co-parent may hurl pain at each other but the person you are hitting most squarely is your child.

Children experience their parents as intimate parts of themselves. As children grow and develop, they do so in constant dialogue and response with their parental models. At certain times they will identify strongly with their mothers, at other times with their fathers. If a child is brought up by two parents of the same sex, he will internalize both as fundamental parts of himself, even as he will eventually seek out a person of whatever sex is not represented by his parents to work out some psychological dynamics that have to do with gender. Even if one of the parents is not on the scene at all, the child will project an image of that parent for himself, and he will define himself partly in relationship to what he imagines.

One way of looking at the developing self is that children go from being completely merged with their parents, completely identified with these authority figures, to becoming individuated adults. The process is one that goes back and forth—merging or oneness and individuating or separation. You can notice this drama over the years. The infant doesn't have any idea of where he begins and his father ends. Even a toddler will say, "you hurt me" when he stubs his toe, not differentiating his mother from the outside world or seeing any other causality outside this relationship.

You can even see this drama within the course of a day, an hour! First, your seven-year-old clings to you and cannot go join the birthday party made up mostly of kids he doesn't know. Then, after playing with these kids for some time, he doesn't want to leave them and rejoin you.

Even when you are not physically there, as your child's parent you are a key part of how he's forming himself and his relationships. And so is your child's other parent. When the two parents fight, the child feels split inside. The child feels the conflict—it is as if the conflict is happening within himself, not in front of him.

Children think of you not as husband and wife but as Mom and Dad, their parents. You want the children to feel that it's okay with you that they have a relationship with the other parent.

Be aware that your children will go very far to please you. It may not feel this way when you have to struggle to get your kids to clear their dishes after dinner or put their clothes in the hamper, but these small skirmishes are deceptive, because in the biggest ways, your children will do your bidding, or will do what they think you need. Children are very accommodating and will accept the role of messenger until they are older.

Letting your child deliver messages or other communications between you and your co-parent has several negative effects. One is that the child stays located in your former marriage—the union in which at one time you communicated more or less freely is now a space occupied by your child. Obviously, your child can't get over the divorce if one of his main points of reference with regard to his parents is their former relationship.

Then there's the old confusion between the messenger and the message. A child who has to give one parent information from the other which may not be met with glee becomes responsible for that parent's displeasure. And that is very unfair. Additionally, the child is lonely in this role. Remember that the child of divorce really does have some hard truths to swallow. One of them is that he can no longer be fully and completely himself with either parent, because another part of him is loyal to the other. This is a loss he has to bear. And you make it much harder for him to bear it if you are constantly putting him between you.

Related to loyalty issues, kids will sacrifice themselves to please you or to try to help you with your emotional struggles. Children are very protective of their parents. This can feel sweet and in fact it is, but as their parent you must be vigilant that it doesn't go too far. The girl who doesn't separate from her mother because she's responding to her mother's need for her is skipping a phase, and she'll pay for that later (so, very likely, will her mother). Kids will try to act as mediators—they want to keep things whole whenever possible.

Parents need to differentiate their own needs, to own them, even if they can't solve them. You can say, "Yes, I'm really hurting that your father left me, and I don't always know what to do on Saturday night, but I'll figure it out and it will get better." Your child may offer to stay home with you, and it's important to acknowledge his good intentions, but let him go. The child needs to learn to differentiate his own feelings and needs, to understand that he is responsible for himself and that he can stand on his own two feet. He needs to see you doing that. Your children need to hear that YOU will be all right.

At Some Point or Another Over the Years, Kids Feel Frustrated at Having to Move Between Two Homes

It's not easy to have two homes, although adjustments can be made and with time there can be pleasure in having two spaces. There's a phenomenon that happens with teenagers—they quite often suddenly balk at having to move between domiciles and may refuse to do it. You may respond to this by gently but firmly insisting that they keep doing it. You may allow them to change their visitation so they are with you half the year and your co-parent the other half (if that's possible) rather than going back and forth during the week. One thing to beware of is that the child may say he no longer wants or cares about seeing his father, for example. The child quite often is just fueling his argument that he should be allowed to stay put. He's appealing to you on an irresistible level—you knew it all along, your co-parent is no good! Remember, that's likely not what is going on. And your child, through the teenage years, will do best if you keep up his regular contact with both of you.

The best way to make having two homes a positive thing is to really set up each space so the child feels welcome and comfortable. At first, he may sleep on the couch in an apartment, but eventually, it becomes important for him to have his own specific space. So if it is still the couch, there is a shelf nearby for her favorite books. Make it easy for your child to move back and forth even if it is a pain for you. One woman had her kids bring her their laundry when they came back from their father's. He just would never do their laundry and she cared about having them in clean clothes, even at his house. She decided that was worth it to her.

Even Very Young Children Who Would Seem Not to be Aware of Status Issues Feel Shame or a Sense of Not Belonging Among Peers from Intact Families

One of the strongest social drives we have as people is the need to belong. Divorce can often be devastating to a person's social life. Social life is not a frivolous thing—we identify who we are not only by our individuality but also by the people we move among. Divorce is often perceived as a way to expand oneself as a person, to move beyond a limiting relationship. But when it happens, it's easy to feel left high and dry. It's common to feel that people who once had you to dinner no longer do—that somehow being a single person is threatening to their couple-filled world. There is some truth to that. It's important to connect with people going through what you're going through. Also, join groups or take classes according to other interests, like painting or film or books.

For your kids the situation is twofold. When parents divorce, it's often like kids don't belong in their own home anymore. Even when they stay with one parent and aren't disrupted, kids still have a loyalty to the other parent. This means they can't be fully expressive around either parent without betraying the other. Kids can feel like strangers in their own home. Help them feel more grounded. Try to keep them in the same school, try not to move for at least the first two years. Your language matters. Instead of "a broken family," refer to yourselves as "a restructured family." Kids who come from a "broken" home feel worse than kids who have two families.

Kids feel dropped out of the social fabric. Different than other kids. They can feel shame, embarrassment, jealousy of intact families. One of the very best things about a divorce workshop or program for kids is that they can connect with other kids who've had the same experience. They can identify with their peers and feel okay about this "divorced" status.

Help your kids by letting them be kids. Let them off the hook about the divorce—which means facilitating their life so it isn't over-influenced by the fact that their parents are divorced. Divorce can be much harder on the child who has to stop playing on the soccer team because one parent can't pick them up that day. Or they live in a different town half the week and it's too hard to get them to the other town for friends' birthday parties and so forth. Kids need their own social identity.

Normalizing Divorce

"Normalizing" divorce is about taking the concept out of the world of broken homes and damaged goods and letting kids know that their experience is pretty common and shared by many others. In fact, really feeling comfortable about being divorced is an important goal for everyone in the family. This proposition may sound problematic. It's one thing to get a divorce because you feel you have to, or have no choice. But feel good about it? Divorce is wrong, right? Divorce is for people who made bad choices or had some kind of midlife crisis or want to shirk responsibility in some way, right? Nobody's advocating divorce here. No one thinks divorce should be as common as sneezing and that the social contracts we enter into should be easy to break. Why divorce has become so prevalent is not in the scope of this book. But the fact is, that children who accept the divorce do better than kids who feel that something has been irreparably wounded in them. Yes, losing their family of origin is a big blow. But it can be overcome and moved on from. The goal of healthy, lasting relationships is one children of divorce should hold for themselves. They have to feel good about themselves first.

There are some social factors that mitigate against normalizing divorce. Many people's parents are from a generation that frowned on it—one woman's mother, after knowing blow by blow how her son-in-law lied, cheated, and stole from her daughter, still encouraged her to get back together with him. She firmly believed in "for the sake of the children," and furthermore, she really couldn't conceptualize her daughter without a husband. No matter how good this woman felt about getting rid of a deadbeat husband, her mother's feelings affected her own self-concept.

Make an inventory of how you feel about the divorce, and the attitude your family and friends take toward it. This will help you assess how much support you are getting—it is very likely you could use more support.

One way to help normalize the divorce for yourself and your kids is to become mindful of your language. The way we say things is often a value judgment on the content of what's being said.

Instead of Saying... Try Saying...

(Based on work by Dr. Isolina Ricci)

Visiting	Living with
I have children but they live with their mother/father	I have a family
The childrens' mother/father left us	I have a family

The children are seeing (or visiting) their dad/mom	The children are at mom's/dad's house, with their other family
Motherless, fatherless, split home, broken home	The home, family
The children have one home and their father/mother visits	The children have two homes
The marriage broke up, failed	The marriage ended
Wife, husband (ex-wife, ex-husband)	Childrens' mother, childrens' father
Custody and visitation agreement	Parenting agreement
Remarriage, reconstituted family, blended family, combination family	Family (or second family, third family)
Where do you live?	Where do your mother and father live?
Where do you live?	Where is your other home? Where does your other family live?

What you want is to encourage and support a sense of wholeness for yourself and your kids. Phrases like "reconstituted family," and "blended family," are not bad. But the words do implicitly refer to a previous family organization. Especially while a family is in fact reorganizing, these are fine phrases. At some point, you want to move on and characterize the present situation as something whole in and of itself. Most of us have become pretty sensitive about asking kids where they live or who they live with— we understand that the answer is multiple. But it is good to remember to try not to make assumptions, especially when talking to kids.

The Truth—But

It's difficult to communicate to kids that the world is good and safe if they aren't feeling that way themselves. But most of us can recognize that the way to deal with life's blows is enhanced considerably if you feel confident and feel an inner confidence in yourself that you can make it, that there's a place to come clear. If you yourself aren't feeling that way, you can still theoretically understand it, even provide your kids with support you probably didn't get as a child to help them have better tools than your own. It's important for a child to understand that he has his own life, that what happened to his parents happened to someone else, that there are things to learn from it (if the child is a teenager and can understand such things). Tell your child the truth about what's going on, but remember to use a positive framework. As a parent, continually focusing on encouraging your child keeps you in the moment. Naturally, you will go back over the relationship and how and why it fell apart and you'll be mad and sad, but you can also keep your focus on what your child needs now. Not only will you help your child, you'll help yourself move on.

Good parenting through divorce involves some pretty specific directives, like:

1. Don't fight in front of your kids.
2. Keep your child's contact up with both parents.
3. Don't use the child as a mediator.

But there is an overall environmental factor to the deal as well. The quality of the home and in many cases, homes, is ultra important. A relaxed, "normal," life-as-usual tone to your parenting will help your kids a lot. Honesty is a true virtue—honesty tinged with discretion. You want to be clear with your kids about what is going on, without being brutal. Kids can adapt remarkably well to adversity, but there is no sense in burdening them with information they can do nothing about.

Focus on the divorce as a transition. Speak of it as the way to a new arrangement, towards two homes to live in—an expanded world, rather than a crippled world.

Ways to Stay in Touch with Your Kids
1. The phone can be a wonderful way to keep contact with your kids. On the other hand, if your former partner is answering the ring and you don't want to even hear that "hello," there may be a better way. Faxing is great. For kids who don't read or write yet, faxing pictures you draw is just as good. Encourage your child to fax you back. Keeping the back and forth of a relationship is a high priority. Of course if your child is old enough, by all means use e-mail. Their e-mail account can be a child's own private terrain of connection with you, and this can make them feel masterful and special all at once.
2. If you don't see your kids much, collect souvenirs from your week

for them. These don't have to be expensive gifts, just little mementos that keep your kids informed about your whereabouts and let them know you were thinking about them while you were in the Denver airport, for example.

3. School-age kids who are not yet blasé about their parents will love reading a book in tandem. You can agree to read a chapter of *Charlie and the Chocolate Factory* at the same time and then have a conversation about it. You can separately rent *Willie Wonka* and compare the book and the movie. This is a way to share an experience without being in the same room. Some kids are really into nonsense rhymes or poetry like Shel Silverstein's. You can easily share some reading of these over the phone—then fax, mail or e-mail a copy of the poem afterwards.

4. Teenagers may not welcome reading the same book as you at the same time, even if you volunteer to read something they are assigned at school (it's worth asking though). However, teenagers do love being respected and treated like adults. If there's a controversial television show or movie out there, ask their opinion of it. DO NOT use the occasion to forbid them from doing something or to preach about something. Questions are your friend with teenagers—teens don't want to be told anything, but they like to be asked.

Stories

Theresa's Altar ✍

THERESA FANTES HAS built a shrine in her father's house. In a recessed alcove in the bedroom she shares with her brother, Theresa juxtaposed smiling photographs of her parents so it appears they might just join hands across the frames. Most prominently displayed is a photograph of Theresa at her first Communion, smiling in frothy white clothes, flanked by her mom and dad, grandmother, and little brother. Theresa's shiny dark hair and liquid brown eyes are evident in her pretty mother. Her deep olive skin draws a straight line to her father's Italian heritage. This homage is filled out with souvenirs from Disneyland, birthday party favors, and school craft projects in meticulous array. But only in this special space is Theresa's family serene or whole.

"She wasn't acting like a wife or a mother," Theresa's father Michael says of his former spouse. "The judge saw it that way too." Michael is explaining his unusual custody arrangement, in which he has the kids a full half of the week. Michael is still angry, still struggling with his ex-spouse over money issues, over schooling for the kids, over the way she lives her life. "It isn't right!" he says, describing how Theresa and her little brother share a room with their mother's boyfriend's child in their other home, the apartment near Michael's house, for which he pays half the rent. "If they want to live together," he says of the boyfriend, "why don't they get married?" Michael is convinced that his co-parent and her current partner "want to beat the system out for a few bucks."

Or rather, his bucks. Currently Michael is his ex-wife's sole support. She hasn't worked since they got married ten years ago. Now she doesn't want to take a low-paying job, which she feels is all she's qualified for, and which would provide bare compensation for taking care of Theresa after school and her three-year-old brother all day. Michael, who gave his ex-wife $90,000 when their divorce was finalized a year ago, doesn't sympathize. "Hey, break even on your dime, not mine." What he wants is full custody of his children.

When asked what about his former wife's point of view, Michael is forthright. "She says I'm a teenager and just expected her to babysit the kids while I did what I wanted." As if to substantiate her claim, he admits, "She's very attractive. I thought she would help my career, have dinner parties, be a good hostess. I thought she'd be family-oriented." They don't seem to have discussed these issues before they were married. "I was dead wrong," says Michael.

The full expressiveness of Theresa's shrine is unexpected testimony to her inner life. Upon meeting her, Theresa is shy and withdrawn, hardly able to speak it seems. Very quietly, very gently, it is actually easy to make friends with her, and then Theresa is full of whispered confidences. "My mother doesn't make my bed,"

Theresa says, "I do." She is fond of cats. She doesn't mind brushing her long, long hair everyday. "My mother wants me to keep it," she says. Would she cut it otherwise? Theresa is somehow struck by the question. She looks down, and a wave of remote silence follows.

Although she is obviously bright, adept at drawing, and a good reader, Theresa was held back a year at the elite private school she attends. A learning specialist and a child psychologist were called in. "She has a short attention span," Michael says. "They told me to keep the divorce stuff away from her. It's like she has something else on her mind, and she shouldn't."

3

How Divorce Affects Your Child's Development and How to Support Your Child's Healthy Growth Over Time

What Is Development?

ALL OF US with children marvel at the moment when suddenly a toddler can pronounce "elephant" instead of "eh-funt." Or when a six-year-old says, "Mommy, you're prejudging." Both language acquisitions and conceptual leaps are related to actual physiological changes that occur in a growing child. Child development is definitely a science—experts have mapped out time periods in which a child's brain becomes capable of something more than it has been before. Children crawl, walk, talk, and toilet train at their own rate and according to their gender. Trying to get them to do these things before they're ready just adds tension and expectations where there should be none. Reading is another one of those brain-switch moments—you can make a child memorize the alphabet, but you can't train a child to read with comprehension. Some kids are going to do it at age four and others at age seven. It's important to support reading as an activity from very early on, but not to actually expect the child to read. Sensitivity to the child's ability within a normal range makes development a bit of an art—and that's where you come in.

Developmental changes are not just neurons firing, they also present opportunities for new learning. There are some key times when a child is able to comprehend new information and make it part of her purview. Development can be looked at as a series of attainments, but it is also a series of gateways, further opening the child to the world and her place in it. The process is flexible and gradual—it represents a measured transformation of the past to the present. While it is useful to look at development as a series of building blocks adding onto one another to create a whole self, it is important to know that if a piece is missed, there is always the chance for repair or replacement later.

One important reason to have an understanding of development is that your child is a living, growing being—where she is today is not where she'll be tomorrow. It helps when confronted by mystifying and difficult behavior to have a sense of what your child's developmental task is at the moment. "My seven-year-old seemed to become afraid of everything," says one father who became concerned that his co-parent's late-night lifestyle was somehow disrupting his son's sense of safety. "I mean, his mother works late and then always goes out to dinner. So a babysitter is putting my kid to bed. No wonder he doesn't feel okay!" This man has a fairly equable relationship with his co-parent, and she disagreed that their son was upset because his sitter puts him to bed. "She's the same nanny he's had since he was an infant—she's like another mother to him."

Seven-year-olds are making some enormous leaps in their understanding—it's roughly the age where children realize the world is not just about them. This can be pretty disquieting—there's a universe of stuff to now look at and try to understand. Younger children experience the world as coming to them and now they are beginning to understand that they have to move out into the world to interact with it. The imagination of the seven-year-old is also growing—along with wonderful creativity, fears can be activated as well, and nightmares are not uncommon.

This father talked to his child's teacher and read some childhood development books. It put his son's behavior in perspective. "I could cool my jets when I understood this was a natural thing he was going through and not related to his mother or to the divorce necessarily. And when I relaxed about it and accepted his fears, my son seemed to make some progress with them too."

On the other hand, divorce does present a particular kind of disruption to your child's life. That's not the end of the world if you are aware of it and handle the situation mindfully. Divorce is experienced as loss, and a certain amount of energy the child would be using to achieve developmental milestones is going to be diverted to grief, and to coping. The time your child spends making initial adjustments isn't time lost, however, if you can be there to give her a leg up when she's ready to refocus. Most children are able to get back on track with where they were going.

Where a child is developmentally when you separate or divorce is going to affect how she reacts to the divorce. An infant is going to respond on a survival level and a toddler might exaggerate the separation anxieties she's already having; a school-age child will try to get you back together and may disbelieve the divorce is really happening; an eleven-year-old on the verge of adolescence may try to substitute the pursuit of perfection for the anxiety he's feeling; and a full-blown teenager may start to break all rules everywhere. It's important to understand the developmental framework so you can gain some insight into where your child is and where she is going when you divorce. For every parent, a developmental understanding of the childhood journey is a key support in the project of helping kids realize their full potential.

It is also critical to understand that your child will review her experience of your divorce at every major developmental milestone she goes through. So if your five-year-old sails through the divorce with no perceivable fallout, you are not home free. Now, don't groan that this divorce is a huge boulder you have to carry through every change your child goes through. Just be aware that issues relating to trust, loyalty, intimacy, and commitment are likely to come up again and again. Keep in mind that when your child seems to be having a turbulent time with relationships later on, you might have a word with her about your divorce, and acknowledge all over again that this was a difficult loss and maybe she'd like to talk about it. One woman was very concerned that her thirty-year-old son, who had been living with his girlfriend for five years, was phobic about getting married. Her co-parent had become a very absent father once their divorce was finalized. "I said to my son, 'Don't let this girl go because your father let you go.' I don't really know how he took that, but just bringing up the subject seemed to do him some good."

The Unwritten Rules of Childhood Feel Broken

Children lose something fundamental to their development when a divorce occurs: the family structure. Even if you keep things consistent (which is really important), and even if you keep your child's contact with both parents a priority (also critical), the world the child has known is gone. The external breakdown of the family is going to be experienced by children as an internal event, and depending on what developmental stage they are at during this time, they are going to take a hit there. This can be healed by time and attention.

Children are on a continuum of development—from adjustment to maladjustment. Rather than label or even pathologize children (does every single boy out there have attention deficit disorder?), what you want to do is identify areas of concern. Kids are going to regress for all sorts of normal reasons. Many parents have seen an older child regress when a younger sibling makes a new attainment, like walking or talking. In that case the older child feels threatened, but with support can expand her view of herself to tolerate the competition. She can learn over time that her self-worth is a constant thing and doesn't depend on her brother or sister being less or more immature than she is. The level of regression and how long it lasts is more to the point of concern and if it is too disruptive or prolonged, that's a clue that the child's inner security system is not bouncing back.

Remember that developmental tasks are more beginnings than endings. The project of becoming a person is ongoing, and when something doesn't get done right the first time, there's opportunity for catching up later. Children are amazing and most will find the good in a situation.

The family is like a building foundation and frame. The child is developing from infancy to adulthood supported by this foundation and along the lines of this frame. The marriage itself has been a strong part of this structure, not only providing guideposts but also maintaining the fact that the mom and dad are the grownups, the authority figures who set rules and negotiate with the outside world. Kids are not only going to grieve the loss of the family as they have known it, they are going to be angry, too. They have an implicit understanding that parents are supposed to make sacrifices for their children—not the other way around. Anger is a difficult emotion and some kids will hide theirs for years for fear of upsetting their parents or getting punished for their feelings. The best thing for you to do for a grieving child is hear her out, give her space, allow her room to have those difficult feelings. Angry feelings need to be acknowledged and allowed also, but you have to provide an appropriate venue for them. Punching pillows is a great one and so is screaming in the car on the freeway (unless this is going to get you, the driver, in an accident). With anger goes a sense of frustration, powerlessness. The child has no say in this event, and his impotence in this matter can extend to other areas of his self-concept.

Just saying, "I know this is hard for you and not how you want things to be," can help a lot—you are treating your child with respect, and she will feel that.

The divorce reshuffles the way things are supposed to be for a while. Kids want rules, and they don't want to make them. Many of the impulses a child has organized into productive play or in participating with the other family members at mealtime get sprung out of their box. The family structure has also been a control on the harder-to-handle impulses children have (and don't we all). Again, the reference point is the child's inner security system. When they are insecure, children will compensate. Some will become like adults themselves, providing reassurance in a false way, since they are essentially trying to elicit what they really want from an adult source. This is a "mature" child but one in danger of sacrificing her own developmental path to skip straight to the adult stage. The pain comes later. Other kids will respond at the other end of the spectrum. They will cease to respect any rules. Doing so will also get them a lot of attention at a time when the focus has moved very far away from them.

The child's response can last for a few months to several years. It can also last a lifetime. It's important to note that there's a difference between a child experiencing pain and a child reacting with total dysfunction. As with all dimensions of parenting, you have to make an ongoing judgment call about where your child is on the spectrum—if she's experiencing too much pain, if she can't handle it, or if she is able to cope. Again, there's an immediate response to the divorce and a long-term response, and as a parent, you have to keep both in mind. You can help with the whole trajectory by reestablishing a regular schedule and comforting home parameters.

You can see that both for the overcompensator and the rebel, it is important that you set firm rules. There will naturally be a transition period as a new set of rules is established in each household. Along the way, be sure to spend one-on-one time with your children. It will help ground them, keep them connected. As long as children feel alone and frightened, they will find some outlet for their distress. Their reaction may be hidden—they may squash something in themselves in order to get by.

Custody and Visitation Decisions Should Be Influenced by Development

Developmental considerations are absolutely critical when deciding about custody and visitation. Children have different needs at different ages, and knowing what these are can help make both their lives and your life easier—more in sync with what's going on for them. You want to figure out what's best for now and what might change down the road. What your one-year-old needs at this moment is going to change when the child is ready for school. And will change again when your child becomes a teen.

Below are some of the key elements of development. Basically, you want to get a sense of the parameters of the task: development is the process of building a self. All of the key points in this task are highly influenced by your interaction with your children—their relationship with you is how they explore the world. Following this discussion is a break-down by age of what kids are going through developmentally in several broad age categories: infancy to three; four to seven; eight to eleven; and twelve to young adult.

Supporting Healthy Development

1. **Keep the home fires burning.** Provide a warm, safe, comfortable environment for your child and keep your routines consistent.

2. **Pay attention to "a-ha" moments.** These are opportunities, when your child is relaxed and interested in something, or when she asks you a question. Educators call these "teachable" moments, and your child is showing a readiness to learn something.

3. **Rather than tell, tell, tell, ask questions.** With teenagers, this is paramount. There's a very important distinction to be made, however, about what kinds of questions you ask. Teenagers hate to be cross-examined. You want to ask their opinions of things, not ask them what they did today. Communication is much more about listening than talking. Show genuine interest. Even with younger kids, asking questions invites their participation in their own learning, which increases their buy-in and establishes an excellent habit of taking an active role.

4. **Be careful about failure.** Kids want to succeed, they want to please you. At certain points they will want to give up activities they feel they aren't good at—chess, for example, or ballet. Of course it's okay to let some of these things go, but be careful to emphasize participation and enjoyment over winning or being the best. Life gets too narrow too quickly when we only pursue activities in our comfort zone.

5. **Try, try again.** Show your child you are willing to learn too. When you make a perfectly inedible pie crust, laugh and start over. Completing even one project around the house (easier said than done!) will show your own willingness to follow through. Your children will internalize this as the way to be.

6. **Take a straightforward and relaxed approach to body issues.** Bodily functions and changes are part of nature and kids need to be in a good relationship with their own, not clouded over with embarrassment or false ideas.

7. **Protect kids from excess stimulation.** This is a necessity in our day and age, when kids are utterly barraged by sights and sounds

most of which are intended for adults. Kids are naturally in tune with themselves in a way we have lost, partly because we respond so continually to the outside world—we forget how to follow inner promptings. Allow children the space to respond to their own spontaneous ideas and impulses—these are partly developmental imperatives. A three-year-old boy, for example, may want to run around in a cape. He's not only imitating cartoon characters, he's acting out a "magical-thinking" part of his development. Satisfying it, he can move on to the next developmental prompting.

8. **Keep play toys simple.** One really loud mechanical gizmo is more than enough. Kids are naturally creative and you can help stimulate their imaginations by giving them more mental room to build with rather than more stuff.

9. **Keep television time to a minimum and be aware of what they're watching.** Especially the commercials need some adult explanation, if only: remember, someone is trying to get you to buy something here. It's more important to teach your kids to observe and to think twice than it is to prevent them from seeing what they are going to see anyway.

10. **Problem-solve and brainstorm when things get rough.** Sometimes the "solution" isn't to be found and kids just need to be supported and heard. When you are the bearer of bad news, give them some power in the situation. Allow them to make as many decisions for themselves as can reasonably be accommodated, without going overboard and giving them all the control.

What Is the Self?

You can see very young children get fixated on their image in the mirror. They are utterly enchanted by the idea: that is *me*. Philosophers continue to puzzle over exactly what the self is, so it's no wonder your toddler laughs delightedly at himself reflected there. What a mysterious, wonderful thing. And that image is the outline of the vehicle for the child's experience of the world, the place where she takes everything in, the means by which she expresses inner compunctions and desires. Until they are around four, children don't really understand the idea that other people have a point of view. (Of course we all know and have to deal with adults who seem to cling to the toddler's self-absorption. Many of these adults did not get to fully experience their feeling of "me" when they were children, and this infantile need searches in vain for satisfaction in the adult world—which is a good example of how a developmental disruption can have persistent effects throughout life.) Children are self-centered, but they're supposed to be. They have to solidify this vehicle of theirs, and that's what development is all about.

One reason for discussing development at length is that this seed of a person reflected back in the two-year-old's reflection is ever-present. Even you, right now, wizened and weary, still operate from a fundamental self that has been yours from the get-go. It's one of the reasons early childhood intervention and education are so paramount—because what happens now for a child does have future effects.

Childhood is about developing and maintaining a sense of self. Children have a very wide range of similarities and differences, and they are engaged in expressing their individuality. Most of having a healthy grip on oneself is gained through positive relationships with the world around the child. What are the rules at home, in school? One child's mother says, "Our family rule is: shoes stay on in the playground." The child says, "But Emily took hers off!" The mother says, "Our rule is that they stay on." Despite the disappointment in the barefoot department, there is something reassuring and focusing to the child about *our* family rule." As adults we take it for granted that we understand that everybody's family is different, that there are different rules and situations. Orienting the child to the world is a big part of being a parent.

When a child is really obstreperous and commits some very disruptive act, you can be sure she is trying to assert herself, to be somebody. Kids will try to be somebody in a negative way if positive venues aren't open to them, or if they feel constantly like a failure. Part of what is challenging about a kid who acts out all the time is that it's hard to interrupt the cycle and find something positive to respond to in the child's behavior. Children are in a constant dialogue with you and with the rest of the world about who they are, discovering themselves; if the dialogue isn't positive, it's going to be negative. The child won't rest until she's responded to, which is why, even when you are dead tired and want to sit alone in a dark room, you will actually do yourself a favor by connecting with a child who wants your connection. If you just bark from the next room to keep it down, it's likely that the behavior will escalate until you actually get up and interact with the child directly. A moment of positive, one-on-one acknowledgment can save an hour of frustration.

As mentioned earlier, society has only recently become widely aware that children are people, too. Just how much full agency a child has is still under discussion—look at legislative battles over prosecuting minors as adults. Whatever your opinion about the responsibility children may or may not have, they definitely do observe, mimic, take it all in. What goes on in childhood most assuredly matters. Even if we say, "Ralph is more physical and Joey is good with his hands," we view these as sort of charming attributes of people in waiting—waiting to grow up, to see if Ralph's current facility turns him into an athlete or a sports medicine physician.

Divorce and Self-Image

THE YOUNG CHILD'S developing self is a delicate thing and can be hurt easily, but it is also an elastic thing and can be repaired. Divorce is often felt as an assault on adult self-image: you may feel rejected or like a failure. It's hard to keep these vulnerable feelings separate from your kids, who constantly take cues from you. Kids can feel out-of-it with their peers from families that have not undergone the same kind of change. When they aren't feeling strong among friends, the ordinary slings and arrows of play can be felt much harder. A downward spiral of low self-esteem can result. A divorce workshop or group for your kids can help them connect with other kids who have gone through what they have. Schools can put you in touch with such programs, as can community centers and churches. Kids of most ages will also experience the divorce as their fault, and they can feel that a piece of themselves is bad, has ruined everything. This requires constant reassurance that the divorce is not the child's fault. Kids also experience divorce as an internal event—two parts of themselves have gone asunder. This requires patience and time to heal, as well as continued contact with both parents. A healthy self-image is fundamentally based on being recognized truly—when a child does something positive, makes a real leap, you notice it, you remark positively on it. Constantly praising a child doesn't do the trick, because after a while they understand that you aren't differentiating one set of their actions from another. Notice their real accomplishments.

We know that what we see now in a child will undergo change. This makes it even more paramount to be sensitive to the oblique ways children are responding to themselves and the world—nonverbally, below the surface, through play. Children are sponges, and they absorb tone, habits of optimism or negativity. Young children have no way of differentiating outer events from inner reality. Dreams and fears alike cross the boundary. Your job is to be the adult, to be reassuring, and it is critical. If your child sees you falling apart or terrified, she's not going to know how to cope with it, or where to place it in her mental model of what the world is all about. She's going to get a vague, persistent feeling of fear or dread and she's going to store it away. Again, the seeds of adult anxiety are often planted in such childhood moments.

Attachment Is the Key Overarching Concept in Developing a Healthy Self

So we have the child's self—a unique, discrete identity starting out on its path toward maturity. It is very important to view your child as having a significant individuality, to understand your child's need to be self-focused—indeed, her inability to be anything but—and the subjective, often wordless way she takes in everything around her. It is equally important to understand that the health and potential of this self do not stand alone. All human beings have a fundamental need from infancy to have at least one primary relationship with another person to depend on—ideally a positive one.

Psychologists call this "attachment." The attachment relationship is the main vehicle through which parents teach their children how to adapt to the world, respecting their own biological needs and the desires of their personality in balance with what society expects. Temperament, emotions, intellectual abilities—all the various attributes making up a personality are moderated, balanced, and focused through the attachment relationship.

That the child needs healthy attachment relationships through divorce is widely understood by the courts. It's why for many years the mother almost always got custody of the children. There's an increased recognition that the child needs multiple attachment relationships. There's also much more cognizance of the need for the father to stay in the picture. Healthy attachment to the mother is important, but the relationship with the father turns out to be more critical than previously supposed. Research has also shown that, depending on their temperaments, many children can tolerate being separated from the primary caregiver, the person with whom they live most of the time, for longer periods of time, or more frequently.

Attaching to at least one other human being in a healthy way provides a constant feedback loop for the child—the information back is: I am a fundamentally good being in this world, and I feel good. As the child gets older, this consistent responsiveness helps her understand that who she is today is who she was yesterday and who she'll be tomorrow. In other words, it allows her to not have to reinvent herself every minute, but to rely on a solid base without thinking about it. This relationship helps her feel like the world is a good place too, full of opportunities to play and learn and interact. This attachment relationship is internalized, so the child can comfort herself during separation from the family. It's based on the feeling of being valued and loved. It fuels a positive attitude toward the outside world.

The Perfect Is the Enemy of the Good

An element of this feedback loop of the attachment relationship is called "mirroring." Children need admiring mirroring from their parents, but not excessive praise. As with so much parenting, discretion and balance are required here. When your child does something like paint a pot, you praise it. It's more effective for your child if you praise the effort, noticing some of the details, rather than give an overall: that's great. You want to encourage their process over their results, so that they will do the same. One common trap to avoid is the overcorrection impulse. When a child shows you a letter she wrote, you might correct the spelling—leave that to the teachers at school. When she sets the table for dinner, you might go around refolding the napkins. While you do want to require a certain level of effort—you don't want to accept the child just throwing the napkins on the table—if she's tried, then it's best to accept the job as done. The message is that she is an important contributor to the family life. If you constantly correct she will get the message that she doesn't please you, or that she isn't competent.

A child who feels mostly bad about not pleasing her parents may compensate with a strong desire to be perfect. The impulse toward perfection is something of an escape hatch—feeling uncomfortable, the child retreats to a fantasy world where everything is under control. Every effort you make to positively connect with your child, to give positive mirroring, will be stored up in the child's savings bank of self-esteem. When the child does fail or is faced with some unpleasant turn of events, that savings of esteem will help her accept it, cope, and try again, rather than escape to a fantasy of control.

It's natural to long for control, and indeed can be a powerful motivator toward any variety of achievement and success. But a more balanced view should be at the heart of the child's self-concept. The child further knows that everything she does is not, in fact, so good. It's important to be honest about transgressions, to point out certain mistakes. Respect your child, even when you are disciplining her—she will understand the essential esteem at the base of the interaction, and that esteem will help her deal with her troubles.

Children Use Defense Mechanisms Too

The whole perfectionism thing is essentially a defense mechanism—in general, the child feels too much stress to tolerate it and finds a better state of mind for herself (better in the very short run—not so good in the long run). What happens to the bad feelings she's covering up is that she represses them—pushes them away to where she doesn't think about them consciously. Of course you can't get rid of feelings this way. The trouble with pushing the feeling into the unconscious is that it gets merged with the world of fears and dreams and magic, the land of no-time, no rationality. The unconscious is also a wonderful place where originality percolates and ideas spring up to deal creatively with problematic situations. But when a piece of information is lodged in the unconscious, it's really hard to connect with it again, to bring it to the surface. Those buried feelings will influence the child but it won't be clear what's prompting her.

Moreover, it takes a certain amount of energy to repress feelings, and this energy isn't being used to master those developmental milestones. Again, all is not lost when a child is repressing something. In a safe environment, with a supportive and trustworthy person, the child can grow to tolerate those awful feelings in balance with positive feedback. When the child can stand the feelings, when she can name them, she can take in new information about them (like, "my mother was sad but not because I'm bad"), and then she can move on from them.

And Kids Have Control Issues

Who has what control over what is a balancing act for you and your children. Obviously, you have to be in control always of many important facets of their life, like the car and the stove. It's very important, however, that children develop a sense that they can function independently and responsibly. It's a good idea to really pick the scenes where you must keep control, and try to hand over as much choice and free will as possible to your children, within their capacity. Trying to do things just a bit beyond their abilities is how they learn. This attitude of allowance does mean putting up with a mess, if you're letting your child mix cookie batter, for example. It's well worth the extra trouble to clean up, or the extra time that has to be built in to whatever project you're undertaking.

If you are overcontrolling and constantly interrupt your child's desire to do something and fulfill a task, the child will learn that it is not pleasurable at all to be assertive. With healthy respect for others and for authority, you want your child to have a healthy sense of internal control. You want your child to feel that her ideas are good ones and to get the satisfaction from following through on them. Give your child plenty of opportunity to have control, especially during a divorce, where the whole thing is out of her control and she is having to adapt to the agendas of others.

"My daughter was telling me she did not want to see her father anymore," one woman said of her nine-year-old. "She said, 'I only want to be with you, Mommy,' and because I needed to feel loved, and because I was so mad at her father, I really got stuck on this idea that she wanted to be with me, so she should be with me." This woman's co-parent was not so happy to hear about this. The nine-year-old girl had a six-year-old brother, and he had no problem with seeing his father. "Some part of me knew it really was that she hated the drive to his house, because it takes two hours, and she gets car-sick," the woman said. It took a mediator to point out to the mother that she needed to put her feelings about her former husband aside and to recognize that it was more important for the girl to continue her relationship with her father than it was for her to avoid car sickness. "But we had this power struggle for several months, where I had let my daughter think that because she wanted something, she was going to get it." In many, many divorce scenarios, kids wind up getting to exercise control where they really shouldn't be able to.

"I had to tell her I had made a mistake, and that she had to do the visitation our way, not her way. So I made it up to her by allowing her to paint her room a new color, which she chose." The girl's father also told her point-blank that he was sorry she had to travel so far to see him, but that he thought the world of her and wanted to make her stays with him more comfortable for her. Together, they decided she could rearrange the room she stayed in at his house to feel more like hers. The girl also piped up with her own solution to the car ride, which was travel-sickness pills. Many of us don't realize that just addressing the children directly helps them work out their issues. It's more important that they participate in the process of addressing their needs and less important that they get what they originally wanted.

Little, daily ways of giving your kids control really help when it comes to the big issues. So if your daughter wants to go to one playground and not to another, and a change in plans is doable and not terribly disruptive, you let her call that shot. She grows to feel powerful in relationships in general. Of course we've all seen this go haywire, in households where the kids seem to be calling ALL the shots. Or every time your son says he doesn't want to go to T-ball practice, you cave. Too much outer control is no good either, and disrupts the child's sense of himself in the wider world. Remember, you're preparing him for relationships other than with yourself.

It should be mentioned that it is a common issue for moms in general to feel guilty about the divorce and to frequently give in to their kids. (Dads tend to fall on the other side of the fence, and have more trouble with listening and empathizing.) So, if you are one of those moms, don't be afraid to set limits. You aren't depriving your kids, you're helping them through a transition.

Some kids, especially faced with parents who are continually falling apart or not functioning well as adults, adapt "too well." This is the child who reminds her father to get his hair cut, decides what everyone is having for dinner, and puts her younger siblings to bed. What's wrong is that all her energy is going to making the external world work; she's not spending time and energy on her internal development.

High Conflict Can Affect Development

A CHILD'S MENTAL, emotional, and physical growth all take energy. If you are in a high-conflict situation with your former spouse, you will have to take extra measures to shield your children. Kids who are scared all the time are not growing—they are using all their energy to survive. You may feel, hey, that's ridiculous, we yell at each other, not at the kids, but that is not how your kids experience it. Your roadblocks become their roadblocks. Keep your child's exposure to conflict as low as possible. Be realistic about what happens when you are in contact with your co-parent—if the interaction is always stressful, do it when your kids are not around.

Other Relationship and Self-Image Issues

If there is a healthy, relaxed connection between child and parent, the relationship is likely to be productive. Both parent and child respond to each other, allow themselves to be influenced by each other. The parent listens and responds to the child as much as the child does to the parent. This is easier for both parents and kids when there's a natural fit between their temperaments. If you love hiking and rock climbing and your kids do too, there's no problem—we know what we're doing this Saturday, and we're all looking forward to it. Sometimes parents and kids who have opposite kinds of temperaments still mesh well. Your bookworm child loves going to the pool with you while you do your laps, because she can sit there and read uninterrupted for an hour. Just don't ask her to take a swim.

A poor fit between child and parent can make both suffer, but particularly the child, who is forming herself in relationship to you. If your daughter learns that her needs are not acceptable to you, or that your needs are more important than hers, she will try to suppress herself. What you can end up with is a kid who doesn't want to swim, but does it because you insist. She doesn't swim well; she feels like a failure. If you could respond better to her, and let her read instead, you encourage her natural inclinations and she will be able to use them to succeed—perhaps academically. Of course this is another area full of judgment calls (aren't they all?). If you have an overall understanding of your daughter as a bookish couch potato, and you really want her to have some physical activity in her life, it's perfectly reasonable to insist that she choose at least one sport to pursue. That's called balancing her life. If she senses your support of her in general, she'll be more apt to give it a try.

Here is one of the developmental rubs of divorce. Keeping the attachment relationship with you going is at the heart of survival for the child, and she will sacrifice herself to do it. If you find yourself slipping into a needy, childish role with your own child, it's a sign that you need more help than you're getting. Parents need to give more emotionally to their child, to be more responsive to the child—the relationship is unequal in this way, because the child does not have a fully formed self as yet. Later in life, when the child is an adult, there is more equality, and it is more appropriate to ask for a more equal investment of effort.

Growing an Independent "True" Self

Paradoxically, the twin needs to have healthy attachment relationships and to be independent go hand in hand. Children need autonomy—hang out with a two-year-old for ten seconds and you'll see how strong that drive is. But the next second the child is looking for Mommy's or Daddy's hand—

it's a constant back and forth between attaching, and separating. Children develop a self in relationship, and this relational aspect of emotional life turns out to be just about the most important element to mental health.

The primary drama of the infant/toddler, which is to learn to experience herself as an independent entity with a secure base, and which can be described in terms of oneness and separateness, continues as the child develops. People have a tremendous drive to be accepted and to be safe, so a child will do practically anything to insure these things for herself. The tasks of growing children are to adapt themselves to others—to get along with the people who have important places in their life—and also to assert the independence which is part of a healthy self, and from which a person operates at maximum potential in the world.

The question of how much a child should learn to obey and conform and how much a child should learn to be independent and to take risks is answered differently by different cultures. One Caucasian boy who went to school with other children who were mostly Asian would not let his mother put two phone numbers on the "phone tree" set up by his teacher to give the parents in the class a way of communicating effectively with each other. "Two phone numbers meant his parents were divorced," his mother explained. "And among the kids he goes to school with, divorce is just not part of their lives. They don't even know what it is." Not only divorce, but also many other iterations of individual assertion are often discouraged by cultures that place the family structure above all else.

But by and large, in the United States—melting pot that we are—we do emphasize individual freedom above other sets of values. Success in our society is more often based on the ability to innovate and to be independent, to be entrepreneurial, than it is in other cultures. And to be individually strong, we have to be able to access our true strengths. As reflective adults, we can look back and understand how we adapted ourselves to other's expectations and needs many times at the expense of what would be best for ourselves. Yet our children are in danger of doing this for us as well.

A psychologist once explained her profession to a skeptical listener. "You go to a trained professional, and you tell them about yourself. Much of what you believe about yourself was taught to you by your parents. If you're running into trouble, it's likely that some of that information they gave you doesn't really work for you—maybe what they were saying had a lot more to do with who *they* are and less to do with who *you* are. The therapist gives you some more useful information about yourself." She perfectly describes the therapist's role as "mirror" for the self, usually a corrective mirror after we've carried around a distorted view of ourselves for too long. As a parent, you are the original mirror for your child.

Another consideration in the relationship drama is how much to protect your child. Too much protection and the child gets the idea that any autonomy will threaten the parental relationship. In other words, if the child ever steps away from the parent, she'll never get back, she will have no protection at all. An overprotective parent is usually in fact overdependent on the child. When an adult doesn't feel too good about who she is on her own, a child can seem to fill in the blanks. Paradoxically, this parent gives the child the overt message that the child can't survive without her; actually, it is the parent who is leaning on the child to get through the workaday world. Particularly when adults feels lousy about being divorced, they can compensate by being an over-involved parent. The opposite of course is also true—a parent can reject the role completely and jettison the whole family concept along with the marriage. These are all examples of how developmental issues are impacted by divorce.

Some children may present themselves as utterly independent—not needing you, anyway, thank you very much. A child who emphasizes being autonomous may be rejecting his own need for connection because his parents treat this need with distance or even contempt. The recent (and excellent) books on raising boys all emphasize our society's tendency to push boys to separate from their parents too young, to not be "attached," and connect this habit with the widespread unhappiness of boys and their tendency to violence. Children are malleable and will do what's required of them, even if it means being more independent than they're ready for. But such a child will hit a roadblock later. A child who doesn't have those "warm fuzzy" feelings of attachment to draw on will have trouble with intimacy later— because he won't know what it is.

If your child seems to be rejecting *you*, don't be fooled. Again, children do have an innate need for independence, and one way to assert that need is to say "NO!" to the parent—witness the two-year-old again, who has a fit because she wants to go down an enormous slide by herself and you won't let her. But if the behavior is persistent, and the child is older than a toddler, it may be that she in fact feels insecure in her attachment to you. Children are dependent on us and they know this in the cells of their bodies even when they are acting in ways we might call obstreperous or ungrateful or oppositional. A child who is fighting you every step of the way may be trying to negotiate a different relationship with you—but it does not mean the child thinks she'd be better off without you.

Listen to your child. Spend one-on-one time with her and try to follow all her cues rather than providing them yourself. Do things her way for a whole hour (that's much harder than it sounds). Get past the usual humps even if that means letting some bad behavior go for a little while. Take the high road, and try to figure out what's going on beyond the conflict. It takes time and patience to do this but saves much more time in the long run.

Kids Need to Be Kids:
Play and Pleasure Are a Part of Healthy Development

Sometimes it's hard for adults to take children's play seriously. In the Maria Montessori system, children's activities are referred to as "work," even though someone else might call what they're doing play. Montessori, like many other childhood education pioneers, recognized the importance of what children are doing with crayons and blocks, and rightly connected these activities with the adult version we get paid to do much later. Children's play is a kind of industry in service of a goal.

Children have three primary forces driving their activities: their body, their developing self, and the social world at large. Play is critical in helping children integrate these three areas: physically, they learn to focus and direct their energy; they learn to express the unique promptings of their burgeoning "I"; and they learn to get along with others. Moreover, these different processes go on at their own rate, and play helps children reconcile where they are with all three at any one time. In play, the physical, the social, and the individual come together.

Children need to spend some time initiating and completing their play without adult involvement—unless something dangerous is about to happen, of course. When you're spending a fair amount of time with kids it does help for you to present them with new choices of play—as long as you are operating as the helper of the play and not the master of ceremonies. For smaller kids, you might say, "Here, try your blocks" when a windup toy has ceased to amuse; for older ones, you might say, "How about drawing a picture?" But you should let them choose the offered activity or not choose it—don't push. It creates anxiety for kids to have to perform their playing for us and defeats the purpose of their play. They are trying to develop mastery and when we push them we take over an important executive function. To initiate is a great skill kids developmentally want to obtain. If they don't get to initiate, it makes them anxious and passive. This is a consideration to be taken moderately, of course. Sometimes you have to say, "Well, you can color or you can use the clay and these are your choices." Those are normal boundaries and without them we would all be a little less sane. But if a child is in the midst of an activity, don't interrupt unless you have to. Discretion again is necessary, and the balance to be sought is between freedom for the child and learning to abide by social considerations.

When children are playing they are creating model situations, they are experimenting, they are planning. These are all activities necessary to dealing with experience in a useful way. A creative attitude toward life gets its start in the spontaneous play of childhood. Children will move from one thing to the next—they are driven to try something new, because the emphasis is on new information, new learning. Remember this the next time you're in a mega toy store and your child wants this, that, this, and that. Toy-makers know full well how to capitalize on the allure of the new. Which lasts, oh, until you get to the car. Maybe longer, maybe till after dinner.

It's common in a divorce to forget to have fun. But pleasure is important to kids. It reassures them, it helps create a positive ground for their growth. Pleasure is also associated with learning. When a child is happy, pleased, relaxed, she's open to new things, can tackle a new concept.

Temperamental Characteristics of Children and How They Influence Custody and Visitation

What's a temperament, and why is it important in custody decisions? Temperament is basically the overall way your baby is oriented to the world, whether she's jumpy or mellow, needs more reassurance or approaches new situations easily. We all have a temperament—when we talk about "type A" people that's one way of looking at it. Temperament is biologically based and is evident from the very beginning of a baby's life.

By assessing your baby's temperament, you can build a schedule that works better for her, creating less disruption and acknowledging her needs. Remember, what works best for your baby works best for you, too. If your child has difficulty making transitions, you'll likely encounter tears, tantrums, and plenty of stress if you ask the child to make them too often. By responding to your child's temperament, you make her life more comfortable. When a child's life is more comfortable, she can spend her energy on attaining the developmental milestones appropriate for her age, she can learn and grow with greater ease.

Children whose circumstances challenge their emotions are constantly struggling with themselves. Say you have a two-year-old who shies away from strangers, who doesn't want to join her peers on the playground until she's had plenty of time to warm up to them, and who gets overtired and hysterical if she doesn't eat at pretty much the same times each day. This kid is going to be burdened if you have her going to her father's on Thursday nights, returning back to her mom's on Friday mornings, then spending the weekend every other week with dad. She's going to spend so much energy adjusting and readjusting to the changing environment, she's not going to have enough time to relax and play. Moreover, she's going to cry and scream and drive you crazy, so that your time with her is stressed. This child would do better to have an extremely regular visitation schedule, so that every Tuesday she goes to the same play group with the same parent, and every Saturday morning she goes to the aquarium or on an outing with the other parent.

On the other hand, you could easily have a very adaptable, low-key child who isn't bothered at all by changed venues. This child says, OK, here I am, let's have a go at it. This child makes the transition between caregivers easily. So if the mom works in sales, and has an erratic travel schedule, and the dad is a nine-to-fiver with a fixed routine, this child is fine with going to mom's for odd and varying lengths of time.

A couple of things to keep in mind: temperament is not bad or good. As mentioned, we all have temperaments. While the mellow, easygoing kind sounds really heavenly, most children are going to have areas where they are less flexible and more uptight. If you have a high-strung child, that's a particular challenge. But you can, and should, approach it positively. "Spirited" children often grow up into interesting, innovative adults, especially if their caregivers have responded to them with sensitivity and encouragement. Regardless of what the temperament of your child is, the more you adjust to the way the child is the happier both of you will be. This goes back to the "goodness of fit" issue describing the match between caregiver and child in the matter of personal style. There's no doubt that if you are an athletic, high-physical-energy person, it's going to be relatively easy and gratifying for you if your kids are too. But if you happen to have a shy bookworm type, what a pleasure to observe the different way this child approaches the world—you can learn something from her. And if the opposite maintains, and you want to sit quietly reading while your child wants to play ball standing on her head twirling a baton, take that with some humor also. Maybe you want to run that child ragged on the playground before going home to dinner, so that the house stays in one piece along with the state of your mind.

Temperament + Development + Situation = Behavior

THIS WHOLE AREA touches on behavior—when you stop to evaluate your child's temperament, you're going to be asking questions about how the child behaves. If you have a six-year-old who cannot complete a task because she is such a perfectionist, and who demands more time and attention from you than your other kids, and if you hear from her teachers that she has a hard time moving from one activity to the next, part of this is likely due to her temperament. Part of it, however, is a style of behavior she's employing to get a particular kind of attention. What she needs depends not only on who she fundamentally is, but also what is going on in the moment for her. In chapter 6, different behaviors, their underlying causes, and how to approach them are discussed more fully. Use your sense of your child's temperament to help you judge what's really going on and how best to help her through it.

Temperament and healthy development go hand in hand. Children grow best when they are comfortable and presented with challenges within the range of their abilities. And be advised, your child's temperament can definitely change over time.

With an infant or baby, there are basically two aspects of temperament that are most relevant to assess. You want to look at "approach-withdrawal," which is whether it is easy or difficult for a child to enter a new situation, and "adaptability," which is her ability to be relaxed when the setting or the caregivers have changed. If your child withdraws from any new situation, you can anticipate she's going to have a harder time with your separation than a child who is more easygoing. When you pick your baby up from your former spouse, and she kicks and screams, it is not that she's rejecting you. Rather, this child needs more help in making the adjustment from one caregiver to another. This baby probably needs fewer, longer visits with the non-custodial parent, whereas a baby who can pretty much fall asleep in a strange room given her blankie and a pat on the butt can probably tolerate shorter, more frequent visits. Although there are nine scales of temperament, in general you can look at three broad types to figure out what kind of child you have.

Easy, flexible children are biologically predictable and regular—they want a bottle of milk at the same time every day, and you are fairly certain that you'll be changing a poopy diaper at roughly the same time every day. This child adapts easily to change, and her mood is mild, mostly positive. This child doesn't ask for it much, but deserves special attention sometimes, too. Check in regularly with this child and make sure she gets special time with you.

A *difficult, feisty* child has intense, mostly negative moods. She is biologically unpredictable, withdraws from most new situations, and makes changes very slowly. Especially when this child is a toddler, approach her negative behavior by redirecting her energies. She's not going to understand a time-out. Even the word "no" is an abstraction. You do want to put firm limits on unacceptable behavior, so if she throws sand in the playground, remove her from the play area immediately so she gets the picture. While this child can be very challenging in the moments of "bad" behavior, she'll benefit mightily from a lot of physical reassurance from you, and from time spent building her relationship with you. Most toddlers need stimulation during part of the day and quiet time during another part of the day—try to read this child's mood and give her what she needs in the moment. The more comfortable and confident she is in her world, the easier it will be for her to learn to master her emotions.

Slow-to-warm, fearful children respond negatively to new situations and are slow to adapt, but they can have good biological regularity and mellow moods. You are the base of security for this child. She needs to be free to come to you when she's feeling fearful, and needs time, time, time. Patience is required for this child, regularity and reassurance. Transitions are very hard for her and continuity works best.

Handling Custody and Visitation When the Conflict Level Is High

THROUGHOUT THE DISCUSSION of custody and visitation, continued, regular contact with both parents is emphasized. For example, if possible, it is best for babies to see both parents every day, and that would likely entail one parent visiting the house of the other. There is a very large exception to this rule of thumb, and that is if the conflict level is high between the parents. It is better in this case to go longer between visits in order that they be made in safe, neutral surroundings, perhaps with the help of a third party. If you are in high conflict with your former spouse, DO NOT go to their house even if they are not there, and don't have them come to your house. It can be super difficult in our world to find friends, neighbors and family to help with this, but make every effort to do so. If you are really without resources in this area, go to a social support agency and ask for help. A church is another option. A social worker may be able to help you pick up and drop off a baby without exposing you to the other parent.

The Ages of Childhood: Developmental Time-Blocks and Custody and Visitation Issues

Newborn to Three: Who Do I Trust?

Babies need:

1. Security.
2. Consistency of routine.
3. Sensitive transitions.
4. At least one attachment figure—the primary caregiver.
5. They will also bond with a noncustodial parent.
6. Regular exposure to all attachment figures, including both parents is best for them.

Dangers at this age:

1. Separation problems can result if transitions aren't handled well.
2. Babies may not be confident enough in their attachments to let the primary caregiver go even for short periods of time.
3. Insecurities bred at this stage may lead to relationship capacity shortfalls later on, and troubles with healthy attachment in general.
4. Many people forget that babies are people, too. They are constantly responding to and interacting with their environment and their caregivers. Babies should be given the same conscious consideration as older children when working out custody and visitation.

Custody and Visitation Suggestion:

Easygoing babies can tolerate two consistent residences quite well. Babies may actually adapt to two living spaces more easily than an older child will. If the child does stay in one home all the time, the ideal visitation is for the noncustodial parent to visit every day. Of course, if there is a high-conflict situation, one parent should not be entering the other parent's home. It is always most important to keep the conflict to a minimum, even if that means one parent does not see the child as much as would otherwise be possible.

Parents of newborns know how incredibly demanding this phase of life is for the caregivers; it's ironic that until very recently infancy was more or less dealt with unilaterally in custody proceedings. The baby stayed with its mother, period.

It makes sense in one way: babies need a primary attachment figure above all else, and because of cultural attitudes, we are used to this being the mother. But babies do have responses beyond the mother, right from the beginning of their lives, and a divorce is likely to bring them a feeling of loss of contact with one of their primary caregivers.

For many years, the idea that two people would share custody of a baby seemed foreign—of course the baby needed to stay with its mother and would hardly know the difference if he or she wasn't exposed to the father. What we know about attachment needs is that most children really do need at least one consistent caregiver—whether this is a woman or a man is secondary. Contemporary thought has also changed to acknowledge the emotional needs of both parents—not just mommies, but many men want to stay intimate and attached to their babies in the event of a divorce. Attachment works both ways, and it is undoubtedly better for the development of a lifelong bond with a father that the child is regularly exposed to the time and care of this very central figure even in the very first months of its life.

There's been a fair amount of discussion into how custody and visitation arrangements affect babies, for better and worse. One side of the debate maintains that consistency is of the utmost importance for infants, and they should always be put to bed in the same crib in the same house. On the other side, there's evidence that many babies are more flexible than previously thought. Some babies can adapt readily to different environments and should be exposed to two homes from the get-go. It should be noted that this "flexibility" is generally within a very consistent framework, and doesn't mean that babies don't need regular schedules and familiar surroundings. They do. It's just that many of them can adapt pretty well to a weekly change in primary caregiver, and a weekly change of crib.

However, while the custody and visitation arrangements you make for your school-age child will depend largely on your own schedule and your child's school schedule, and while your teenager's arrangements will reflect not only these factors but other, emotional needs as well, the arrangements you make for your baby should more keenly incorporate the child's temperament.

Up to eighteen months of age, infants aren't able to differentiate between what is happening now and what is a memory. Time is a major concept that takes several years to develop fully—toddlers hardly know how to wait, and asking them to is tantamount to saying no to whatever it is they're after. A big task for babies is to sort between the external world and the subjective "I" experience of it—so they eventually learn that people continue to exist even when they are not right there in front of them. Because they don't differentiate between internal and external doesn't mean they aren't experiencing the outside world though—they are. Furthermore, the way babies develop conscious memories seems to be based on the overall emotional state associated with the memory—so the baby's environment is very important to the positive associations that fuel the building of the self discussed above.

The drama of an infant/toddler is oneness and separateness. Their understanding, which is felt more than thought, travels between being an individual and being part of the parent/s. Three-year-olds are unable to understand that their self-centered perceptions are different from others' perceptions. They construct a reality in which they have an omnipotent view and insist that mother or father also has omnipotent powers—to do whatever the child wants them to do.

Infants need to build trust in their environment. The world is brought to them, so that makes it of the utmost importance that all caregivers approach the child with consciousness and care. As for moving kids around—some kids stay part of the week with their grandparents as a matter of course and no one thinks badly of this at all. In fact, in greater adaptability, in a wider circle of loving caregivers, such a setup is viewed quite positively for the child. And a mild-tempered baby may have no problem being moved at night. For all temperaments though, it is ideal for the child to have continued contact with both parents. It's harder for babies to develop a relationship with someone they don't see regularly—because out of sight is out of mind.

Toddlers have heightened separation issues. They are really working out the "I" and the "you." Consistency is of the utmost importance for this age group. If this age child is moving between two homes, the environments at each should be orderly and pretty much always the same. A transition object, a blanket or a stuffed animal or doll, helps this child immeasurably. As with infants, toddlers need pretty constant contact with both parents. A week without the other parent is too long—it will be hard for the child to "connect" with the parent she sees after seven days of not. When a child this age doesn't have a strong, immediate connection with the noncustodial parent, it can feel like a rejection. That's not the right way to look at it. The child lives in the moment. As the child gets older, she'll be able to understand better that her relationship with you continues over time periods where she doesn't see you. Some parents feel hurt at this juncture and spend less time visiting their child—the answer is to spend more time.

Toddlers:

1. Are becoming independent.
2. Are learning to understand themselves as separate entities from their primary caregivers.
3. Are helped by symbols of comfort—which provide continuity across change.
4. Need consistent routines and plenty of reassurance.

Dangers at this Age:

1. As with infants, security issues are paramount with toddlers and the same attachment and separation concerns maintain.
2. Toddlers are more aware of themselves as an "I" and are more invested in routine. They need even more consistency than infants do to make sure they feel confident and secure.
3. Toddlers are more aware of loss and need to have their grief addressed.

Custody and Visitation Suggestion:

It may be harder to introduce a toddler to a new sleeping situation. Separation issues are heightened for toddlers. It may be easier to have the child visit the new home for a period of time before sleeping there.

Four to Six: Who Takes Care of Me?

Four to Six-Year-Olds:

1. Need safety and security.
2. Believe that they are the cause of the separation or divorce.
3. May fear that someone will be hurt by inter-parental hostilities—themselves, their parents, or all of the above.
4. Have frightening fantasies of what will happen or has happened to the parent who moves out.
5. Fear being left by the parent with whom they primarily live.
6. Can be overwhelmed by intense emotional reactions.
7. At some point or another will have problems or fears around visitation or transitions.
8. Fear being replaced—they worry about parents' remarriages, potential step-siblings, life being further disrupted.

Dangers at this age:

1. This age child can internalize the pain she feels at the divorce—this will contribute to an overall self-image problem where the child feels bad and wrong.
2. The natural fearful reactions, if unaddressed, will become part of how the child views the whole world—as an unsafe place.
3. As with children of all ages, healthy attachment is threatened when one parent leaves.

Custody and Visitation Suggestions:

This age child can understand better that he or she will see the other parent again—so can tolerate longer intervals between visits—a weekly schedule is okay. A four-year-old will have more trouble with this than a six-year-old, and bringing along a favorite stuffed animal or other transitional object will help. This child can appreciate and understand her own room in two separate houses. Shared custody is best. The schedule should be very consistent. The child is beginning to have a sense of where she will be at any point during the week.

From about age two to approximately seven, children are acquiring language and concepts—they are classifying and putting reality into categories of time and space. Everything can be accounted for. They are self-centered, but by the close of this phase they are taking the measure of the person facing them. Language is egocentric and doesn't take into account the point of view of the other (this changes by the end of this phase).

Four- to six-year-olds are able to conceptualize the absent parent. They are beginning to regulate their feelings, their physical functions. They will increasingly identify with the same-sex parent. Conceptualizing their agency in the world, they start taking responsibility for the divorce. They understand themselves as the center of the universe—can't really understand it any other way. Who will take care of them becomes of great issue to them. They use a primitive logic: if one parent left, maybe the other one will too.

This age child is likely to regress around the divorce—maybe to reclaim a security blanket or toy, to stop using the toilet, to increase clinginess, to increase aggression. It's important to remember that their inability to understand the divorce means that they will fantasize simple but dire causes for it—that they are at fault, that since their parents don't love each other anymore they will potentially stop loving their children. These kids need clear and frequent reassurances that they did not cause the divorce, that they are still loved by both their mother and father, and that they will be taken care of. Acknowledge their fears and correct them. This age child needs to see each parent as much as possible—a two-week break is too long.

Kids at all ages fantasize that they are the cause of their parents' divorce—and this is damaging for them, because they feel intrinsically bad, less worthy. The preschooler will also compensate for a lack of personal power through "magical thinking," a kind of blurring of reality and fantasy in which super powers, through action figures or magic figures like fairies, do what the child wishes to be done.

Over this time period children are differentiating between magical thinking and reality-oriented thinking. A toddler with no sense of time and a belief that both she and her parents are omnipotent gradually learns the constructs of temporality and the world of limits. She becomes more concrete. However, she still feels no self-sufficiency and understands that she is at the mercy of others—this contributes to her fears. Children this age respond to the change in the family by being afraid. They need reassurance. They have a primal fear of being orphaned. If one parent can leave, so can the other. By about age five the child uses compensatory fantasies to express or to deny her anxieties.

Even children in very secure home situations are going to have this nagging, outstanding worry that they can't quite put into words. This issue opens the door to deeper reassurances that the child is valued and will be cared for, and leads to the idea that kids can have a home in two different places. This age is ready to understand that and talking to her about it will help.

Seven to Ten: In the Middle

Seven to Ten-Year-Olds:

1. Have a strong internal identification with each parent. The divorce feels not only like a rift on the outside, but also like a rift on the inside.
2. Parental hostilities are intensely upsetting to this age group. Their divided loyalties mean that they just can't stand the polarizing of their parents in opposition to each other.
3. This age group will try mightily to reunite their parents. They will try this by acting out and becoming a focal point for the two parents; by behaving well in the belief that if they are good, their parents will get back together; by acting as an intermediary and recreating a sense of a three-way relationship.
4. This age group will consciously feel that they caused the divorce.
5. They will try to please and protect you.

Dangers at this age:

1. This age child will sacrifice herself in the service of a weakened parent.
2. This child will act as an intermediary between parents, but this puts her in a terrible position. If she is asked to relay information that is greeted with negativity, she will feel responsible for it.
3. This child's divided loyalties create an internal logjam that will be hard for her to get over.

Custody and Visitation Suggestions:

This age child can understand different points of view. You can explain to the child why you are getting a divorce, in an appropriate way, of course, and she will take that in. This child needs regularity and a feeling of belonging at each home. Her school schedule and social life need to be respected and maintained. As she gets older she can be consulted about the custody arrangement—what works for her, what doesn't. Longer separations from the noncustodial parent are OK. As with all children, the more contact with both parents the better.

The young school age child is developing a moral sense, understanding the difference between right and wrong. She's developing empathy, physical mastery, and a sense of self: I am somebody who can spell. This child is ready to begin to understand the divorce and that the family is to be reorganized, not lost. Try hard not to criticize the other parent to this age child. She needs reassurance and love from both parents. Let it be OK for her to love the other parent. This age child will show grief, through crying and sobbing, especially boys. They will deeply yearn for the other parent. They will feel this way despite the quality of their previous relationship with that parent—they will feel the loss. It's common for this age child to repress anger against the father (if the father, as is usually the case, is the one who moves out). But she will show more anger toward the mother. If this age child doesn't see the noncustodial parent much, she will commonly feel that parent doesn't love her anymore.

Especially children in this age group need to be protected from their parents' disappointment and anger. Putting this child in the middle is devastating to her growing sense of self. This age child has a well-established sense that her parents are part of her and she is part of her parents. But this is based on them being together. Something inside feels lost or broken when the parents split, and she wants to feel whole again. She'll try to get her parents back together. She'll behave so very well, in the belief that if she becomes a better girl, the problem will go away. Or, she will behave very badly so that her mom and dad have to come together to deal with it.

This age child will try to undo the divorce. She will also feel very angry, and is more likely to be fully aware of her anger. With her developing moral sense, she may take umbrage at what she perceives is a double standard in the parents' behavior—you told us to get along and make compromises and now you aren't doing that at all. When adults act out around the divorce, become more self-involved or behave inappropriately, it will not be lost on this age child.

The main drive of this age group is to keep everything whole. They aren't always overtly angry—blame comes later. They are reaching outward a bit to school and friends and overnights. Their security and confidence in the world is knocked out by a separation and a big change. They will go into tremendous denial, needing to keep things together until they can face it.

Children in this age group will try to mediate between you. Partly they do it to keep some semblance of connection between all the players. They also deeply want you to be OK, and they are trying to help. They are also trying to fix the situation—if things can work smoothly, maybe you'll get back together.

Six- to eight-year-olds in particular have real loyalty conflicts. They show ambivalence and distress about hurting either parent. They are highly invested in trying to please, to placate, to confirm parent's separate views. A child this age will tell you what you want to hear about the other parent. It's very important to take it with a grain of salt and to identify what your child is trying to do, which is protect and please you.

Children this age are beginning to understand just how complicated and incompatible their parents' views of each other are, and they worry about where they stand now. "How will my mother feel about me if I have a good time with Dad at the ballgame"—dad, whom she hates? The child is really stuck. That's why really supporting the time they spend with the other parent is so important, and also why it's really important to not bad-mouth the other parent.

Eleven to Fifteen: I Am Alone

Teenagers:

1. Feel alone. That's normal, it's part of the job of being a teen. A heightened sense of their uniqueness is tinged with sadness and alienation.
2. Are separating from the family.

3. Are solidifying their own identity.

4. Value their peer group above almost everything else. There's a developmental reason for this. Teenagers are preparing to enter the world by themselves and need to learn from a group with wider and more diverse aims than the family provides. They learn not only from their friends, but also from the different families and home situations their friends come from.

5. Still need their parents in an authoritative role.

6. Push you away when they really need you.

Dangers at this age:

1. Because teenagers are verbal and can understand the situation, they are in danger of being treated too much like an adult by you.

2. In separating from the family and in feeling alone, teenagers are already engaged in the bittersweet process of saying goodbye to childhood. The divorce compresses the experience and can hasten adulthood when they aren't truly ready for it.

3. Teenagers can place their peer group above the family in a hierarchy of importance. It's common for a teenager to tell her parents she wants to live with the parent within the closest proximity to her friends, but of course she won't put it this way.

4. Teenagers who are treated too much like adults not only lose the family as they have known it during divorce, but they also lose their role as the child of Mom, the child of Dad. This much loss can be overwhelming.

5. Many teenagers are, shall we say, difficult to deal with. Oppositional or unresponsive teens are looking for a way to relate differently to their parents; they are in danger of being dismissed or given up on by a parent who is affronted by their behavior.

Custody and Visitation Suggestions:

Even teenagers with their burgeoning independence need to see both parents frequently. They are much more able to participate in a visitation schedule that works for them, but their desires should be received within the context that you are still the authority figure. Teenagers at one point or another are likely to refuse visitation, to say they no longer want to go between two homes. This should not be taken to mean that they are rejecting one parent, even if that's what they say. Teenagers bristle under having to do things according to other people's agendas and their lives feel very complicated to them. They need to be encouraged to see both parents regularly.

The teenage years are the time of individuation. Kids this age naturally feel lonely and the divorce takes away a crucial grounding. The task for this age group is to separate from the family—divorce makes this less of a choice for them that they accomplish on their own time and makes it more of an enforced march. Losing the family structure can lead to despair for this age group—the feeling is: I'm really alone.

Teenagers will assume adult responsibilities greater than their years. Teenagers often relish the power their parents de facto give them when they rely on them too much during a divorce. Because teens are pretty capable and verbal, parents fall into the trap of treating them as confidantes, and leaning on them to help pick up the slack with home responsibilities. Parents of kids this age need to distinguish between cultivating responsibility in their teens on the one side, and switching places with them on the other. Many teens become more adult than their parents during this time.

Many teens resist your attempts to help them through the divorce. This is because you have already imposed on them by having this problem, and they don't want to have to involve themselves in your business more than they have to. They resent what they feel is an imposition on their life. Because they resist help doesn't mean they don't need it. Teens need to feel that they are not alone. Peer support groups are ideal for teenagers, if you can get your kid to participate in one.

People sometimes say when kids are teens they need their parents as much as they did when they were infants. There is a point to this. Infants get their cues about the world from their immediate surroundings, and their relationship with attachment figures literally creates their world. Teens need to have this world created by attachment figures also—but in a different way. They need the structure in order to have a point of reference, the point they are departing from and coming back to.

It's never too late to improve your relationship with your kids, but you will do much better with your teens if you have a healthy relationship with them prior to their adolescence. If they are accustomed to your authoritative concern, they will continue to respond to it even when the hormones are raging. If you haven't laid down the tracks of respect before this time, however, you are going to meet with resistance and opposition.

Peer relationships and social life are paramount. Adolescents who don't have a firm home life will substitute the peer group for this structure, and that can mean trouble. It's one thing when kids are experimenting with their own level of response to the pressures the peer group puts on them, but if friends are all a teenager feels she has, she will be much more likely to be sexually active young, to do drugs, the whole nine yards. Teenagers are pulling away in many senses, but it's important not to push them away. As with the obstreperous toddler, teenagers can be pretty aggravating. Just remember they are developmentally driven to be somewhat obnoxious to their parents. Keep them aware that you still feel they are part of a unit with you. They will respond to that.

Teenagers are self-aware—what they're good at, what they're not good at. They can conceptualize other viewpoints. They're likely to develop empathy or condemnation of one parent. When you talk to this child, he or she can see right through you. Children this age can see both sides of the conflict, but are also likely to cover up their distress. They also tend to see things in black-and-white, which results in finding one person the villain and the other the good guy. Again, minimize your conflict with the other parent and encourage a relationship with that parent.

Sexual feelings are coming up, and kids are looking for ways to handle them. The sexuality of parents becomes more evident. At the same time, the rules and regulations of society are of interest to them. Give honest answers to adolescents. Be very sensitive if you are pursuing a new love life—keep it discreetly apart from your teens. In the first place, it is hard for them to face you as a sexual being when they are wrestling with these feelings themselves. Second of all, they will feel doubly betrayed by you—the divorce is one betrayal, and then this new person represents another.

Children in this age group have certain advantages over younger kids when it comes to divorce. They understand more cognitively. You can speak pretty frankly with them about what is happening and why, and about your plans for the future. Indeed, they can participate in these plans. However, teenagers are very likely going to experience the loss of the parent-child relationship. So, not only are they losing the family structure they're used to, they are also losing the more individual feeling of mother-child and father-child.

Teenagers are individuating and separating from the family. These are necessary and natural developments, but ideally occur over the course of several years. Divorce speeds things up. Many adolescents respond by acting a lot older than they are—alcohol, drug, and sex issues come to the fore. Maintaining a healthy authoritative relationship with your teenagers will help them navigate these stormy seas with more success and fewer dangers.

Many divorcing adults regress in their own behavior, begging the question of who in the family is the grown-up. Even support groups for teens are likely to help the teen take on an ever more mature standpoint. Often teenagers are left high and dry by their parents during a divorce—it can be harder for parents to understand how much their teenagers still need them. One leader of a support group for teens said: "We spend a lot of time helping the kids figure out how to get what they need. We try to empower them to figure out how to see one parent when the other one is trying to prevent that." It's a trap adults fall into. Most understand the need for smaller kids to see both parents, but don't appreciate the vulnerability of their teenagers. The sad thing is that even these teens who are being "empowered" are being coached to act even more like adults. Suddenly, for these kids, it seems there are no truly mature adults around at all.

Teenagers are engaged in trying to figure out their potential place in the adult world. They absolutely need their parents in an authoritative function. While the balance is under construction, so to speak, with the teenager gradually taking more responsibility for herself as she gets older, this process will work best for her if her parents maintain their stability and their role. Discipline and family rules are very important to teenagers, even if they balk about them.

Stories

Toughing It Out, Keeping Cool ↜

THE MARRIAGE BETWEEN Michael and his ex was a thing of brevity, less than a year long, and broke up soon after their son Leroy was born. Both Michael and Leroy's mother went on to establish other families, Michael in a smallish town near the utility he works for, his former wife in the city. "I don't know, now, looking back, if I treated Leroy as well as I should have," Michael says. Michael remarried when Leroy was five and shortly thereafter he and his new wife got pregnant. "He's always had a tough time getting along with my wife, and when we had the twins (girls now eight years old), she really gave up any attempt at having a good relationship with him." Leroy spent about half his time with Michael and half with his mother; the trouble was, his mother's life was fairly turbulent. "She's been married like three more times," Michael snorts. "Now she's living with some guy and his four kids and there's Leroy and a mess of her other kids from other marriages." Michael likes not one thing about Leroy's mother, and their conflict level is high.

Now fourteen, Leroy has decided he wants to live with his mother full-time. "I can't stand it," Michael says. "He wants to live there because there's no supervision. He's been arrested three times for stupid stuff, breaking into a car, joy-riding. Always on her time. She doesn't care. Now, he's not only flunking math, he's flunking P-E. P-E! I mean, the kid doesn't care either. Why should I care? I'm on the verge of letting him go."

In a situation like Michael's, one thing piles on another to make for a real pressurecooker. It's not uncommon for fathers, especially, to want to escape the whole situation. Particularly when conflict is high, the ability to walk away is tempting. No, deadbeat dads are not looked kindly on in our society, and yet it is not exactly an uncommon phenomenon either.

"Why shouldn't I just put on the Bad Guy hat? She wants me to wear it anyway. She says I'm too strict with him, he's bored living in a small town, he doesn't get along with my wife and she favors her own children." Michael winces and acknowledges that his current marriage puts a strain on his relationship with Leroy, and sometimes he feels he has to choose between his wife and his son. "When he's a brat, when he disobeys, man he makes it easy to get mad, to say, you wanna go? Then go."

The trouble is, a fourteen-year-old does not really want to say goodbye to his father. Leroy needs help, he needs counseling, and Michael does too. Whatever resentments are seething with his current wife need to come to the surface—not with Leroy around, though. But one thing is certain: for Michael to wash his hands of Leroy is a mistake.

A couple of issues are highlighted in this situation. First of all, with teenagers, priorities often have to be readjusted. Leroy's trouble with the law and his poor performance in school are real problems that have to be addressed. But for Michael, they shouldn't be the primary focus. The primary focus is the relationship between Michael and Leroy. There has to be an understanding that this is the most important thing for Leroy, an incredibly crucial factor in his chances at picking up the thread of his life again.

"I mean, he doesn't understand yet, he's throwing it all away," Michael moans. "He thinks, what do I need high school for? College doesn't even enter his thick skull. But I know what happens next. Next he's twenty-one years old, got a stupid job that pays nothing, got no hopes of a better one. Then he'll end up in jail."

But telling the future to a fourteen-year-old is like talking to a wall. Another shouting, disapproving voice isn't going to make Leroy wake up and smell the coffee. A positive relationship with his father will help his self-esteem. Leroy needs self-respect not built from threats but built on pleasure, shared experience, quiet, good time together. Out of self-respect comes a natural desire to do well in the world—with the idea that he is capable of being a contributing part of it.

How to Connect with Your Children through Better Communication and How to Manage Communication with Your Co-Parent

COMMUNICATION IS THE key to parenting. Hearing your kids, responding to them, creating an environment in which it is easy for them to hear you—these are the tools that help build strong, healthy kids. During a separation and after a divorce, communication is the way to integrate the past and the present so that kids can acknowledge their experience and move on. Good communication is also the key to good behavior. Children who are heard are less likely to act out. When they do act out, healthy communication habits help prevent escalating conflict and also turn the situation into a learning opportunity (sometimes!).

How to Connect with Your Children through Better Communication

As a concept, communication covers the mundanities of life and also its finest, richest qualities. People, and indeed all animals, function largely through communication. We respect many rules and guidelines around how we communicate in the social realm, from traffic lights that dictate who goes first to complex business laws. We know people who communicate badly—the way they get their needs and desires across always elicits a negative response. Do you work with a yeller or a whiner? Are you related to one? Do you ever really remember what it was they were after, or do your ears just ring when they finally leave the room?

The way we communicate is the way we are in the world. Art, science, medicine are all partly about communication—they are common languages that rely on received bodies of meaning, from which we learn and invent new meanings. Communication is not a nicety conveyed through memos and e-mails, although the word has been co-opted by marketing and human resources departments. Communication is the heart of human interchange, and how we do it matters.

In relationships, when you "hit it off" with someone you find yourself understanding much about that person that is never explicitly stated but is conveyed through a thousand subtle and unseen signals. And you feel understood by that person, too. Parenting is an interpersonal relationship of the most important kind, and we communicate to our kids that we love and care for them in myriad ways, from feeding and clothing them to sharing our deepest held beliefs with them. The way we talk to them, say "yes" and "no" and everything in between, not only teaches them about our expectations of them, which in turn shapes their self-concept, but also teaches them how to behave with others in the world, from school to work to their own intimate relationships.

Communication is about being clear—putting out what you need or require and getting a satisfactory response. Yet the normal transactions of life between intimates are quite often not clear at all. When you ask your child to pick up his room, you want him to respond to your request, and often he doesn't. What occurs between the asking and the doing (or not doing) is often a whole lot more involved than getting some dirty clothes off the floor and the bed made. Getting at the unstated content behind a child's action or lack of it takes patience and some strategy.

Then there's the communication issue around dealing with your co-parent.

Communication between divorced people has very likely broken down some-where along the line—many relationship problems are effectively communi-cation problems. Lots of interesting books have been written about the different ways men and women express themselves, and the ways we miss each other's meanings. Even if you were mutually agreeable about getting a divorce, it is likely that frustrations and resentments down the road put up new impediments. Sometimes people are almost willful in their miscommu-nication, or in their hostile communication. It's as if they want to keep it clear: I don't get along with you.

Be that as it may, it's important to have more or less clear ways of com-municating with your co-parent about your child. Getting there can be very hard. On the one hand you have to really focus on the moment, on what's being said. "What does he want from me, under all this invective?" You have to try not to respond to the feeling being conveyed, but to the content. On the other hand, you ask yourself, "Why should I take this?" And so you have to keep yourself emotionally planted firmly outside the conversation. You have to keep your eyes on the prize and always remember, you are mak-ing your absolute best effort to get along with this person for the sake of your kids. Your goal is to keep communication open with this person so that you can more effectively parent your children together, from two different and perhaps utterly opposing perspectives.

Most of what follows is a discussion of communication in terms of con-necting better with your children. So-called reflective listening and active listening strategies are explained, as is the use of "I" statements. Difficult communication situations are discussed. Concrete exercises for productive interaction are provided—how to hear, and how to be heard by your kids. Finally, there is a discussion of communication strategies using the same techniques for dealing with your co-parent.

Communication Begins with Acknowledgment— Start by Recognizing Your Own Feelings

In a fundamental way, communication is more about listening than about speaking. And the first place many of us don't really listen is to ourselves. When most of us are hungry, our response is simple. Get something to eat.

Maybe it's broccoli and maybe it's a hot fudge sundae, or maybe we say to ourselves, I'm hungry but I'll wait an hour until dinner. However, when many of us are angry or sad, we don't have such a clear response to those sensations. Without saying, "Gee, I'm angry," we let the feeling take us by the seat of the pants. We cut someone off in traffic. We scream at someone for a minor infraction in the workplace (or we take it out on the kids). We don't say, "I feel sad," but instead try to think about something else.

When you take a minute to actually accept and acknowledge your own real feelings, you go a very long way to handling them in a satisfying way. When you recognize and name your feelings and ask yourself, "What do I need right now?" quite often you can complete the cycle of the emotion and move on from it. It's important to practice acknowledging and responding to your own feelings because when they aren't recognized, our own needs stand in the way of hearing anyone else's. When your emotions are engaged but below the surface, they are simply not available for empathizing with anyone else, even your children.

Of course, we all put aside our own feelings all the time to respond to the situation at hand. But when there is too much going on inside us we can't very well focus clearly on what's outside. As much as you need a relationship of trust with your children, you need to have a relationship of trust with your own self. So that if you are sad and need to talk to a friend, you can say, "Well, I'll make sure and get some meaningful contact for myself later. Right now I'll focus on the kids." If you trust yourself to take care of yourself, you can put those feelings on hold for a bit. But if you are in the habit of not listening to your own needs, they will insist on permeating all your doings. And if your children are expressing needs, they will feel you as fundamentally unavailable to them, which will cause a negative response in them, like anger or despair.

The Screamers

OK, so let's say there are some people out there who are balanced and calm and never scream at their kids in order to put an end to some conflict. Praise be, and let's thank them for setting us a goal. Most of us have heard ourselves losing it with our kids. Maybe yelling at them is a habit, in fact. It bears some thought.

If you are a person who yells and screams to resolve conflicts—well, why do you suppose that is? A minute of reflection will probably yield some uncomfortable fruits. Did your parents yell at you? How did that make you feel? "I felt nothing," you might shrug. "It's just what they did." But what if you really sat down and brought yourself back to how it actually did feel when your parents yelled. Did they respect you? "We were just kids. What's to respect?" Many of us have internalized angry or dismissive parents and accepted their judgments of us from long ago. The fact is those feelings do indeed prompt the way we treat our kids now. Do you respect yourself? "Oh, of course!" But, actually, do you really respect yourself?

In a deep way being a parent also means bringing yourself up all over again. This is just one of those situations. You don't have to get all involved in thinking about your own parents if you don't want to. But if you are a screamer, it is likely that you were screamed at. It is likely that you don't actually respect your own needs and desires very well, or employ very good tools in dealing with them. Not only are you passing this negative self-concept onto your children, you are helping to create your own unpleasant, conflict-ridden household.

One woman said, "My friend made this off-the-cuff remark about how sarcastic my daughter is. I was sort of offended but it made me look at that. I realized, yes, she's sarcastic and it's unpleasant. It also gets her into trouble at school. The mouth on her! On the other hand, I'm totally sarcastic with her. My home life growing up was one harsh crack after another, and here I am continuing it. It's so obvious, but I just didn't even think about it, it was like the air I breathed. When I stopped with the sarcasm, so did my daughter."

What Happens When Kids Aren't Acknowledged

What is dinnertime like at your house? Do you sit down with your kids and talk about the day, about whatever is interesting everybody at the moment? When do you take care of business—hear about an upcoming field trip, remind everyone that you'll be out of town next Sunday? It's important to have some regular time in which you address each child's life in a direct way, asking about what's going on. It's very hard to keep everyone's schedule straight (a big calendar on the wall helps), but it's very important that all the little pieces of what's going on in everyone's life are followed up on—not just because that will get you to the church on time, but because everyone feels more valued when they've been accounted for. You want to keep an open flow of information, large and small; your kids aren't going to come to you with the big stuff if you don't make time for the small stuff. The overall atmosphere of a household sends a message: you can be yourself here, or you must hide and suppress yourself here.

Communication is at the heart of this. Remember the mother in *Ordinary People* who just could not say "I love you" to her son? It was like the inability to speak had been bred so deep in her that she could not step outside that behavior pattern even when her son was withering away in need of her expressed love. Kids need to hear it, they need to speak it—communication is vital to them. Children develop by watching and absorbing information from you about what you truly value, how you make choices, how you cope with difficulty. You let your children know you are there for them when you communicate directly with them—they implicitly understand that you are open to their needs and desires. They are also forming a self-image partly based on how you respond to them.

Kids get super-frustrated when they aren't heard. When kids aren't heard they develop a negative relationship with their own feelings. They may keep on and keep on in a destructive behavior pattern, maybe at school. They won't feel right inside, because they need to be recognized—it goes back to the healthy mirroring discussed in the chapter on development. Kids who don't feel right inside don't act right on the outside. Furthermore, constant discounting teaches them that their feelings are not valid. They may simply not understand themselves at all and so do not know how to regulate themselves in the world, how to manage their anger or sadness. In the worst case, they dissociate from themselves and remain out of touch not only with their uncomfortable feelings, but also with their greater intellectual, social, and creative abilities as well. All of these expressions are tied to feelings.

Mirror Mirror on the Wall

WHAT IF YOU looked in a mirror and saw only bad things? What if every time you looked in a mirror you saw something that pleased you? What if you looked in a mirror and saw absolutely nothing? How would you feel about yourself—who would you think you were?

You are the primary mirror for your kids. How do they see themselves in your eyes?

That's certainly not to say that your child's every sensation has to be treated like a grand incantation calling down your complete response. Part of healthy communication with your child leads them to a better place to handle their own feelings. Children's discomfort often stems from not feeling competent. Good parenting helps kids discharge negative feelings, restoring them to a feeling that they are the ones with mastery over their emotions and not vice versa.

Kids Want Connection, Power, and Reassurance

Sometimes it isn't clear at all what your child is wanting from you, if anything. One nine-year-old kept telling her mother she did not want to talk about the divorce. "I tried to respect her wishes. She would just put her hands over her ears when I sat her down to talk about it. But months went by and I realized something major was not being addressed." The girl's father had moved out and gotten an apartment, and a makeshift custody arrangement was worked out pending the more formalized divorce proceedings. This girl was old enough to fully realize that her parents were divorcing. "Finally I put it to her this way. I said, 'We *have* to talk about the divorce. But you start. You tell me how we should talk about it.'" The girl hung her head. "I don't want you to say bad things about Daddy," she said.

What the mom did in this case was tell her daughter that she would *listen* rather than tell. Asking questions is a great way to get some conversational flow going when it isn't easy otherwise. You could ask your kids if they have questions about what's going on and by their response you can learn a great deal about their fears and misperceptions. This nine-year-old told her mother a lot about her own feelings when she said she didn't want to hear bad things about her dad. She didn't want to take sides. She didn't want to think badly of her father or have to protect her mother. Between them, this mother and daughter found a way for the girl to express an objection to the way her mother was dealing with the divorce—clearly, she was "saying bad things about Daddy." The mom had to be ready to hear this objection, to put aside her anger at her co-parent because it was upsetting her daughter.

In general, you can be sure that somewhere in their television-glazed faces your children do really want three important things, in addition to love: connection, power, and reassurance. Connection is another way of saying acknowledgment. This nine-year-old needed her mother to acknowledge her feelings about her father, and when the mother did so, it gave both of them a feeling of being connected more closely to each other. With the acknowledgment goes respect. The mom had to follow through on the girl's request. Doing so gave the daughter some power in the situation—a sense of being important enough to be listened to. And the need for reassurance lingers over the conversation also. Even if your kids don't say it, they need to be told you love them and always will and, to the degree you can say it honestly, that your co-parent may have moved out, but will continue to be in their lives.

Honesty Is the Best Policy

Another thing to look at is the overall way you relate to your kids. Are you honest with them, or only to a point? Often in a divorce values get distorted or out of whack for a while. One grown man still recalls a conversation he had with his mother when he was eleven. "She said she and my father were having trouble but would not get divorced. Then they got divorced." Thirty years later, it's not the divorce per se that bothers him, it's the perceived breach of trust between himself and his mother.

Now, we all understand her position. She was stressed, probably hoping that her disintegrating relationship would not, in fact, end in divorce. An eleven-year-old is looking for reassurance—and when she broke her word, it felt like his mother betrayed him. Somehow that compounded the hurt, or perhaps it defined the divorce for him. He may have felt, "Now I not only don't have my family, but I can't trust my mother anymore either."

We are all going to be put in the position of this man's mother one day, whether the issue is divorce or something else. Her son's memory might be very different if she had been able to sit down with him and say, "I told you we would never get a divorce, and now I have to change that. I'm so sorry to have to break a promise to you. I'm sure you're disappointed. But this is what's happening."

That would be hard enough to do. But then, ideally, she would have been able to let her son cry, to let him get angry with her. Many times we don't really let our children have their feelings because we can't bear to see them, to receive them. We feel guilty about hurting our kids, want to deny the fact that we are hurting them. Or, life is just so overwhelming we're not thinking at all about how our kids are feeling.

This man's mother would have created a very different experience for her son if she had followed through on the discussion. He would probably still remember that his mother had once promised that something wouldn't happen that did indeed happen—and he would have learned the painful truth that sometimes the all-powerful parent is not totally in control of her life. But a follow-up conversation would have taught him a few more things. That his mother was strong enough to admit a mistake and to move on from it. That she valued his trust, cared that she hadn't been able to keep her word. She would have provided a container for the awful feelings he had about the divorce and the underlying fears it raised—not the least about his trust in her. By following through she would have demonstrated integrity.

Seeing, feeling, and knowing that his mother had integrity, her son would have been able to move past his disappointment in her. He would have found something deeper in her to trust, which would then translate into a greater feeling of pride in himself, in who he is. Kids feel wounded when their parents divorce, and recourse to good feelings about themselves helps them heal.

Your child will respect you for maintaining your integrity. That respect will lead to a better relationship with your child across difficulties. That respect will also translate to the child's self-image—he will intuitively feel that you value him and that you value yourself.

The point is not to live some flawless life where you never have to go back on your word. The point is to acknowledge and value the whole experience, with your children. They will get it. They will understand and respect you for saying, "Hey, I did my best. I had an idea and I really pursued it, but then I realized I couldn't keep going on that track." Basically, you want to keep a dialogue open with your kids. The best way to do this is to make observations and ask questions. Perfection is not the goal. Wholeness is the goal.

Kids are always noticing and calibrating how you are treating them, what you think of them. They are also noticing how you treat yourself and other adults. They take their cues in all ways, not just verbal. The way you approach discipline (discussed in chapter 5) is a case in point—you are not just guiding their behavior, you are communicating your expectations of them. And that in turn tells kids how highly you regard them. These are the small transactions that build up to a healthy self, a person who takes responsibility and relishes a challenge. These transactions are essentially communications. Remembering to follow up a conversation is a communication. Not only is the content of the conversation continued, but you also communicate to your child that you are thinking about them all the time, that emotionally you are prepared to follow through for them.

Reflective or Active Listening to Your Kids

Reflective or active listening is a way to communicate with your children with the goal of understanding what they are feeling, and validating those feelings where that's appropriate. Reflective listening responds mostly to nonverbal cues, and active listening is verbal. Both nonverbal and verbal strategies involve mirroring back the child's emotion to acknowledge it.

Let's say your son falls down and cries a lot and you're afraid he's a crybaby and you want to discourage that. So he falls and cries and you say, "Oh, come on that couldn't have hurt." He's kind of stuck—he was trying to tell you he felt hurt, and now he has to cry louder to make the same point. Try, "Gee, it's hard to fall like that." And move on. Chances are he'll move on too.

Or your daughter is throwing a fit. Instead of saying "Just get over it and go do your homework," you calmly say, "You are angry that I made you turn off the television." Reflective or active listening lets your child know that you acknowledge her feelings, that you are paying attention. It helps her define her own feelings, express them fully, and move on from them. "Yes, I'm mad!" she answers. She glowers, she fumes, and then it's on to something else. She'll be able to let go of the conflict over the television if her integrity—what *she* wants, *her* control—is not at stake. When she feels acknowledged, she isn't losing any piece of herself in the tussle with you.

If in this situation your daughter did not want to let go of the conflict, you have two choices. One is to explore her feelings a bit more, if you suspect that something else is going on. "You are still angry…?" you might offer, giving her space and time to fill in the blank. Maybe she doesn't know why she's mad. If she's old enough and has learned a bit about her own feelings, she may be able to stop and say, "Well, I'm mad because I don't have enough time to do what *I* want to do." That can open a much larger conversation about the pressures she feels from school and other responsibilities. If she seems angry all the time, this may not get resolved in one conversation.

On the other hand, if she just wants to see how far she can get with the television issue, you may want to curtail the conversation. Sometimes the line blurs between true communication issues and the garden variety negotiating a child will do to get what she wants. One way to discourage these negotiations from going on and on is to state your child's feeling and follow it with a firm "But…" "You're angry that I made you turn off the TV. I understand. But you have to go do something else now." She may not get what she wants but she'll feel respected and heard, even if she disagrees with your decision about the television.

Reflective Listening with Younger Kids, Active Listening with Older Kids and Adults

WITH BABIES AND toddlers, reflective listening focuses on reflecting back messages you are receiving from the child's nonverbal behavior. When a two-year-old is having a hissy fit, you might say, "My you are frustrated," but saying it is going to have more utility in helping you keep cool than helping the toddler. You want to give small children space to have even difficult feelings (unless the situation is dangerous, like in the bathtub, and then you have to intervene regardless of the emotion) and you want to try to satisfy their frustration or soothe them or both.

With older children and adults, active listening is a verbal tool. You repeat back exactly what you are hearing from the child or the adult, in their own words if that isn't going to sound condescending or angry. Or you can paraphrase, repeating back what you perceive is the general feeling or content of what you heard them say or what they seem to be expressing. Ask clarifying questions. Clarifying questions are aimed at getting a better understanding of what's at issue.

Active listening is a strategy where both parties come away feeling that they got something out of the situation. Make sure your kid feels satisfied at the end of the conversation and that you do too. It may take some time.

I-Messages

I-messages are a way of expressing yourself to your child in a way that respects you, your child, and the situation. You say what you are feeling, what caused it, and what the outcome of your feeling is. "When you scream at me about the television, it makes me feel bad. Then I don't feel like we can have a nice dinner together." "When you scream at me, it's very hard for me to understand what you really need and neither of us is very happy about that."

When you use "I" it makes your kids perk up their ears and listen. Say they're fighting in the back of the car. You are asking them to stop, and asking them to keep still, and saying, who started it? And essentially, it's a three-ring-circus. Try saying quietly (just loud enough to be heard) "It makes me angry when you hit each other in the car." It works because there's this moment where the kids become aware of what they're doing and that little sliver of awareness, and the fact that they are having an impact on you, gives them an opening to stop.

Reflective listening and I messages are strategies for minimizing the extra emotion that can get larded into a conflict. If your child is throwing a fit, and you throw a fit in return, nothing is resolved. You have merely used your own anger to trump your child's anger. You have essentially taught your child that the way to reach your goals is to be bigger and louder.

You have also sent a message that you don't respect your child's feelings. It's natural for the child to take that further—my parent doesn't respect me. This of course makes for low self-esteem.

Some examples of I-messages:

Child is interrupting while you are on the phone, or speaking to someone at school or in the store. He's tugging on your sleeve and expecting an immediate response.
YOU: Stop interrupting! You are so rude!
BETTER YOU: "When you interrupt me I can't think. I'd like it if you would wait until I'm finished and then I'll listen to what you have to say."

Child demands to be taken to the store.
CHILD: Take me to the toy store!
YOU: What, you demon seed! Don't tell me what to do. I will not be spoken to that way—you might order your father around like that, but not me.
BETTER YOU: It really puts me off when you talk to me like that. What if you asked politely about when we might go to the toy store?

Parent comes home and the kitchen is a mess, with dirty dishes on the table.
YOU: What lousy, piggy children! I slave all day and I come home to this?!
BETTER YOU: I feel so discouraged when I work all day and walk in to a sight like this.

Communication Goals and Guidelines

1. Basically, you want to keep your kids talking to you.
2. Kids will keep talking to you if they feel you listen to them.
3. Make observations: "I see you're kind of down today..." "I can imagine it might not be easy to remember whether you're going to my house or your father's house each day after school."

4. Ask questions: "Could I put a note in your lunch to remind you about bringing your homework from your mother's house?" "Is there something I could do to help you with your sad feelings?" "Are they the kind of feelings you'd like to talk about now or maybe you want to tell me about your day first?"

5. Don't contradict the feelings when they are expressed. If your child says, "Mom said I could go to the movies with my friend and then she didn't let me," you might be tempted to say, "She's always changing her mind." But that doesn't address the child's feeling, and in fact cancels it out. Instead, say something like, "You didn't get to go to the movies."

6. Using discretion according to the child's age, don't jump to solutions. Kids need to state their feelings more than they need a course of action determined from them. Even a seven-year-old can brainstorm some of his own strategies for his problems, and if you always take care of them, he'll get out of the habit of trying.

7. Practice non-blaming. Find a non-blaming way to reframe the situation, to state how it makes you or the child feel. Instead of "You never make your bed," try "It discourages me when you don't make your bed. I feel like I have enough to do and I want you to be the kind of kid who remembers to make his bed."

8. Let some stuff go. If you and your child are going through a time of being out of sync and you are finding him constantly at fault, try to let minor infractions pass. A child who is constantly messing up may have something on his mind and if you can approach him in some other way besides harping or reminders, it might get to the heart of the situation more effectively. As he's going to sleep you might sit by his bedside and say, "Things don't seem to be working that well for you these days. Do you feel that?" Be prepared for silence, and wait as best you can for a response or an opening of any kind.

9. Kids will escalate their behavior until they're heard.

10. Give kids the space to have their say. Quite often they know what you're going to say and how you're going to say it—if you expect their participation, they will be less likely to tune the whole conversation out.

11. Wait to discuss a situation when feelings are not hot.

12. Give an older child more space. Give a younger child more assurance. Remember, kids go at their own pace. Younger kids need more time.

13. Change what you can and know what you can't.

14. You don't have to agree with your child's feeling or desire to show you understand it. If you have a different agenda, you can direct your child to it more effectively if you first show you know where he's coming from.

15. The more you understand your child, the more he will trust you and trust himself. You will have a better relationship with your child.

Divorce Will Tempt You into Poor Communication with Your Child

You may feel like you never put your kids in the middle between you and your co-parent because you never explicitly ask them to carry a message for you, or give them mail that is still coming to your house, or because you make a big effort not to talk about your co-parent in front of them. If you are making these efforts, you deserve a lot of credit and you are very much helping your kids.

But there are sneaky, almost irresistible ways any bad feelings you have about the separation and divorce will get into your relationship with your kids. It is very hard for parents to separate out their own feelings about their co-parent from any issue the kids might be having with the co-parent. Consider the following:

KID: Dad said he would take Ralph and me swimming after soccer practice.

YOU: That didn't happen?

KID: No, we played at Ralph's house. Ralph has a new basketball hoop.

YOU: How did you happen to be at Ralph's house, when your father was supposed to pick you up?

KID: Dad never came. We called Ralph's mom and went to his house.

Now, what on earth are you going to do here? You are absolutely livid at your co-parent. You know the guy is a louse, but to neglect his child like that! While it is *possible* that there was a miscommunication or a change of plans, while it is *possible* that your co-parent took care of the situation and perhaps even arranged for Ralph's mother to pick the kids up, you just know that the utterly self-absorbed S.O.B. is guilty of negligence and in fact you should look into getting complete custody and not letting him have any more of this damaging contact with the child.

That's one way for your thoughts to go—and fear and concern for your child can push you in that direction. But first things first. Notice how fast the focus actually moves off the child in this situation. You go straight to anger at your co-parent.

YOU: (Carried away by a reaction to your co-parent) "Oh my God, I'm going to call Ralph's mother and that's the last time I let your father see you on a Saturday."

Instead, ideally:

YOU: So you didn't get to go swimming.
KID: No, but we played basketball.
YOU: It sounds like you're disappointed about the swimming but the basketball made it okay.
KID: Yeah. Can we get a basketball hoop?
YOU: I'm sure you can play with Ralph's quite a lot. Were you concerned that your father didn't pick you up?
KID: I was worried that we were forgotten.
YOU: It was a good idea to call Ralph's mother.

In this scenario you put aside your flip-out for a moment and complete the conversation with your child. Your child may in fact be confused and with so many plans and arrangements, a lack of communication may have occurred between your co-parent and your son. Your son brings his confusion to you and de facto asks you to straighten it out with him. If you fly into a reaction, you don't straighten it out with him, you just amplify his distress. In the scenario above, you step in as a rational adult, you hear your child, you reassure him, and you let him move on in his child-world, with the assurance that you will take care of the adult world. *Then* you go and kick your co-parent in the keister!

(Actually, you read further in this chapter about how to communicate productively with your co-parent and so you wait until you feel calm before picking up the phone).

Don't Build a Coalition against Your Co-Parent

IN THE ABOVE scenario, you may move quickly to call Ralph's mother, to find out what happened from an adult point of view that is not your co-parent's. If you do this when you are alarmed and angry, you are likely to vent about your co-parent to Ralph's mom or whomever. While you do need friends to vent with, it will be better for your child if those adults are not the parents of your kids' friends. When people take sides they build coalitions that can distort every action. If you build a coalition of your children's friends' parents against your co-parent, you will make it harder for your co-parent to participate in school functions and all the myriad activities kids do together. That's a way of pushing your co-parent out of your child's life. It may feel satisfying, but it is not good for your kids. It is best for your kids if both parents are involved in as many aspects of their lives as possible, especially those that are school-related.

A couple of other issues are highlighted in these scenarios. One very difficult issue is raised when one parent really does drop the ball all the time and the other parent is left to pick up the pieces. You can find yourself being drawn into a dynamic over and over again that you steadfastly don't want to be involved in. This requires setting some firm limits with yourself. Again, keeping your focus on what your child is stating can help you as well as him.

In the moment, your job is to respond to your child, not to your co-parent's actions. One woman was in this exact dynamic and her daughter, who was five, was always very upset when her father was scheduled to pick her up and didn't (he wasn't leaving her at playdates, but with her mother). "Sadie gets really mad at me, hits me, takes it out on me, and I find that so hard. Now she's using her words and saying, 'I'm so disappointed that my dad didn't come.' All I can say is, 'I understand.'"

She's exactly right. It is not your job to make sure your co-parent is a good parent. And it's going to be hard to witness the fallout when your co-parent lets your child down. But all you can do is keep up your own end of the bargain with your child, and support him in his feelings.

Of course you have to ensure your child's safety and if your co-parent is chronically flakey, you should not allow the child to be in a too-vulnerable position. You can give your child a cell-phone so he doesn't get stranded. You may have to take the matter up with a mediator.

One of the main tenets of this book is that children experience their parents as part of themselves, and the divorce feels like an internal split even more than an external split. Your kid may ask you leading questions that have a subliminal desire to get you re-involved with your co-parent. The child may feel reassured by what he perceives is your connection with your co-parent, even if that connection feels uncomfortable for you and is mostly negative. By keeping the focus on what the child is actually saying, by not immediately going back into the feelings of your relationship with your co-parent, you can help keep your boundaries firm. You are also sending a message to your child that you are separate from your co-parent and you are not going to jump back into a negative stew, but instead are going to proceed rationally.

Another common response kids of all ages have to divorce is "Who takes care of me?" When a parent flakes out, that question is at the core. It may be that your child's insecurity about that very issue is coloring his own interpretation of events—because it is still possible that your co-parent arranged with Ralph's mother to have them picked up but didn't adequately brief the child about the change in plans. Although pick-ups and drop-offs are baroque and involved under the best of circumstances, in the divorce situation it is even more important that the child feels very secure with all arrangements that involve him. You and your co-parent will probably have to make an extra effort to be very clear about those kinds of plans.

Some other examples of bad feelings sneaking into conversations with your child:

KID: Dad promised to take me to McDonald's and he didn't.

MOM: Your father wouldn't know how to keep his word if it had a million dollars attached to it.

A better response:

MOM: So you didn't get your fast food fix.

KID: Mom said if I didn't do my homework I couldn't go skateboarding. I love to skateboard, and she wouldn't let me do it.

DAD: Well, I guess you didn't do what you were supposed to do.

This is a tricky one because the mom's deal with the kid is fair, and the dad is more or less supporting it. The language used could be improved, however. The child seems to be stating, in fact, that he didn't do what he was supposed to do and may feel bad about it. You don't want to just compound his feeling of failure. It would be more helpful for the dad to say: "Why didn't you get your homework done?"

Kids will also play parents against each other and the trick is to get beyond that to the core feelings the child is struggling with. "Mom won't let me…." "Dad won't let me…." Part of these statements are questions about the maintenance of authority. There's a simple rule of thumb here. "Your mother makes the rules in her house." "Your father makes the rules in his house." This takes some discipline on your part, to not get into how things are done on your co-parent's watch. For more on all this, see chapter 7, "Sharing Parenting."

Kids Elicit Emotions about the Other Parent

IN THEIR COMMUNICATION, kids will say things about their other parent that make you respond emotionally.

1. They will do this naturally just in talking about this other part of their life.
2. They will also do it to reinvolve you with your co-parent.
3. They will do it to indirectly ask who has more authority.

In all cases it is important for you to keep your emotions about the other parent out of the transaction with your child. Come back to your child each time: what is he asking me? What does he need from this? Remember kids need reassurance, power, connection. They need to know that they will be taken care of. They need to know that you are OK.

FOURTEEN-YEAR-OLD: Dad says you let me stay out too late.
MOM: Your father thinks I'm a lousy mother.

I bet you can figure this one out. The kid is questioning the authority of his father against his mother. She makes it about her. When the child makes a leading statement like this, the best thing is probably to say nothing, to let it go.

Communication and Behavior Are Linked
—The "Ah-Ha" Moment

One of the most effective results of active or reflective listening is that it eventually helps put the child in touch with himself. Kids go on and on with their behavior, and it's like they don't even know they're doing it. Sometimes they have to be disciplined for behavior, and then they get a cause-and-effect message from you. Say you have a four-year-old boy who throws sand in the playground and you give him a time-out, and then he comes back to the playground and hits somebody with a shovel. You remove him from the premises. The cause and effect of consequences is absolutely appropriate in this situation, but sometimes you need to reach the kid on another level. He needs to check in with himself, recognize his frustration or anger, and find a way to manage it.

In raising a child you are helping a whole self grow and mature. Mature people, in general, are able to observe themselves—they don't just act. They think about their actions. Thinking about your actions is a kind of communication with yourself. You can help teach your child to do it by leading him back to himself through active listening.

So your son throws sand and you give him a time-out. You can see he's still on a tear—his mood hasn't changed much after five minutes. "You are frustrated." "He won't let me play!" "You're angry." "I wanted to play with the kickball and he…." And it will go on. "So when you're angry, what can you do about it?" This may stump your child and he may go back to "I had the ball and he took it and…." So then nod and say it again. "When you're angry, what can you do about it?"

When a child is in full-swing active play, and his energy is high, you want to help him find an equally attractive and energetic outlet for that energy as an alternative to hitting his friend with a shovel. It may not help him to suggest that he go down the slide by himself. But it may help to tell him to look around and find someone else to play ball with. As these playground dynamics go, the villain in the case will very likely want to join in a new game of ball, and your child will have the deeper satisfaction of resuming play with the person he was struggling with.

And kids will struggle with each other. It's more important to support your child's feelings and to bring his attention to them than it is to find a solution to the problem at hand. Some kids are working on some major power issues, and you will exhaust yourself with other people's children if you get into it too deep.

How to Show Understanding

How to reflect a child's feelings:

1. Listen to the child's expression.
2. Identify the child's feelings. Phrase a statement that conveys acceptance and understanding. Give the feelings a name—happy, sad, angry, disappointed, scared, hurt, etc. ("You are angry about that missed play date.")
3. Parental attitude is very important. Take the time to listen with full attention, or wait for a better time.
4. Genuinely accept the child's feelings.
5. Have confidence that the child will find his own solutions.
6. Remember that feelings are often temporary. A child will move through them much more if his feelings are accepted.

Things Not to Do When Reflecting Your Child's Feelings:

1. Do not criticize the child.

2. Do not reassure or sympathize with the child. This sounds harsh— but your reassurance at this point sends a message that the whole transaction is over, and that the conflict being expressed is not solvable by the child. The best the child can hope for is a kind word from you, and that doesn't help him learn to deal with his feelings.

3. Do not suggest a solution to the child's problem.

4. Do not moralize or tell the child what he "should" do.

5. Do not threaten a child with punishment because he has negative feelings. This comes up when your child is angry. Often you want to put an end to his feelings of anger immediately—because they make you uncomfortable (this is understandable!). You CAN say something like, "I want you to express your anger in a normal voice. Otherwise it's very hard for me to listen to it. And you are allowed to be angry, but you are not allowed to throw things."

6. Do not put down the child's feelings. We do this more often than we think. "You shouldn't get all huffy about such a little thing!" While you want to acknowledge their feelings, you of course don't want to encourage them to dramatize every little incident that comes along. By calmly saying, "Hmm, you sound upset," and letting it go, you encourage your child to move on and solve the feeling himself. It's important to remember that if a child is doing something over and over again, he has a goal or a need that he's trying to meet. He's going to keep trying until he gets there. Often a child has an overall sense of insecurity that you can address holistically. This includes communication, expression, behavior, and plenty of positive reinforcement. Sometimes a regular time spent with the child alone several times a week will give him what he needs.

Roadblocks to Communication

(Based on work by Dr. Gordon Thomas)

THE FOLLOWING TYPES of statements often prevent honest communication of feelings and make the other person defensive.

Type of Statement:	Examples:
Ordering	"Don't you dare talk to me that way!"
Warning	"If you do that again, you'll really be punished!"
Preaching	"Don't you know you're supposed to obey all adult authorities?"
Giving Solutions or Suggestions	"If you would act nicer, these things wouldn't happen to you."
Lecturing	"Anything you get in life must be earned."
Judging	"I would never have done anything like that when I was your age."
Praising, Agreeing	"Yes, you're right. You can go there whenever you want."
Ridiculing	"Why are you being such a wimp?"
Interpreting	"You've always been jealous of him, haven't you?"
Consoling	"There there, it isn't so bad."
Interrogating	"Did you ever stop to think they might be right?"
Humoring, Diverting	"How about an ice cream?"

Listening for Understanding

"I hate it at Dad's house. He never reads me a story before I go to bed."
Feelings: Disappointed, angry.
Response: "You wish Dad would read you a story before bed." OR "It makes it hard for you to go to bed at Dad's house when you don't have a story."

(Note: In the case of something like this, and depending on your child's age, you may want to speak to your co-parent about the situation. If the child is old enough to ask his father for a book before bed, you can let that go. They have their own relationship to work out. It also depends on your relationship with your co-parent. If you're on good terms, you can discuss this. However, don't tell your child you'll take care of it. It's important to acknowledge his feelings and let that be enough.)

Mother has invited child to her company picnic at a time when he's usually with his dad. Both parents had discussed this earlier and agreed on this plan if the child wanted to do it—and he said he did. But when it actually came time to leave his dad's for the picnic, the child was reluctant to do so.

Feelings: Ambivalent, unsure, torn, pulled apart.

Appropriate response: It's hard to decide where you want to be when both choices sound good to you." OR "You want to go to the picnic because it sounds like it will be fun, but it's hard to say goodbye to me right now."

The inappropriate response to this is something like: "Go ahead, you'll have fun." But at some point, if the child continues to object to going, you do have to set limits. Children need to be acknowledged, but they also need to honor their agreements and fulfill their responsibilities.

A child may use a situation like this to bring attention to their ambivalence, which is fine, but those mixed-up feelings cannot be solved by allowing him to not go to the picnic. Further conversation in this scenario might go something like: "I understand you changed your mind, but your mother is expecting you and you said you wanted to go. I'm sure it will be fun, even if you don't think so right now. So let's go."

Fine-Tuning Listening for Understanding

1. Tone of voice is very important. Do not parrot, mock, laugh, overemphasize or underemphasize what the child is saying. Convey

genuineness and honesty. The tone we take with our children often sounds like a tape recording of the tone our parents took with us. Sometimes it takes a major effort to catch yourself in the act of impersonating your own parent. Becoming conscious of how you were parented will bring up some big feelings in yourself. It will help you become a better, more conscious parent.

2. Use words appropriate for your child's age. There are plenty of occasions to use words your child doesn't already know, to expose him to a varied vocabulary and so increase his own. But when feelings are in the forefront, use words your child already knows well.

More Examples:

"I don't want to go to Mom's. Everyone hates me over there."

Feelings: Lonely, left out, discouraged.

Response: "You're having a hard time at Mom's house these days."

This is a case where you definitely want the conversation to go on a bit longer. Are there some specific people at Mom's house who create a problem for the child? The hard part right here is to wait for what your child says next.

"Mom always makes her boyfriend whatever he wants for dinner, and she doesn't care whether I like it or not."

You could do some active reflecting here and acknowledge these feelings; you could say, "Why don't you talk to her about it?"

One thing kids are doing in these kinds of complaints is trying to get a sense of where they have more power—with mom or with dad. What you want to foster in them is a feeling of power in themselves; that they have the wherewithal to discuss what is going on with both parents. You might be tempted to say something like, "I'll make you whatever you want for dinner the next time you're here," but that's giving a wrong message. You may want to console your child, you may want to get out of the conversation quickly, and the offer seems like a solution. But it just encourages more testing on the part of the child, and that doesn't serve him in the long-run. He needs to feel secure with both parents to the extent possible. His feelings of security reside in himself, and that's where you want to help him get stronger.

"I'm afraid to go to sleep at Dad's because I might have bad dreams."

Feelings: Fearful.

You want to say: "Does being at Dad's make you have bad dreams?" OR "There's nothing to be afraid of. Just go back to sleep."

It's better to say: "Bad dreams can be scary." OR "You're worried about how you'll get back to sleep if you wake up from a bad dream."

"Jimmy's dad is taking him fishing. He always gets to do neat things with his dad. Why doesn't my dad do things like that with me?"

Feelings: Disappointed, sad.

Ouch. This might really hit home—you may harbor thoughts that your co-parent is a neglectful father who doesn't do enough positive activities with his child. You may wish heartily that things were otherwise, for the sake of your child. But you can't change the situation. The best thing you can do is help your child name his feelings, of disappointment in this case, and get them out there. By hearing his feelings, you're helping hugely.

It's best to say: "You wish you and Dad did more things together."

"Mom lets me have Super Blastos at her house!"

Feelings: Angry at Dad.

You want to say: "Your mother may not care if you play with violent toys, but I do!"

It's better to say: "You're angry that I won't buy this for you. You wish I had the same rules as Mom."

You can't really know from your child's strategy whether or not his mother DOES let him play with Super Blastos, or whether the child is just trying this method for guilting you into getting him what he wants. Either way keep yourself out of the ugly feelings. State the child's frustration, and move on. You could get upset over what you deduce is bad parenting either way, but your child will learn much more from you about how to behave if you model calm rationality. It's not the time for a "lesson" about guilt-tripping or even about violent toys.

"I hate the divorce! It's all your fault. Dad says you left him and didn't want to keep our family together. I hate you! You are selfish!"

Feelings: Angry, resentful, sad, disappointed.

You want to say: "Oh yeah? Did he tell you what he did that made me finally leave him?"

It's a million times better to say: "You are really having a hard time with the divorce. You feel it's all my fault and wish I would have stayed with Dad so you could have the family together."

Now we're hitting home. "Did your father tell you that?" might pop out of your mouth before you know it. It's really, really hard to hear this kind of stuff from your child. Since most people go to a kind of Neanderthal way of behaving around divorce, it's quite possible below-the-belt sorts of things like this are indeed getting said by your former spouse.

Not only is it important for you to stay out of the conflict that is being set up for you to fall into, active listening will help you do it. Just don't go there—keep your focus on your child's feelings, on listening to the feelings your child is sharing with you and not so much on the content of the complaint.

It definitely gets tiring to be the one taking the high road all the time. In many cases, your child is testing your boundaries, testing how much power he has in the situation. Try hard not to give in to this testing by taking the bait. Remember, taking the bait is not a healthy thing for your child. Your rage and reaction in this case would not be about your child's feelings at all, and your child would end up being stuck with those feelings, compounded by confusion about yours.

"Why do you take so much money from Dad? He can't even take a vacation this year."

Feelings: Angry at Mom, protective of Dad.

You want to say: "What? Look at how he spends his money. He just bought a new car and he's sending his girlfriend's child to camp. Those are his choices."

It's better to say: "You're worried about your dad. It seems like you're having some feelings about things between your father and me not being fair."

"Mom's going to have another baby. I can't wait!"

Feelings: Excited, testing the waters of your reaction.

You want to say: "What? How's she going to pay for another child? I hope she doesn't want any more help from me because I'm not giving it to her!"

OK, let's say you are utterly flabbergasted when you hear this. You can't possibly reflect your child's feelings because you can't think straight. Your child is probably wondering how you'll take this information anyway, and in effect may be asking you how you feel about the news. There is an appropriate response, of course, which is something like, "You're excited about becoming a big sister!"

It's really okay to say, "Wow, that comes as a surprise to me," and let it go at that if you need to process the information. Later, you can say something to your child about her excitement in having a new sibling—you want to make that okay for her. It's alright if you can't be the perfect listener every time—when you can't reflect back with equanimity, it's best to wait for another occasion.

Positive Communication with Your Co-Parent

This whole topic may elicit a deep sigh. You just can't manage to have a conversation with that such-and-such without it devolving into nasty recriminations. You've tried to be rational and calm, but your co-parent is totally invested in letting you know, at every possible juncture, how unhappy he is with you, how wrong you are about everything. Furthermore, even the smallest arrangements go awry. You simply asked your co-parent to pick your kids up early on Saturday so you could fulfill another obligation—instead, he didn't pick them up at all and you had to renege on another responsibility. As stated previously, many separating and divorced people seem almost to relish their miscommunication with each other. Somehow missing the boat all the time reiterates the idea that the marriage didn't work. The renewal of anger and frustration keeps the issue of who has power over whom alive, and when people are feeling wronged and aggrieved they may resort to negative strategies to make themselves feel strong.

You can get into this discussion of the whys and the wherefores for years. Indeed, many people who have been divorced for decades will still tell you with passion why their former husband or wife was always difficult and obstreperous. You don't have to resolve all your feelings about the person you were formerly married to in order to be an effective co-parent of your children. But you do need to make every effort to communicate well. Because it is across the lines of these communications that much of your childrens' lives get lived.

Checklist for Communicating with Your Co-Parent

1. Eyes on the prize. It's worth struggling through difficult conversations and plans with your co-parent because you are doing it for your kids.

2. Develop a deaf ear. If your co-parent is in the habit of goading you, don't take the bait. You don't need to teach him a lesson. You don't need her to understand your point of view.

3. Use active listening to acknowledge your co-parents' needs and feelings, even if you disagree with why they are having them. People don't move on in the conversation when they don't feel heard.

4. Avoid a placating tone or sentiment. "Yes, dear, it's hard to be a millionaire investment banker," or "I know you need time to *get in touch* with yourself," are going to stoke the fires of enmity.

5. Cool off before picking up the phone.

6. If your co-parent is giving you a knee-jerk response, change the subject. Stay out of the dance.

7. Double-check your actions. Are *you* giving a knee-jerk response?

8. You can't control the other parent. Don't try to control the conflict, just get out of it. Sidestep it.

9. If you can't speak with civility, communicate via fax or e-mail.

10. Expect ten defensive answers before you get anywhere.

11. Remember your kids are listening.

12. Work on resolving your conflicts. If you can't resolve your conflicts, how can your kids?

13. The solution has to include both you and your co-parent. You have to give some ground.

Embrace the Idea of Good Communication

The first thing to do to improve communication with your co-parent is to make the decision that you are going to try hard to do it. Take the long view and understand that you are going to be in contact with this person more or less for probably several decades—even when your kids are grown, there are going to be weddings, and grandchildren, and all sorts of occasions where a smooth ground between you will benefit everyone. In the very first place, you don't want to be duking it out with this person for the rest of your life. That's just too tiresome—and you have better things to do.

If it is hard to extrapolate that your own satisfaction is going to be enhanced by communicating well with your co-parent, then go straight to the higher purpose: your kids. Many of the negative effects of divorce result from poor communication between co-parents. Bungled or disruptive custody and visitation schedules, putting children in the middle, children's feelings of being abandoned or not important, all of these fall under the rubric of communication.

Goals of Communicating with Your Co-Parent

1. To make clear arrangements regarding your kids.
2. To model good negotiating and problem-solving for your kids.
3. To make your life easier.

You and your co-parent need to have clear messages about who, what, when, and where to manage your kids' schedule. You also need to treat each other with respect, because your children are watching and taking cues from your behavior. They are learning how to negotiate with other people from the way you do it. They are learning how to deal with difficult feelings by watching you handle yours. This is not to say that every dispute or miscommunication is a disaster—it's not. Your overall effort and good intentions will have the lasting impact on your child. Ideally, they will also work on a difficult co-parent over time, encouraging a good reciprocal effort. However that may not happen, and it isn't your goal.

The High Road Requires Some Blinders

Some of the most successful people in the world have the thickest skins. That may not be something we want to encourage in ourselves in general, but when dealing with your co-parent, it will help to let certain things go, to turn a blind eye and a deaf ear. Don't let yourself get riled up by every little thing. Just forget it—drop it. Say to yourself, "That bozo is always pushing my buttons and that's why we're divorced." Roll your eyes and forget it.

Some people are expert manipulators because they sow the seeds of discord, and you're upset before you even know what hit you. The next time your co-parent upsets you, take a moment to simply realize the fact. "She's done it again." "He said x, y, z and suddenly I feel awful." It can help you see that what's upsetting you is not an objective reality, but a subjective surmise.

One woman's husband liked to criticize her parenting style. "He would tell me that I didn't spend quality time with the kids. I would take them to the movies. He took them golfing. He said he valued time to talk with them and I didn't." It upset her, naturally, that her co-parent de facto called her a poor parent. Was she a bad parent? "No! I spend plenty of time talking to the kids, and we love going to the movies together." What's the true import of her co-parent's comment, then? "He was just saying he's better than I am which he always does and is partly why we're divorced." When she looked at it this way, the woman could see the comment in perspective. She could say to herself, "He's just trying to make himself big by making me small." She could extract the upsetting part of his communication, the part about her being a bad parent, and disregard it. He was just using an accusation he knew would get a rise out of her. Ignoring these kinds of baits goes a long way to discouraging their use—if your co-parent doesn't succeed in getting your goat this way, he or she will eventually stop trying it.

Acknowledge Your Co-Parent's Needs

We're not talking the deep, emotional needs of your co-parent, which you no longer need to pay any attention to at all! We're talking the logistical limitations your co-parent has in relation to caring for your children. If your co-parent is a chef and works from one in the afternoon till midnight, he's not going to be able to pick the kids up after school. You may absolutely need the kids to be picked up after school, and then you need to approach this situation in a problem-solving manner. "I know you can't get the kids at 3:00 and neither can I." This may sound obvious but many people insist on pushing their co-parents in areas where there really is no leeway. If you find yourself doing that, you need to take a step back. What are you trying to prove? And why? Be practical. Approach the situation from what is really there.

Many co-parents are locked in what both parties feel is an unequal balance of needs acknowledgment. "She doesn't realize how hard I work," and "He thinks I can leave the office any time to take the kids to the doctor, but he can never leave to do it." Variations on the theme are endless. One very good strategy to begin changing the balance of the relationship is actually to verbally acknowledge the constraints and wishes expressed by your co-parent. Even if you can't quite get to a solution for the problem. "You don't feel you can leave the office in the middle of the day." Often when people feel they are being heard, their defensiveness and aggression subside and real communication and compromise can begin.

One man divorced for over ten years shared custody of his teenage daughter with his former wife. "I called her the other day about picking Cassie up for the weekend and she was so tense and brief I just thought, 'what a pain in the rear she is, I can't stand dealing with her.' Then later she e-mailed me and told me what was going on for her—changes in her job, her sick mother—and she apologized. But I realized, I still have to be exposed to this person's whole life all the time even though we've been divorced for more than a decade." It's one of the rubs of divorce—neither party is going on from here into a complete vacuum, and both you and your co-parent are going to have complexities and disappointments and all sorts of eventualities that will enter into your discussions with each other. Rather than wish the other person's complications away, just acknowledge them and cut to the chase.

Keep Yourself Honest

Check in with yourself —spend some time thinking about your own sore points and how you are likely to head into rage or confusion once those buttons are pushed, and make every effort not to go there. Cool off before you pick up the phone. Being angry and then initiating a communication is a not entirely honest thing to do—you're loading the dice. You're putting your co-parent on the defensive. You may dearly want your co-parent to pay in some way for his or her actions, but this is something you can't work out while you're talking about how your kids are doing in school. The residual resentments of divorce are not going to be resolved through these communications—they are just going to be tossed back and forth, distorting the situation at hand. If you feel overcome with the desire to wound or hurt or obfuscate, it's OK—just get yourself some help. Vent elsewhere. Don't give your co-parent the satisfaction of meaning that much to you on such an intimate level.

Use "I" Statements and Active Listening Techniques

The same techniques for communicating well with your kids apply with your co-parent. It's a bit harder to use them, because your co-parent is tuned to many possible shadings of the conversation, and may be just waiting to be offended or to disregard your honest attempts at communication. Accordingly, don't use condescension—taking the high road means really trying, it does not mean "Let me show you how much more enlightened I am than you are." The placating platitude will only annoy. It dismisses the issue. Try to be honest with yourself and say, "This is hard for me to hear right now, but we can talk about it later,"or "I'll think about it."

Active listening with the child's other parent can be used to diffuse difficult emotions, to keep the ball rolling, as it were, without getting caught up in anger and accusations. Active listening is one of the fundamental tools of conflict resolution. When active listening with an adult, your perceptions of what the other person is saying will be corrected by them, perhaps several times. You may have to restate what's being communicated several times before they really feel you've "got it."

Remember, getting what you want out of a situation means the other person largely gets what they want out of it also. The solution has to include both of you.

With a child expressing anger, sometimes all they really want is for you to know they are angry. With an adult, there is often a more concrete wish being communicated, but sometimes it isn't clear what that wish is. When your co-parent wants something you don't want to give them, it does help to talk directly about the subject—not around it. Active listening helps you get to the heart of the matter.

Example Exchange

JOHN: Judith, I can't make it today. I know I'm supposed to be there in fifteen minutes.

JUDITH: You always do that. You're always letting JoJo down. Why don't you call me when you've got it together?

JOHN: I don't have to take this! *(Slams the phone down)*.

Instead ... "John, I feel awkward when I have to explain your lateness to JoJo. I wish we could work out a schedule that is good for both of us."

When you are presented with an issue, situation, or feeling, try to summarize it. Say, "Do you mean that you feel that situation was unfair?" Then the person you're talking to can say, "No, I mean this." Put your reaction out there (within reason) so you can feel it out and follow the train of thought. This can be hard—it can be a new way of talking for many people. Your co-parent may quickly try to get you back to a fractious emotional terrain simply as a matter of course. Some of us are actually habituated to stress and strife and paradoxically feel more comfortable there. Watch yourself for these tendencies also. If it helps, sit there on the phone with a pen and piece of paper and make a mark every time your co-parent tries to derail the conversation. Expect it to happen ten times before you get anywhere. If you find yourself too tired by the whole thing, just excuse yourself. Say, "I can't quite think straight right now. When would be a good time for me to call you back?"

You Can't Control Your Co-Parent

Try to work beyond your conflict with the other parent. There is a vicious cycle of attack and defense—and it won't get you anywhere. Once you are in the conflict, don't try to control it, get away from it—change the subject. Later, when you're cooled off, approach it with a problem-solving openness. Invite the other person in to help solve the problem, to collaborate. Don't get stuck in who's right, who's wrong. It's important to try to work on these issues for the sake of your kids. You may want to wash your hands of the whole deal, and indeed, there may be too much between you to really approach productively. Choose a few key issues—the ones that have to do with your kids. If you can't talk on the phone, use the fax or e-mail. Take a deep breath. Try to be positive.

Remember, your kids are watching. Try to project that although you are having a hard time, it won't always be so hard. The more negative you are about the divorce, the more negative it will be for the kids and they will turn that on themselves. At the same time, you can't control how your co-parent is going to deal with the situation, so take care of yourself. Modeling good behavior will turn down the heat on the conflict and send your children a good message.

Another Example

CHILDREN ARE COMING back to Mom's house from Dad's. Dad walks in with them; Mom is uncomfortable with this.

Inappropriate:	"You intrude on my space. You think you can walk in here any time you want, but you don't live here any more. From now on, just let the kids out of the car and don't walk them in."
Appropriate:	"I'd rather that you not come in the house when you drop the kids off. I feel vulnerable around boundaries right now and that would help me out."

Rage and Guilt Are Sometimes Embedded in the Conversation

Why do people escalate into bitter feuding and exhausting manipulations? Often it's because of shame and guilt. Rage and selfish behavior are often strategies to ward off far worse feelings. No matter what the circumstances of the divorce, both people at the very least are going to feel like failures at relationship, for a while. If one person has established another relationship already, that can exacerbate the bad feelings in the other person—you may feel wronged, but deep inside you might also feel, "oh my God, SHE has a new partner; it must be ME who doesn't know how to do this." A generalized feeling of "there's something wrong with me" is tremendously eroding to a healthy sense of self.

Address your own feelings of shame and guilt by talking to a therapist or to a support group. We want to hide these feelings that make us feel less than everybody else—one of the best ways to ameliorate them is to talk them out.

When your co-parent is having a real conniption fit, it can help to remember that shame and guilt might be the source of it. By screaming back, you actually confirm their lousy sense of themselves, which will in turn make them want to "win" over those bad feelings even harder. Screaming louder doesn't do the trick, but people try it all the time anyway. The more your co-parent can make you the bad guy in this scenario, the more he or she is trying to make themselves feel better. There can be a terrible loss of face in a divorce—if your co-parent is feeling abandoned and ashamed of it, he or she is going to try to save face and often that will be at your expense.

The key is to remember this factor. Don't address it directly with your co-parent. Let it inform your understanding of why the conflict gets so bad. But remember, your co-parent's emotional business is not yours anymore. Don't take it on—you have enough on your plate.

Anger Is Not Your Friend

You know how things build when you're angry—you don't just have one complaint about the other person, you have a mountain of problems with how they're behaving and what they want from you. Building that little mountain of rage can feel good—you build yourself a case for condemning the other person, and you feel more right about it the more you add to it. While your co-parent may indeed justify a heap of anger, it doesn't help negotiating with him when a big pile is standing between you. Active listening can be a discipline for you—to break down exactly what the issues are, to deal with just those issues, and to let certain other things go. Sometimes anger has its uses—it can help propel you out of a bad situation, if you happen to be the sort of person who talks himself into staying when you should go. Beyond that, re-consider. Your anger feels good, it feels satisfying to be right, but it really isn't that helpful to you in the long-run. It doesn't help you solve the hurdles that are standing in the way of the best life for your kids. Which is your best life, too.

Another Example

PARENT MAKES AN appointment for the child on the other parent's time.

Inappropriate: "You put the kids in the middle when you plan things for them on my time. It's a setup for me to be the bad guy because then they are mad at me when I can't go along with what you planned. So stop trying to control things!"

Appropriate: "I'd appreciate it if you would make appointments for the kids on your own time with them, not on mine. I feel like I disappoint them when I can't go along with what you planned." OR, "Before you make appointments for the kids on my time I would appreciate it if you would clear it with me first. I feel resentful if I have to change my schedule around after the fact."

Focusing on Outcomes

Focusing on outcomes is a way to get past verbal pitfalls. For example, you might say to your co-parent: "Betsy is failing in school. One thing we can do is make sure she gets her homework done every day. I understand it may be difficult for you to help her get her homework done when she's at your house because of your job and other pressures."

Then you might expect your co-parent to tell you in no uncertain terms how difficult her life is and how hard everything is and she may even complain about not being able to handle Betsy, who doesn't listen to her. Expect your co-parent to name many thousands of complaints and excuses.

Gently repeat your outcome statement. "Betsy needs to get her homework done. I'm willing to listen to what you need in order for us to find a solution for her getting it done every day." Notice that you very wisely and maturely avoided saying, ". . . at your house which is a disorganized mess and you don't care if she flunks school and winds up on the street without an education!" Keep avoiding saying such satisfying things because they won't help you reach your outcome.

If possible, brainstorm several solutions to the situation. Maybe if Betsy got an alarm clock and woke up a half hour earlier each day, she could organize herself better and get the homework done before school. You don't want to use bribery, but you could offer to get her a desk if you believe she doesn't have a space in which to work at your co-parent's house.

When focusing on outcomes, expect to get a long list of defensive excuses and nonanswers before you get anywhere. Remember, if your co-parent can come up with a solution that works for him, it is much more likely that he'll implement it and follow through. So be patient. Don't attach too much to your own solutions—remember that what works is much more important than what's ideal.

If both of you can agree on using a mediator to help with these issues, that's a great idea. You could pose the possibility of a mediator by disarming your co-parent with your candid self-assessment: "Gee, I can't seem to let go of my own opinions enough to listen to yours. It would help if we could get a neutral third party involved. Would that help you?"

One father was extremely frustrated with his ex-wife because in school conferences their daughter's teacher said the girl was always falling asleep in class. "My ex just does not get it that our daughter needs to be in bed at eight o'clock. If there's an interesting program on television, she lets her stay up. I don't care if it's PBS, sleep is more important to her!'"

This man approached his ex-wife on the subject in a way that didn't exactly help things. "I couldn't help it, I'd get so frustrated. Miranda would fall asleep at the dinner table once she got to my house and I'd call her mother and say, 'What the hell? You're seriously hurting our child. If she can't stay awake she can't learn!'"

The father's position and concern were very clear. The mother's were a little less distinct. Because Miranda's father took such an active role in his daughter's education, her mother kind of left that part of her life to him. So when Miranda was at her house, she was looking for other ways to enrich her life, like opera specials on television. "I can say my wife looks for ways to get my goat, and imperiling Miranda's education is one sure-fire way," says the father. But by bringing the full freight of this conflict between them into the discussion of Miranda's bedtime, he wasn't helping matters one bit.

This man and his co-parent used a mediator to help them through this and other conflicts. "We came up with an outcome statement we could both agree on: Miranda needs to go to bed earlier. I can't tell you how long it took to get to that!" The mediator posed a solution: since it was hard for the mother to get Miranda to bed during the school week, maybe she ought to live with her father Monday through Friday. "Well that got her attention—she doesn't want that at all. So for the time being, our child is getting to bed on time. I'm sure it'll slack off eventually, and I'll have to drag us both back to the mediator again."

It's easy to get fed up with the constant battles—but your child is worth it. This man and his former wife had always clashed over issues of practicality—it was part of what made them get divorced. Yes, it is so tiresome that getting a divorce when there are kids involved doesn't free you up from these conflicts. But since you are no longer married, you can look at the ongoing dialogue with your ex as a business partnership, in which you perhaps have to deal with a very difficult, but vital, partner—your co-parent.

Outcome Checklist

You need to resolve an issue or make a request of your co-parent. Before you see or call them:

1. Write down what you plan to say. Write it out very fully, including all the feelings that you have surrounding the issue.

2. Go back and read what you've written. Look at everywhere you've called your co-parent wrong, implied that they are stupid or mean, and so forth. Examine your words for any implication that they are bad in any way. Cross out all those words. Rewrite what you plan to say. Hone it into one declarative sentence that contains no blame and doesn't pick a fight or vent any feelings whatsoever.

3. Cut the sentence out and hold it in your palm. When you speak with your co-parent, stare at the sentence. Remember, this and only this is the agenda of this conversation. Anytime the conversation veers away from this piece of information, stop.

4. If your co-parent has an issue of their own to bring up, make sure you feel the issue you raised is resolved first before moving onto it. If sticking to this one point has been draining, ask politely if you can reschedule another time to talk about their issue.

5. As you negotiate, do not say "no" to anything that comes up. Say, "I'm willing to consider your solutions to this situation. I'm writing them down." Write them down. As your co-parent feels that he or she is being heard, it is likely that defensive, hostile reactions will subside. When they are done with their solutions, go back over the list out loud. Ask for some time to consider these. When you talk again, be methodical (but not annoying): "Here are my responses to your suggestions. Would you consider them?"

6. As you keep talking, remember at roadblocks to repeat, "I'm willing to keep working until we come up with a mutual solution." Mean it.

Stories:

Making the Connection ॐ

As a LICENSED social worker, Katie Stimac had all the buzzwords down. "I know the stuff. I know about active listening, about creating healthy boundaries. Everyday I work helping people put their lives in order, trying to make an orderly world for them. But my own life just kept falling apart at the seams."

Not yet thirty, Katie and her husband, Jake, have four boys, aged three to ten. Jake has substance abuse problems and their marriage has always been volatile. In a drunken rage he put her head into a wall and she had him arrested; an antiviolence program in the court system led Jake to Kids' Turn, which the whole family participated in.

"I recommend divorce workshops to people who think they know what they're supposed to be doing, because you can't help yourself, you get caught up in your stuff, and in fact, you are not doing what's best for you or your kids. One day in the workshop I just realized, it's not just my awful husband who's creating this situation. It's me, too."

With four kids and limited income, day-to-day exigencies are always stressful for Katie and Jake. Jake is emotional and very attached to his boys, who adore him, yet he is never consistent about his visitation. "It was my worst problem," Katie says. "The boys just love him, and I know they need a father. Jake is out of control in many ways but not with them. When the kids come back from being with him they're happy, they went fishing, I can see they feel better about everything. But I couldn't live my life around whether he would show up when he was supposed to or not."

When Jake didn't show up for a scheduled visit, Katie would become more and more agitated. The kids would be sitting and waiting, faces pressed to the window. The oldest boy would shut himself up in his room—sometimes even forgoing dinner and certainly refusing to talk to his mother about his disappointment. "So then I would pick up the phone, scream at Jake. The next time I saw him,

I'd be tearing my hair out." While the oldest boy became withdrawn, Katie and Jake's seven-year-old would try to make the situation better. "Don't worry Mom," he'd say, "Dad is here now and it's OK." "It's not OK!" Katie would scream. Then it seemed like the tables were turned and Jake would be the calming presence in the room.

"I just realized, I have problems. I have problems! Somehow I am participating in this awful chaos and making home an even more unsafe place for my boys." Katie joined Al-Anon. "It's free!" she laughs. "Going to a self-help group like Al-Anon provides just the interruption I need. Instead of having the whole, crazy reaction to my husband I hold my breath. I'll talk about it in my meeting later. I'll be heard."

Meanwhile, Katie took her problem to the mediator assigned to her and Jake by the court. The mediator basically told Jake that if he didn't show up and didn't give advance warning, he was going to lose his rights to see his boys at all. "It's logical consequences for adults," Katie says, smiling at her mastery of the buzz words.

With four kids, it was virtually impossible for Katie to respond fully to each child's needs all the time. "A friend had great advice for me," she said. "You know how the pediatrician tells you not to worry so much that your kid gets all the food groups at every meal, but to look at a whole week's worth of nutrition? My friend basically told me to make sure that I heard each kid at least once a week. That sounds ridiculous, but it really helps me. In fact I keep track of it in my date book."

Doing this led her to see that while she was in constant contact and response with her youngest kids, especially the middle ones who were seven and nine, she had virtually no meaningful conversation with her oldest, who was twelve. "I noticed this over the course of several weeks, and this lightbulb went off. He was the one who cared the most that his father didn't show up, but part of that was because I was ignoring him! I didn't do it on purpose—it's just that he's pretty self-sufficient and the other ones are always in my face, needing this, needing that."

Essentially, she caught up with her eldest son just in the nick of time. "Because he is older, he could understand and accept that we had to make a special effort to have time together. I made a date with him to hang out for an hour before he goes to bed every Sunday night. It's like a big treat because he gets to stay up. And the deal is, he gets up and gets dressed *tout de suite* on Monday morning or the time gets shorter the night before. We read or talk or whatever. He likes it because it's this extra time—I didn't take anything away from him. I'm so glad I got this together before he really becomes a teenager and turns off from me altogether."

5

How to Support
Your Child's
Expressive Self

I F COMMUNICATION IS the key to connecting with your child, expression is the key to your child's connection with *herself*. Just as it's hard to underestimate the importance of healthy, fluid communication between parents and their children, expression is a barometer of mental and emotional health. What and how your child expresses herself really shows you where she's at. Expression helps her move through her feelings and let them go. Artwork, fantasy play, reading, and talking it out are tools your child will benefit from using her whole life.

Kids are physical beings and part of their task through every stage of development is to express and control themselves through growth spurts and other changes. Just as you bring crayons and paper to a restaurant to give your child an outlet while he otherwise has to sit still, drawing and playing acting games can not only help your child say and understand how he feels, but blow off the pressure from those feelings also.

Even highly verbal kids who seem able to tell you exactly how they feel may actually be holding something back, and when kids are holding something back, they probably feel it is a "bad" or otherwise unacceptable feeling. Those, of course, are the feelings you want flushed out for them. Giving your children a wide range of ways to express themselves can help provide unexpected outlets for some unexpected truths.

Expression is a direct line to our emotions, but it plays critical physical and intellectual roles as well. Expression is about more than venting —it's about activating the full panoply of human abilities. When we say "creative expression," you might think, Mozart, or O'Keefe. But also think, Michael Jordan and George Soros. Expression is the activation of the self through various forms—music, art, basketball, and finance among them. Moreover, it is through expression that a child learns to initiate, to persevere, to reinvent, and to complete a task. A block in expression is a block to learning and to future attainments.

The ability to express oneself is bound up with the very mechanisms of learning. A four-year-old's picture of the house she lives in looks very different than an eight-year-old's rendering of the same exact domicile. The maturity expressed by the older child reflects cognitive advances, a deeper understanding of the way things work and go together, and a much greater ability to match an inward idea with an outside depiction of it—she can really control a pencil. An eight-year-old has a developed memory and can retain details like shingles, or paint color. There is also by this age an emotional overlay to the illustration. A child who actually draws a lot from age four to age eight is both grasping concepts by depicting them and mastering them at the same time.

To foster and encourage your child's expressive self requires some patience and self-knowledge on your part. You have to be in a space to actually hear what they have to say or see what they have to show without shutting them down, or giving any signals that what they are feeling is unacceptable. If you aren't in a space to do this right, then let it go until you are.

Along those lines, there are some benefits kids get from divorce support groups that you can't really provide yourself. A major part of expressing yourself is finding the words to say how you feel—and kids often employ an internal censor around their parents. In a divorce group kids get to see that their peers have the same or similar experiences. Divorce often changes a family's social orientation, either through moving to a new neighborhood or school or just in the vagaries of shifting alliances. People you once socialized with as a family may feel they have to choose sides or drop you altogether— they are cowardly scoundrels, and you didn't want to be their friend anyway, but boy does it hurt when that happens. And it does happen. A divorce support group gives your kids another peer group to belong to, and that is immensely reassuring.

Also, no matter how good your intentions or how well you receive painful information about how your kids feel, they are not going to share everything with you. The divorce creates divided loyalties—even if your child seems not to have a relationship with the other parent, that person is internalized by the child and some part of himself will protect that internalized part. The only way a kid can really talk about the whole experience of the divorce and find an advocate for both the side of himself that identifies with his mother and the side that identifies with his father is with an outside person or group. Therapy is another option, of course. But if you feel your child is adjusting reasonably well, a kids' divorce group is of incalculable benefit.

The remainder of this chapter covers:

1. Why expression is intimately tied to learning and growth.
2. Suggestions for fostering creative expression in kids of different ages.
3. How to respond to what your kids show and share with you.
4. Declarations from the Kids' Turn newsletter written by kids to their parents. This encapsulates what kids want their parents to know about how they feel about the divorce and is written at the end of a six-week workshop, when the kids have become familiar with the divorce concepts and have worked through drawing, puppetry, and role-playing to connect to their feelings.

Expression Is Intimately Tied to Learning and Growth

It's a point made in the previous chapter: how we are in the world is largely a matter of communication. Expressing yourself is the home base of communication. And learning to express yourself is learning to read, to write, to understand words, which are symbols, and other symbols as well, like in science and math. Psychology says that for a concept to be truly understood, language must be involved. That means if you can't explain it one way or another, you don't really know it. Do you remember that experience from school, when you had to write a paper on something you thought you knew well? The act of actually having to explain it might have revealed that you actually didn't know your stuff as well as you thought. But by the time you've *written* that research report on the humpback whale, you *know* about those creatures. As the journalist James "Scotty" Reston put it: "How do I know what I think until I read what I write?"

This idea that to be understood a concept needs to be spoken or written is fundamental to why it is important for kids to express their feelings about divorce. If they don't say it or write it, the feelings remain more amorphously part of their general emotional weather, and it is much harder for the child to deal with those unclear feelings. Additionally, language, because it is expression, is the primary connection each of us has with the outside world. Working out problems using language is a way of working out problems in a wider context. If kids keep it all inside, the world they are willing to move in becomes very inhibited and small. An important part of themselves is hidden, is not participating with others. Support groups like Alcoholics Anonymous are built on this knowledge—that to heal, people need to talk. Furthermore, writing is the most "integrative" task of learning—kids who write well demonstrate their ability to organize their thoughts and present them sequentially. They are also controlling their physicality at a high level.

Once words are spoken or written, they can be let go of, and the child can move on. Of course younger children do not have the words yet— because intellectually they aren't developed enough to put feelings into concepts. That's where drawing comes in, and puppet play. Kids of all ages benefit from playacting and drawing because through these media they can show themselves and also hide. There's a risk undertaken in revealing your feelings and if a great horned owl puppet can express them for you, so much the better. Drawings are blessedly open to interpretation, so they don't have to "mean" anything the child doesn't want them to mean—and you should never push them on that. Speech and writing are wonderfully direct but are also more susceptible to defense mechanisms. Ever have a clearly miserable person tell you how happy they are, just insist upon it? They can say such things, but they probably can't draw them.

The Habit of Talking

IT'S A GOOD IDEA to talk to your children a lot. They may not always understand what you are saying, but they get bits and pieces of it. At some point, you'll hear an older child use a sophisticated word with understanding—her understanding begins with exposure. Children eagerly reach out from every corner of their being to absorb the world and participate in it, and they will work on understanding you if you approach them with patience. Engaging in conversation with your kids not only stimulates their cognitive growth, it also connects directly with their ability to express themselves as they are already familiar with open lines of communication with you. We all know people who talk all the time and never say anything and never hear anything you say in response—so just talking is not the answer, but it is a good beginning.

A two-year-old with a crayon makes a rapid tangle of lines called "sensory motor scribbling" which is aligned with her internal state, and she does this without knowing it. (The Jackson Pollock difference is that Pollock knew what he was doing. In fact, one could argue that his greatness comes from the strong connection he made between the two-year-old primitive self and the self-reflective adult.) The growing child moves from scribbling to representation; what begins as unconsciously expressive of a subjective state becomes more about the objective world.

Kids are highly personal and their awareness of the outside world dawns on them slowly, over the course of years, but even a five-year-old drawing a fairy princess is borrowing from a reality outside herself to show her blossoming self-concept. Another five-year-old may spend a great deal of time drawing action figures, guns, and battles—he's still expressing an internal reality using some of the symbols he resonates with from the world at large. By the time kids are about seven or eight, they may still be drawing princesses and war machines, but the drawings will be more elaborate, will tell a story, may even include thought bubbles or other kinds of verbal labeling. You may think, "Hey, we're just talking kids' drawings here," but they show an enormous amount about how well the child is attaining language and concepts.

In learning to read and write, the child is organizing a spatially perceived world of information into a linear, sequential manner. When kids have learning "differences," they are often having difficulty with sequencing—with decoding a word from its beginning to its end, with following a sentence from start to finish. Some kids need to grasp the whole of something before they can master its parts; other kids have an easy time with the parts and trouble with the whole.

Emotions interact at every point with learning because the energy they take is diverting. When a kid is anxious, it's like there's a roadblock to learning, and you can show her and show her but she can't see. Learning styles also have an impact on a child's social life—some kids are overcontrolling with their friends and insist on certain rules. The child may be putting parameters around what she understands, making herself comfortable enough to proceed with whatever game. But peer interactions are fluid and depend on the kind of integrative process that this child is having trouble with. When other kids don't recognize or want those rules, she's going to meet rejection, and that will compound her woes. Thus the child's whole life, from cognitive development to emotional state to social life, are intertwined. An event like a divorce, which causes a disruption in one area, can have repercussions in these other dimensions as well.

And where these developmental hurdles are particularly damaging is over the long-haul. You can see there's a domino effect to a child's sense of failure— not reading well, perhaps feeling sad, not getting along well with peers. Kids who meet with frustration often stop trying, become avoidant about risk-taking. It's not that a child's areas of difficulty become worse and worse, but as they get older they are asked to perform more and more tasks. The foundation needs to be solid for her to proceed with enthusiasm. As the child enters the teen years, she decides more firmly that she is one kind of a person—maybe she says she's good at sports but not at academics. When the truth is that she has academic potential she simply doesn't want to risk getting near, because she doesn't want to fail.

Certainly not every child of divorce follows the negative trajectory to avoidant, limiting behaviors. You can see that when they do follow this trajectory, the disruption to the family life has crossed over into a disruption in development, and development plays itself out through expression.

The Positive Role of Loss in Expression

Expression can be used as the vehicle to healing, and it can deepen and widen many avenues of endeavor for a child. In the first place, loss is part of life. The recent research showing that kids from divorced families can sometimes do even better than their peers from unchanged families makes the point that children who learn to cope young use that ability to great effect throughout their lives. Adaptation is the key to evolution, and children of divorce get an early dose of its importance.

In another sense, loss opens up a new kind of awareness. If that awareness is acknowledged, and treated with care, it can open the doors to greater compassion and even intellectual understanding. Even if a divorce happens when the child is under the age of five, at some point as he or she gets older and understands the family circumstances, there is going to be an awareness of this loss of a potential wholeness. The breaking apart of one kind of wholeness, however, creates the opportunity to find new growth, a new wholeness. There's a saying, "What's bad for the ego is good for the soul." In drawing on inner resources to cope with feelings of loss, a child can develop a soulfulness she might not be prompted to discover for quite some time otherwise.

One loss is extrapolated to other losses as well. Maybe the child's sadness at the changed family translates to a feeling of inner emptiness—such is the proving ground for new artistic endeavor. Invention fills the void. Expression is the way we bring together the various parts of ourselves, the way we integrate opposed pieces. It's the way we restore ourselves when we feel depleted. One reality is gone and another must take its place. There's a basic life principle of eternal regeneration available to all of us, and expression is the way to employ it.

Creative Work Can Help You Too

PROCESS-ORIENTED CREATIVE work is a wonderful way for you to work through your loss as well. If you live in a major metropolitan area, it is likely you can find a class at a university or community center that focuses on painting or writing to work through emotions, or one that puts it another way and takes the emotional life as the springboard to expression. On your own, there are some good books to guide you. *The Artist's Way* by Julia Cameron is a classic in the field and focuses mainly on writerly ambitions; *Life, Paint and Passion: Reclaiming the Magic of Spontaneous Expression,* by Michelle Cassou and Stewart Cubley, uses paint as the medium. Both are excellent and user-friendly.

Suggestions for Fostering Creative Expression in Kids of Different Ages

Talking is one of the most natural and organic ways to open up lines of expression with your kids. As discussed in the previous chapter, talking is really about listening. In this case expression is really about allowing difficult feelings to come out into the open. With older kids, you can ask them point blank how they feel, and use active listening techniques to respond to what you hear. With younger kids, you'll want to use reflective listening, to respond to their emotions in the moment. "You're frustrated. You don't want to go in the car to Daddy's right now. It's hard that Daddy lives in a different place." You want to acknowledge the underlying issue without making too big a deal out of it. It helps to draw a child's attention to the fact that she is having a difficulty or showing an emotion, so that she learns how to observe this in herself. That inner connection made by the observing ego is a key function of expression.

Make-Believe is Serious Business

For kids three to five, pretending with them and encouraging them in their pretend games is right on their level. This is the age of fantasy. Kids will gladly pretend to be a hopping bunny or a purring kitty, or a dirt-digging trac-tor. Giving kids the tools and space and time to pretend may not address the divorce issue per se, but it gives them the opportunity to try on different ways of being, to discharge different emotions. Let a child this age use plastic or light metal containers from the kitchen to bang around with, to sort dried beans into and out of (if they are relatively contained, orderly kids, which some are and some aren't). What you are letting them know is that their activities and experiments are welcome. At the end of the play ask them to put the containers back, if that's physically possible for them. Even if they just get one plastic lid back in one drawer, they are learning that they are competent and have a participatory role. This kind of message eventu-ally widens in the child's self-concept so they are more willing to be expan-sive and experimental. If you are always saying no and disallowing them from adult areas (and some days are like that for everyone), the child can get the idea that she is basically disallowed from the adult world in general.

Play is the way this age child integrates herself with the world, imitating the activities she sees around her, and the various roles of important peo-ple. When small children have invasive hospital procedures, pediatricians routinely recommend getting them a child's doctor kit for home. The child eagerly plays doctor to your patient, reversing the role she so uncomfortably had to play, gaining mastery over an experience that she didn't volunteer for and had to play a passive role in. Use this idea to empower your children: if a major issue is getting into and out of the car going from one house to the other, let the child play Mommy or Daddy and make the couch into a car. Pretend to be a recalcitrant child. If you hit on this game at the right moment, your child will find it hilarious.

Dolls and Other Stand-Ins

Kids from about three on up naturally play with dolls, action figures, and stuffed animals. Through this object the child externalizes her inner being, finding a part of herself in a stuffed cat or a baby doll. Kids use dolls and stuffed animals to rehearse and work out the way their parents treat them—dressing, undressing, feeding, putting to bed—and it gives them the con-trolling role. You can use a favorite doll to try to work out certain problems your child may be having, around the divorce or anything else. "Why won't your baby eat her dinner?" "She doesn't like carrots." "But I think she does like carrots. She liked them yesterday." Even if these interactions don't yield perfect satisfactions in the moment, they still establish a back and forth of mutuality, and give your child an alternate persona to express herself through.

A word about dolls that look like grownups. Some parents are aghast at these dolls, see them as personifying very adult qualities and activities, and disallow them. Most progressive educational systems discourage them, because these dolls present so much detail to the child that the imagination doesn't have anything to provide. These philosophies have a strong point—you want your kids' toys to elicit their imaginations and creativity, not to preprogram them. On the other hand, these dolls do in fact model adult qualities and children are very curious about this realm of existence they are headed into. Girls can experiment with full-fledged womanhood in an exaggerated form by playing with you-know-who, the doll with breasts! Boys can do the same with the action figures they gravitate toward. Children feel their own gender in a strong way and seek to resonate with it, and these dolls in their very specificity provide a certain kind of satisfaction to children. Of course, both male and female dolls should be made available to children of both sexes.

The other contribution dolls and figures from popular culture make is that they provide a binding subject for the peer group. Just as adults talk about the latest film or book together around the proverbial water cooler, so kids talk about their entertainments. Peer pressure is something we all have to deal with from a position of strength in ourselves at some point or another. But for a very small child just forming that self, she can be strengthened in her burgeoning identity by feeling a part of the group. Not to advocate these dolls either—but the subject deserves consideration from all angles.

The same discussion maintains for television and the movies. A certain line of thinking disallows them altogether for children—and there's a point to that. Children are sense-driven, they are like one big sense organ, and they take it all in. When a story is presented on a big screen with loud sound and saturated colors, it can be utterly stupefying. When *Pinocchio* is acted out by puppets for children, there is a physical proximity to a live person, the puppeteer, which the child feels. There is something warm and relational about a puppet play. The level of sensory input is low-key. The story unfolds in a temporal progression that is comfortable for the child—like a half hour or so. When the same story is told on a screen, the child has a different, more passive relationship to the narrative. And, of course, even the movie *Pinocchio* is not the problem—television commercials that show big globs of green goo as delicious snacks are the problem. Kids don't have the same powers of observation and differentiation that adults do—they don't have that little voice saying, "Someone is trying to persuade me here."

Again, though, do you like to be stupefied by the movies? Sometimes that mindless entertainment is a huge relief from the burdens of the day. Kids, too, need a break. Children will have to make their own eventual sense of popular culture. At a certain age—you are the best judge of your own kids—some exposure may not be an evil thing. Sitting in front of the television for long periods of time does promote a disconnect between the child and her own feelings—she's not in her own head while she's watching the tube. But a half hour to an hour a day can help make a transition easier, can function as a breather. The more you can participate in her viewing, the better.

Picture This

Drawing is one of the earliest expressive activities a child is capable of—even a two-year-old can wield a thick piece of chalk. The toddler isn't going to draw a picture of anything, but the very physicality of the activity is satisfying to her. A certain comfort level with drawing from an early age will foster its continued evolution. From about age five, a child can safely handle child-size scissors, scotch tape, and paper, and if you ever have to travel on an airplane with this age child, don't leave them behind. Costumes are a big hit. One mother advises that in every boy's young life there comes a time when he simply must wear a cape. Some little girls dress as Snow White for a year or two before the costume falls apart.

Enter the World of Magical Thinking

Up to about age seven the child has a penchant for magical thinking. This is a tremendously important stage where the child is moving from primary process thinking to secondary process thinking, and understanding the difference between the two. Primary process thinking is the realm of dreams, of fantasy, where time and space do not enclose or limit or define. Primary process thinking doesn't leave us, but by the time of adulthood has become the purview of nighttime and creativity. It's the mental space where solutions are dreamed up, where healing occurs, where crucial adaptations are made. Secondary process thinking is logical and abstract. It's how the business of the day gets done. Kids aged nine to eleven are more involved in secondary process thinking and gravitate more often to board games with their attendant rules. They are more likely to keep their fantasies secret.

While your child still moves freely between the two realms, enter her world of magical thinking. Ask her to draw her favorite superhero and ask her what the superhero is doing. Ask your child, "If this warrior could do whatever she wanted, what would she do?" You may hit pay dirt and get an answer like, "Mommy would move back home," but you probably won't. Go on to ask, "Why don't you wish for something that really could happen." Your child might say something like, "I will get a new stuffed animal." You can then say, "Well, although Mommy and Daddy are not going to live together again, you will probably be able to get a stuffed animal for your birthday."

The child needs to sort out what is and is not affected by the divorce and this will help her do it. This little exercise helps draw the line for your child between reality and fantasy. It helps her understand that she cannot get her parents back together again, but she can still have her desires and needs met.

Making the Transitions

TO HELP KIDS aged four to six make an adjustment to a new living situation, you might ask them to draw something they like to do with Mommy, and something they like to do with Daddy. Of course, the two locations could also include Grandma's house, or if there are not two houses in question, something they like to do with their mother, and something they like to do with their father. An older child can understand some of the logistics about the divorce, words like "judge," "custody," and "court." If your child is resisting the idea of the divorce and you need to show her that this is a real thing, you might make an appointment for her to talk to your lawyer or mediator. Together you can make a list of questions for her to ask. You might want to prepare the attorney for some pretty broad questions, like, "Will I ever go to Disneyland with my father?" Part of the use of this exercise is to actually organize your child's thoughts around the divorce, so she gets a better sense of what exactly is affected by it and what is not affected by it. A good answer to the above would be: "You'll have to ask your dad about that. But you will certainly spend time with him in the future. He cares about that a lot." Open the door to a discussion or awareness that things have changed and that's OK. There are good things about Mom's house, good things about Dad's. Or, there are good things about spending the day with Dad on the weekend. If you know of other families that are not totally traditional, you might bring them up. Like, "Kathleen and her sister live in the city on the weekends. Did you know that?" You are opening up the idea that having a "different" living situation is something other kids have too.

Puppets can be an excellent way to get at issues. You can engage in a puppet play with your children where you or they take the part of sad parents or arguing parents, and then choose a puppet like a lion or an owl to represent a reassuring authority figure. You can let your kid take the part of a child caught between the parents. As the lion or owl, you can reassure the child or ask the child puppet how she feels. Your kid may be able to speak through this persona in a way that's impossible directly. As this play goes on, your kid can take the authority figure puppet and practice saying the reassuring words. You can prompt your kid by taking the child puppet and saying, "Oh, I feel terrible when my parents fight!" If your child is having a hard time going to the other parent's house, you can give her the authority puppet to take with her. "I'll go with you and keep you company," you might say through the owl.

Even if this little exercise doesn't get you anywhere definitively, as in a direct expression of your child's feelings through the puppets, just posing the possibility of role playing will help your child. By taking the part of the child yourself you can show empathy for how your kids feel. This exercise might be something to try more than once. Your kids may warm up to the whole concept and return to it eagerly. They will "get" that they can express certain feelings through the puppets that are hard to show otherwise.

Working It Out with Clay

SOME KIDS ARE in a developmental moment where drawing is too much for them and puppetry is out of the question—these activities require a certain amount of control over yourself, of sitting still. Clay and other soft malleable sculpting materials are generally accessible to all kids. Even if the child just squishes it and makes it into balls and doesn't construct any story and no observations come of this activity, it is good for your child. It's almost as if the clay can absorb some of the unruly emotions the child may have trouble discharging in a positive way.

Storytelling: The Oldest Art

Perhaps more than any other form, stories bridge the gap between the inner and the outer worlds. The key is language. Fantasies help solve inner conflicts, and speaking these or putting them into narrative form gives them a worldly life of their own, gives them a reality that can be pointed to. Going back to the principle that it is through language that concepts are fully realized, so does the story fully encode meaning. If you think about how the child's development follows a progression from the level of action to the level of speech to the level of thinking, stories encompass all three. Stories are a kind of marriage between play and thought.

Children love stories. They love to hear "true" stories about themselves, about you when you were little. They love fairy tales. They love your own (often lame) made up stories. Tell your children stories. Telling them stories about themselves will help them connect their past with their present and trust in futurity even as their current situation is changing. True stories from experience are memories, and they bind what was with what is. Your child will find respite in your memories, just because there is a continuous thread there and they can hang onto it. Make up stories for your kids, even if you don't feel very good at it. Your leaps of imagination may feel played out or stale, but they will resonate with and respond to your creativity—it will spark theirs. Your own spontaneous imagination is catching.

There's a Native American tradition that says Grandmother Spider is spinning a web that is a story and that story is our world. There is a fundamental truth to this idea—culture and identity are stories told from one generation to the next, and they are how we know who we are, where we came from. To a child who says, "I don't want to be from a divorced home," you say, "It's part of your story." Grandmother Spider's web, a story, literally makes our reality. Your child needs to know he is still part of a continuing reality that is holding him. Giving him the idea that *he* has a story puts the divorce in a different light—it's a narrative development, but it's only part of the whole picture, and that whole picture has a size and an importance all its own. Connecting to the place where your child's burgeoning self is questioning itself is immensely satisfying and reassuring for him. It goes back to that fundamental task we all have, of becoming a self.

Fairy tales, red in tooth and claw as they may be, are also very nourishing for the child's imagination. Fairy tales are closer to primary process thinking—transformations are prompted by magic, incidentally, as the result of curses that are eventually undone. The subject of virtually all fairy tales is loss and transformation. In this they are rehearsals for the experience of life. Or they depict the child's experience of loss in a way that is easy for her to take—in the realm of timelessness, of magic, and make-believe. Children have an instinctive understanding of the seriousness of the world, they are trying to orient themselves to it. Many parents want to shield their children from evil and loss and all those bad things, when they would better serve their children by exposing them to these eventualities in contained stories. Kids will let you know what they can stand. A two- to three-year-old who absolutely loves *Snow White* and wants to hear that story every day for two years may turn around when she is five and tell you it is too scary. It has been observed that in fairy tales, evil is the cause of its own undoing—could you put it better yourself?

Reaching Teens

Teenagers are a prickly bunch, half in the world of childhood and half out of it. They will resist being prompted by you to express themselves, but many will welcome the opportunity to take an acting class or a ceramics class. In some way, the teenager does need an outlet for those roiling energies—yes, they may seem to be asleep on the couch during normal business hours, but there's a lot going on in that lump under the afghan.

If your child is at all inclined, get her a diary. With a lock. Pledge, and do not break your pledge, that you will never under any circumstances read that diary. Call it a journal if you meet resistance to the term "diary." Give your kids books like *Go Ask Alice* and *On the Road* to spur them into the form. (Look at these books yourself to make sure you are OK with your child's exposure to them.) Part of the isolation of being a teenager serves a higher purpose—they are understanding in a deeper way that they have a unique, individual mind. A diary can be just the thing to support this development. As with younger children and expression, the act of writing in a diary can both relieve the pressure of their feelings and help them gain mastery over them.

There is a wonderful resource on the Web called The Diary Project, at *www.diaryproject.com*. It is a site specifically for teenagers to write and share anonymously their thoughts on subjects from discrimination to body image to friends to tolerance. One category is: Who Am I? The entries are vetted by a panel before they are posted. There is a companion "Diary Deck"—seventy-five cards each with a teen's anonymous diary entry and questions about the bigger issues touched on. This is simply a spot-on resource for teens and their parents to explore the issues that are sometimes difficult to broach. Both Deck and Web site are intended for kids thirteen and up. But particularly if your teen is on the younger end of the spectrum, take a good look at the Web site before you share it with her. Some of the subjects are very explicit and deal with issues like sex and drug use. It's worth mentioning again that while our impulse may be to shield our kids from these subjects, time and again it is shown that informed exposure with parental guidance protects kids much more than ignorance. This Web site may be the perfect way to answer some of the questions and concerns your teenagers have without risking themselves in asking an adult about them.

We all remember being a teenager—part of the job is being lonely, grappling uncertainly with what to take and what to leave from the world of adults. These days, kids are exposed to much more explicit material than ever before, with far fewer social structures like churches and community organizations to titrate the flow. If only we could put more clothes on those young ladies on television! If only we could take a red pen to rap lyrics! If only we could change the salacious expressions of very young models on bill-boards. But we can't.

One woman with a thirteen-year-old boy found herself totally distressed at the music he was listening to. "It is horrible, let me tell you, by any standard." Of course, this upper-middle-class kid from the suburbs was listening to hard-core rap with virulent aggression against everyone, especially women. "I simply forbade him to have the music," she said. "And that didn't work." Her alarm grew as he smuggled the music into the house. She'd find him listening to it late at night in bed on headphones. "There was really no way I could control it," she said. "If I got stricter with him at home, he'd just spend more time at his friend's house listening to it."

One of this woman's friends, a wise one, suggested she actually listen to the music. "My friend didn't go so far as to think I would learn to like it," she said. "She was saying I should know what it was all about, and try to have a conversation with my son about it. Well, I blew him away one day. I picked him up after school and popped in a CD of the raunchiest, most awful stuff that he adores. His mouth dropped open. And then he began to flinch and squirm, because those lyrics are utterly sexual and embarrassing to listen to in front of *your mother*." And then she made a new rule. He could have the music, but he had to listen to it with her—he could listen to it by himself also, but he couldn't have any music he wasn't willing for her to hear. "I still hate the music. It's ridiculous, it's utterly misogynist, and he's a nice boy. But I decided that the bottom line was I didn't want him hiding anything from me. I want to be in his life. I'll listen to the stuff if that keeps him from shutting down." With teenagers we often have to shift our priorities, and keeping the lines of communication open is more important than controlling what they listen to.

Responding to Your Child's Expression

Encourage your kids with plenty of praise that focuses on their effort, on their inner selves, on how much you love them and love being with them. Try to avoid focusing too much on the accomplishment itself. For example, when they paint a picture, it's better to observe something about it than to just praise it right out. Say, "Hmm, you're using green more than you usually do. I like that." Instead of "Great picture!" It's not bad to say great picture, but you want to encourage the activity itself, keep the child connected with doing it, rather than depending on a final result to win approval.

One child said to her mother, "You just tell me you like my pictures because you want me to feel good about myself." The mother said, "Yes, I want you to feel good about yourself. Because you are good, and I want you to know that. But I also want you to know how much your artwork pleases me." That child was not so much rejecting her mother's praise as questioning it: does she really mean it, or is she just coddling me?

On one level or another kids know fakery, they know shallowness. You don't really get away with anything with them, even if it seems like you do sometimes. If they don't outright rebel against what they perceive as insincere, they will turn the feelings of disappointment on themselves and get the message: no one really cares about me, they just pretend to. The good news is that even if you feel you are failing Parenting 101 all the time, your kids do take in your sincerity, and that helps them build their own integrity over the long haul. Some kids do many things really easily—they read, they get beginning math concepts, and then they hit a roadblock when school becomes more challenging. It's important to teach kids that effort and the long haul really matter, even more than getting an A right this minute. Most of us wish we could be more patient with ourselves learning something new. You have an opportunity to teach your children that kind of patience and interest in the process. It will pay off for them over their whole lives.

The occasion on which you make these particular connections is important. With all kids, you want to be on the lookout for informal, "teachable" moments, when the child essentially creates an opening for you. In other words, you'll have less success if you say, "let's sit down and draw your fears for the future," than if you notice your child is drawing, and you join him. The right situation will present itself for addressing your child's fears and concerns. If you make a suggestion to your child that you are willing to talk about your child's fears, even if that moment isn't right for your child, he or she will remember your openness and will come back to it at a better moment. Remember to choose your time carefully, and let yourself be led by your child's mood and disposition.

Try some of these activities more than once. Sometimes kids take time to warm to a new game, particularly one where there's some emotional content, and you may not be that comfortable with the emotional content yourself. Feel free to improvise if what's suggested here doesn't feel organic or natural to you, but gives you an idea of how to approach your child. The main point is to connect. Kids at different ages require different ways to connect with them, but all of them do want to be heard. Try to be relaxed and calm when you initiate games with your child, and if the moment isn't happening, let it go and try again later.

A Note on Interpretation

Easy does it. Kids indeed are smart, and the minute they think you are looking for "meaning" in their artwork, they will edit themselves to please you, or they will shut down. It's always best to ask open-ended questions rather than make labeling statements. "You made two houses. Why?" Not: "I see you are showing that now Mommy and Daddy don't live together anymore." One of the great pleasures of creative expression is that we reveal ourselves in storytelling, in painting, and we also disguise ourselves in the same work. Don't deprive your child of this function of what she is doing.

Many kids will draw or paint violent, death-filled pictures, but this does not mean they are having deep psychological problems—if they are having serious problems, it will show up not only in their artwork but also in every aspect of their behavior. One of the most useful functions of expression is to discharge negative and violent emotions. Some kids find power on the page that they lack in their everyday dealings.

Children who are drawing out internal conflicts have these in relationship to their parents—one kind of internal conflict can be defined as the desires of the child that seem to be at odds with the parents' rules. Looking at a picture together and talking about it can be a very good way to connect with your child about those problematic desires, but think about how touchy this whole area is—you are the enforcer and when your child exposes herself to you, she may fear punishment. It's important to hear about those fantasies, to see them drawn—you can say, "Wow, that unicorn is really being hurt by that bear." Not: "Who is the bear, who is the unicorn?" Don't try to get an adult translation like "I'm afraid Dad is hurting Mom." Let the child talk about the drawing, and let that be enough.

What Were You Allowed to Express Growing Up?

WE ALL HAVE unspoken and sometimes unconscious rules about what we allow ourselves to feel, and what we allow ourselves to show. Most of this template was formed in our family of origin, where maybe the mother's authority was simply never to be challenged, or a father had such poor self-esteem that any perceived criticism was a total threat to his well-being. What were the rules about how to be and how to feel in the family you grew up with? As you understand yourself more, you'll also appreciate how you influence your children's ability to express themselves.

The Kids' Turn Newsletter

One of the culminating activities of the six-week Kids' Turn program is a newsletter the kids write to their parents. Each age group is asked what they would like to tell their parents, and the leaders write these down. The children are assured that the newsletter will be anonymous. The leaders take the material and edit it a bit—so that if a child says, "I want Fluffy to come with me to Dad's house," the leader will change that to "We wish we could take our animals to both our parents' houses." The entries from each age group are put together in one newsletter and given to the parents, who then have a chance to respond.

You clearly can't do this at home. "Anonymous" isn't going to mean anything when it's just you and your kids. But the amazing thing about the Kids' Turn newsletters is that in over 14 years, the newsletters from each six-week session are practically identical. Kids simply bring up the same wishes, thoughts, and desires over and over again, across ages, across socio-economic backgrounds, across race. So you can read the following with some surety that if you and your child were to go through Kids' Turn, you would receive a newsletter very similar to this one. What follows has been consolidated from representative newsletters created in workshops over the years. Underneath in italics are some parental responses, also consolidated from several years' worth of newsletters.

The Kids' Turn Newsletter

What Kids Want Their Parents to Know

We hate it when our parents fight.

> *We will make every effort not to fight, especially in front of you.*

We feel sad when you don't listen to us.

> *We will try to listen to you better. We would like it if you would also listen to us better.*

We feel sad when our parents try to make us happy. Sometimes we just need to feel sad.

> *We understand that you need to feel sad sometimes.*

We feel angry when one parent calls the other parent bad names.

> *We know you love your other parent, and we will make every effort not to call each other bad names.*

We feel afraid when one parent blames the other in front of us.

> *Sometimes we get angry and say things we shouldn't. We apologize. We will make every effort not to blame each other.*

We want to be happy. We want our parents to be happy.

> *We want to be happy, too, and we will all work on this together.*

We feel sad and caught in the middle. We feel guilty when we have to choose one parent or the other.

> *We will try to keep you out of the middle. Please let us know when you feel you are being put on the spot.*

We want more companionship with our parents.

> *Let's brainstorm some ways to spend more time together.*

We want our parents to get back together again.

> *We aren't going to get back together again, but we will continue to work on a happy new life with two families instead of one.*

Stories

Jamie's Book ॐ

"WE DIDN'T DO screwball things," says Olivia Hammond. "We walked through everything together. We were married for eleven years. Jim and I went to therapy together for the last two. Finally we decided he would keep the apartment, and I would move in with a friend." Olivia is a photographer—she mostly takes pictures of food and restaurant interiors for cookbooks and magazines. Her former husband is an architect and also teaches painting at a nearby art institute.

"From the beginning, we have been completely concerned about doing this the right way for Jamie. Jim spends more time with her than ever. She's absolutely loving that—but part of it is because she's so comfortable at the apartment. There are several rooms at her disposal, her bedroom, a study, Jim's office, the kitchen, living room, dining room." Olivia laughs. It hasn't been easy to take up living quarters with her friend and her friend's child. "Jamie doesn't have her own space there—she shares a bed with me. The other day she curled into a ball and sobbed for like forty minutes, saying 'Mommy, I hate it here.'"

Olivia keeps her good humor about it, and she insists that since Jim pays the rent on the apartment, it's only fair he should live there. "I make decent money," she says. "I'm successful. But I've worked pretty much part-time for all of Jamie's life. I'm having a hard time finding an apartment I can afford that is relatively close to Jim's—like in the same city." Jamie attends a good school that both Olivia and Jim are adamant she should be able to continue in through eighth grade.

Olivia is a pretty woman in her mid-thirties, and while she is clearly brave she is also clearly bewildered. She shakes her head. "I just can't believe how lowered in status I feel," she says. "I never in one million years thought that kind of thing was important to me. But now I'm this nomad, and I don't have a home. And my former husband has like three thousand square feet. He has the career and now that we're divorced, he's this wonderful father. He has it all." She smiles and shrugs her shoulders, looking as if she would really rather not feel any bitterness. "I wonder, if I had never married him, would I have pursued my career differently, so that I would be making much more money now? Of course I would have. But I wouldn't have Jamie." At Jamie's school, Olivia feels self-conscious about the car she drives and the clothes she wears. "I never gave it any thought before, but now I feel exposed. I know it will pass and I'll land on my feet again."

Feeling so very vulnerable and unsettled, it is hard to be present when the nine-year-old Jamie has her own problems. "She's with me half the week, and recently it seemed like she spent every waking hour she's with me complaining. A while ago I asked her to please stop complaining, which I do all the time, but this time it's like she looked at me with these big blank eyes and closed her mouth. She refused to talk to me for the rest of the night."

The two of them were sitting in a spare bedroom on a pullout bed having this interchange. Olivia was exhausted from working all day, had spent an unfruitful couple of hours looking at apartments that all seemed crawling with mold. A little peace and quiet, even because Jamie was angry, was not entirely unwelcome.

"But then it went on. And if she had continued to seem really mad I think it wouldn't have worried me so much. But it's like she became despondent. I would ask if she wanted me to read to her and she'd shrug. Did she want to go out to breakfast? No answer. She wasn't giving me any attitude—she was giving me no affect whatsoever. When I dropped her off at school on Wednesday, she dashed inside without looking back and for the first time in five days seemed like a kid again. Wednesday is the day her father picks her up and she spends the rest of the week with him."

Olivia felt so crushed she followed Jamie into school and asked if she could speak to the school counselor. "I cried in that woman's chair for like an hour and a half. She was very good to me." Jamie had also been having trouble at school and the counselor was familiar with her situation. She and Olivia brainstormed about ways to make Jamie feel more comfortable in whatever situation they found themselves.

"She had this brilliant idea. Since we were living here and living there, why not keep a 'travel journal'? The counselor said that treating our peripatetic existence like a journey would also imply to Jamie that it eventually would end. She reminded me that Jamie had it pretty good because she got to stay at Jim's half the week, which was the space she had lived in since she was born."

But Jamie, who was having trouble with reading and writing at school, looked at her new travel journal and heaved a deep sigh. It was like homework. "I thought about it for a full day after I saw the defeated look on her face," said Olivia. "And then I got a great idea. I put the travel journal away and went to an art supply store." She got a simple sketch book with a spiral binding, and a box of high-quality markers.

"Now Jamie keeps a picture journal," says Olivia. "It seems to really help. She draws like three or four pictures a night. She's so absorbed in it I sometimes get the feeling that she's using the art to block out the circumstances around her. But, hey, if it works to get us through this time, then I'm real happy."

6

Making Peace in Your Own Backyard— The Challenge of Behavior and Discipline

I F YOU HAVE turned to this chapter out of frustration (or desperation) because your child's behavior is driving you crazy, go ahead and skip down to the section on What They're Doing and Why for suggestions on how to deal with it. When you have a bit more margin on your time and mood, come back and read the introductory words, which will help you focus and readjust your basic thinking about discipline.

Behavior Cheat Sheet

1. Time-outs, logical and natural consequences, and understanding the goals of your child's behavior are your best discipline strategies. You can figure out the goals of your child's behavior by checking in with how his or her behavior makes *you* feel.

2. What kind of a parent are you? Another way to gain insight into how your children are acting is to review your own childhood.

3. You have less energy now and yet, more is required of you. Make the extra effort to enforce limits. Establish boilerplate responsibilities around the house and boilerplate courtesies. When your basic rules are not followed, enforce consequences until they are.

4. You have your rules; your co-parent has his or her rules. They don't need to be the same. Your children will learn that different things are expected of them at each house.

5. If your co-parent is allowing your child to stay up too late during the school week or if there is some other issue going on that is having an impact on your child's performance in school or social life, address it with a third party present, like the child's teacher. A mediator is another good idea.

6. If you are in a highly adversarial relationship with your co-parent, focus on maintaining your own orderly and well-run household. Don't worry about what goes on at the other house, unless your children are in danger.

7. A child's temperament influences both how they act out and your best approach for dealing with it. Even with teenagers, check in with your sense of who they are.

8. Acting-out behavior usually has something to do with your child's sense of insecurity. All kids feel insecure as they make new social attainments, grow, and are required to do more in school. Children in divorcing families are also worried about being abandoned and unloved.

9. Remember that "discipline" is an important occasion for meaningful contact between you and your child. It is one of the basic formats upon which your new family is founded. Take some time to review your own expectations and how you can make them more positive.

Behavior Issues Are a Natural Part of Being a Child, and Divorce Creates Special Challenges for You and Your Kids

Problematic behavior is not something only divorcing parents have to deal with—all parents have to deal with it. But there are several reasons why a divorce is likely to result in at least some temporary bad behavior:

1. It makes distracted parents pay attention to their kids, even in a negative way.
2. Kids are genuinely upset, scared, and saddened by the divorce and don't know how to express these feelings.
3. While the household reorganizes, there is a gray area around who's in charge. Children will naturally test these changing boundaries.
4. As the family changes, there can also be new questions about where the child belongs in the world at large. Divorce can feel like a blow to the self, and a weakened self-image may affect how a child feels in relation to his peers. Uncomfortable feelings of not belonging anymore can prompt bad behavior.

> **NOTE:** Throughout this chapter, I sometimes refer to acting-out as "bad behavior." Of course, most children are not doing anything bad at all—they are testing limits, having a hissy fit, finding a way to express themselves. "Bad behavior" is shorthand for talking about the occasion upon which discipline or some guidance is called for.

Time-Outs, Logical and Natural Consequences

A time-out is when you tell your child to go to his room or to another area away from the people he's been interacting with. It is your immediate intervention in response to bad behavior. A very young child gets a five-second time-out. With four- to six-year-olds, you may specify the amount of time: "You get a five-minute time-out for taking that away from your sister." Older kids get longer time-outs—you might tell a ten-year-old to spend an hour in his room, and when you ground your teenager, you are essentially giving her a time-out.

Time-outs work pretty well. They can be the only way beyond saying "no" to get a toddler to associate certain behaviors with a negative outcome. It's important not to extend the time period beyond what the child can understand. Taking away the privilege of playing with friends can be terrific for an older child who on some level may need some personal regrouping. That goes for teenagers, too.

Some child experts have come down against the use of time-outs for the very reason that they isolate the child. There's a point to this. If your child is having trouble getting along with other kids, removing them doesn't teach them how to negotiate or give them better strategies for getting what they want out of a situation. However, even for these kids a time-out can be a very useful tool in your quest to teach him how to behave.

One woman who had learned about using "consequences" to discipline her children said, "Why should I call it 'consequences' when I'm really punishing them?" Sometimes there's a fine line between old-fashioned punishment and what has become widely known as "logical consequences." The fine line is important though.

Basically, logical consequences are related to the misbehavior. If your child acts up in a store, you say, "Stop or I won't take you here again." You give your child a choice and he then decides how to behave. Let's say your daughter is slamming her door to keep her younger siblings out of her room. You've asked her to stop and she keeps doing it. Punishment would entail saying something like, "OK, no birthday party tomorrow." Logical consequences are essentially a warning. You say, "If you slam your door again you will have to miss your friend's birthday party." So if she does slam the door, essentially it was her decision to accept the punishment. (Not that she will do it gladly.)

In general, punishment is something you inflict without giving your child a choice first. There may be times when it is absolutely appropriate. Breaches of other people's safety, or a child's own safety, require swift and memorable deterrents. If you have a school-age child who knows better, and he runs into the middle of a busy street, you don't want to mess with "the next time." He needs to understand right away that his behavior is totally unacceptable.

The trouble with always using punishment is that it doesn't offer the child the opportunity to observe his own behavior and modify it. Essentially, you want him to develop impulse control, to understand that he is responsible for himself and his actions. Logical consequences makes the whole thing a pretty straightforward affair. "If you do this, then this will happen."

The difference between logical and natural consequences is that natural consequences are what would happen as a result of behavior without any adult interference. Natural consequences are only appropriate when there is no danger to your child or to anyone else involved. You would not let a child who ran into the middle of the street get the natural consequence of this action—which might be getting hit by a car. But if he's having trouble playing with his friends and he's being a total control freak so they don't want to play with him, you might let the children's interaction take care of the conflict. "Well, your friend went home because you wouldn't share with her. That's what happens." Although it may be better to say nothing at all. Part of consequences is giving up our lectures, and letting results take their course.

The hard part about natural consequences is getting out of the way and letting them happen. None of us want to see our children writhe in discomfort, or feel disappointed and angry. But we have to let them have those feelings. If they never feel the consequences of their actions, children get a powerful negative message; they can develop the sense that they are not capable of withstanding the consequences, that if they would meet disappointment they would crumble.

Logical consequences are very effective. They give frustrated parents a tool. They give children a chance to learn about their own impulses and behavior. In effect, you separate the bad behavior from the doer—so it is the behavior that is bad, not the child. It is imperative that you follow through on the consequence you've named. If you don't follow through, you will not only set the stage for the behavior to continue, but you will also send your child the message that adult rules don't really count. That will get him in big trouble later.

> **NOTE:** You have to address kids at a level they can understand developmentally. Put a toddler on a protracted time-out, and he will have no idea why he's being isolated. It will not help him learn to change his behavior—it will only scare him. Consequences should also fit the infraction. In general, you want to use privileges like television time as your consequence. Never deprive your child of something he needs, like dinner. That's *Oliver Twist* time. Some kids understand more than others at an earlier age. You know best how to meet your child on her level.

What Kind of Parent Are You?

Whether we think about it or not, most of us have a philosophy of parenting. At the basic level, we believe our job is to provide for our kids and teach them how to get along in the world. Most of us don't love the part of the job that entails discipline—it feels stressful and unpleasant, and we just want our kids to behave.

To a large extent being a parent means disciplining your children. Their behavior is a kind of bridge between themselves and their world, and because they lack experience they need to be taught how to use this bridge effectively. Discipline affects not only how your child relates to you, but how he relates to others as well. Love, respect, and mutuality all travel across this bridge. You want your child to have access to rewarding relationships, and to be able to discern beneficial situations and people from those who are detrimental.

The word "discipline" means "to teach." Discipline is a concrete forum for showing kids what's acceptable and how to manage conflict. Beyond rudimentary rule-following, most of us want to teach our kids to develop self-esteem and to fulfill their natural gifts in sync with the times they live in. It may be hard to remember, but the next time you give a time-out, you are directly influencing how your child perceives the world and his place in it.

Now if that sounds like too much pressure—take it easy! We've all lost our cool, barked at the kids. We like to believe we're enlightened and we really try to be, but sometimes the very same phrases our parents used on us come springing out of our mouths. Like everything else, discipline is a process. That's why it's good to step back and ask yourself, am I an authoritarian, take-no-prisoners parent? Or am I a permissive, anything-goes parent? Most of us are both, at different times.

How you parent has to do with how you were parented. During a divorce, you often have the occasion to think about both, as you reevaluate how you got to this place and as you try to deal with your kids. In many cases, the roots of the divorce can be traced to inherited behavior patterns from our families of origin, in which there were often rigid expectations and not much emphasis on honoring children's feelings. One woman said, "Every time I tell my mother about how my husband ignores my needs, she shows me how I got into this bad marriage. Essentially *she* also tells me to ignore my needs."

If you grew up in an authoritative environment where children's expressive selves were a low priority, it is likely that you are either coming down too hard on your kids, creating resentment and subterfuge, or not coming down hard enough on them. Permissive households are often chaotic and children with too much power at home are paradoxically less empowered in the outside world, more likely to feel like they don't know what's expected of them, and can feel "out of it."

Many of us assume that of course, we are warm, cooperative, relaxed, orderly, and encouraging. And probably, most of us are, most of the time. Where does your rigidity creep in, when does your patience run out, how do you handle your own stress? Do you take care of your anger or do you vent it? You may have let bedtime slide for several days because it wasn't worth the struggle. Did that result in a tired child unable to focus productively during the day? Do you have a regular meal and snack schedule? A hungry child is often spoiling for a fight.

The beliefs underlying the family structure vastly influence how well it runs. There is no doubting that during and after a divorce, your belief system will change. It's a difficult transition, because you don't always know where you're going. The good news is that you have the opportunity to change the framework for your children—it's all up to you now—and give them a better environment to grow up in. You make the biggest difference in your child's behavior. While the divorce itself creates feelings that children need to express, the way you respond to your child's behavior determines whether the child continues, escalates, or lets go of the behavior.

Parenting kids who are acting out is not easy, no matter what. But when you're divorcing or separating, the challenge is bigger. A separation or divorce is a major event that is going to elicit behavior changes in all children—bad behavior, bold behavior, secretive, and sad behavior. You probably feel you're doing your best just to hold everything together and can hardly spare an ounce of energy to deal with it when your kids act out.

The good news is that you can recalibrate your parenting right now to stay in touch with your children's needs and also to address your own. You can take this opportunity to clarify a healthy relationship with your kids that helps them grow up productively, while sparing yourself an ulcer.

Who's in Charge?

Not only are your kids expressing their feelings in ways designed to get your attention, but you have even less attention to give them than before. Add to that the fact that you are likely parenting alone now. The other parent is no longer around to back you up or give you a break. As if that weren't enough, sometimes the other parent seems to making the whole situation more complicated, by parenting in a way that is at odds with your style. It is very common to hear people say that their co-parent lets the kids stay up too late, doesn't give them healthy, regular food, is either too permissive or too harsh. It seems like you have to undo whatever went on while your kids were with your co-parent.

When you are first splitting up, a great deal of coordination is required just to get life accomplished as usual. It may be all you can handle to arrange your schedule to pick up and drop off your kids with your former spouse, now your co-parent. Behavior issues may go by the wayside for a while, unless they are deeply disruptive. If that's the case, try to get help from teachers, mediators, and counselors if your relationship with the child's other parent is too "hot."

One of the things you will have to let go is control over how your co-parent disciplines. Some people remain amicable enough to come to some basic agreement on bedtimes and so forth; many divorcing people can hardly speak to each other and any discussion about doing things one way or another leads to warfare. In the end, you can only control what goes on at your house. With time and support, your children will understand that things are different with each parent.

You will most definitely hear the words, "But Mommy/Daddy lets me...." And in response, say, "Well, that's between you and your mother/father. I do it this way." You may be tempted to be angry and defensive when your child does this, and to blame your co-parent for not doing things your way. Try to think of the situation differently. Your child is asking a question of you—how are you going to respond? Take the occasion to differentiate your way, to help establish your philosophy of doing things. Your child may be squirrely about the short-term result—an earlier bedtime, for example—but in fact will be reassured that you know what you're doing.

Choices To Make

1. An emotionally warm household is more conducive to good behavior than a cold one.
2. A cooperative spirit is better than a competitive spirit.
3. A relaxed approach with limits is better than a strict approach.
4. An orderly environment is more conducive to growth than a disorderly environment.
5. Encouragement works much better than discouragement.

I Just Can't Do It Now

Yes, you are tired and under stress. But it's important to deal with your child's behavior now. So-called positive discipline is in fact a way to remind your children that you notice them and care about them. Make yourself aware of what kind of a parent you are and whether that is the kind of parent you want to be. Are you lax? Do you wince but bear it when your kids talk back to you? Or do you clamp down so hard your kids obey you but feel bitter? Are they withdrawn from you, do they lack trust in you?

In many households, and especially after a divorce, both parents work. There's nothing wrong with this—it's how we live today. One effect of having an "outside" job as well as the job of child-rearing, is that when we get home to our kids we're often tired. At the very least, we've dealt with enough stress and tension during the day that we want to avoid any more of it, and enjoy our kids. We're more permissive with them. And to some extent, just ignoring bad behavior *is* effective! It's a better alternative than getting into a knock-down drag-out confrontation where there's yelling and screaming. However, over the long haul, ignoring or letting stuff slide isn't very effective, because it never teaches your kids boundaries, how to behave, or to be considerate.

For younger kids, consistent rules and routines are paramount now, because they offer a reassuring structure. One of the biggest dangers to your teenager is that because of their relative sufficiency, and because they can relate to you with fair verbal fluency, you will allow them to become cotenants of your house instead of teenage children still under the tutelage of their parents. Teenagers need the structure now more than ever, too, but it's harder to see that. Yes, you are tired and stressed. It's important to acknowledge that and take some extra steps to care for yourself. But this is a critical time for you to take control of your household, and how everyone behaves in it.

Take This Job and...

One of the biggest challenges the divorce poses is the total disruption of the symbolic head of household, jointly held by the mom and dad or their equivalents. Some time will have to pass before each new household settles in and roles are reestablished. There's no avoiding this transition, and it won't be comfortable.

Your kids aren't the only ones responding to this change—you are too. Suddenly you are both mother and father of your household—all the providing and all the disciplining and all the nurturing and all the laundry is done by you. These extra responsibilities come at a time when you may feel something like a child in need of care yourself. There is a danger that in some ways you will relinquish your role as parent, and let things really slide. This is very hard for your kids. They are losing the family structure as they have known it. It is adding to their burden if they also lose you as a trusted authority figure.

The Alien in the Kitchen

When kids are really driving us nuts, we think: oh my God, who *is* this child? I can't control him! He is going against everything I've taught him! He's disrespecting me! And it feels like a Martian just landed in your child's body and green ooze is coming out of his mouth. What's interesting is that in this moment, the child feels really, really separate from you. It's a tricky moment. As mentioned above, ignoring the behavior isn't a bad idea—you are sending a message that this is not the way to assert yourself. Paradoxically, however, you need to know that in your child's extreme energy of rejecting you is in fact a very strong outreach toward you, toward connecting with you. Your child wants something from you—attention, power, to get back at you, to show you he feels horrible about himself, to connect with you, or to define himself.

As children grow up, they deal with their own internal changes as well as a changing world. Every child confronts expectations in school and desires to fit in on the playground. Within the household, kids jockey for power and belonging—building a self and fitting in. It's all part of the question: who am I? We are back to the burgeoning self, being formed in close symbiosis with those around us. Sibling issues add to the mix. Acting-out behavior—disobedience, hitting, talking back, lack of cooperation—all of these are strategies for testing the outline of where a child belongs.

Understanding these motivations may help you approach your child's behavior with love and understanding, along with reassuringly firm limits. There are other foundational questions to ask yourself as well.

What do you expect from your child? Do you expect him to be mostly well-behaved, curious and productive with this schoolwork, and to have friends? Or have you settled into a negative frame for viewing your child—expecting fights, disobedience, poor schoolwork?

Things to Do

EXAMINE YOUR EXPECTATIONS

Are they positive?

Are they negative?

What changes would you like to make?

Your child picks a groove and you can fall into it, too. Remember you're the boss. "My eleven-year-old is using fury all the time," one woman commented. "Finally, my child's father and I said to her, 'We are all feeling sad, disappointed and angry, but you can't use those feelings to extort stuff out of us.'" Her daughter seemed to get enraged at the drop of a hat, to become demanding in every situation. At first her parents, who had a fairly amicable relationship, accepted her behavior as a natural result of their divorce, which they felt guilty about. "But then it became clear—we have to move on from this. My daughter responded immediately when we put our foot down." Sometimes a child's intransigence goes beyond this, but when parents become clear about things, often kids will comply and follow suit.

What They're Doing and Why

The following section discusses broad categories of behavior and what to do about them. They key to responding to behavior is to understand the goal behind it—what your child is after by acting in a particular way. Some of the ways kids display these behaviors and their goals overlap—"snootiness" and "lack of eye contact" might occur in any one of them. The way to identify the behavior and determine what your child is after is to check in with yourself. How does the behavior make *you* feel? Guidelines for figuring it out are included below.

Gauge Your Own Response

There are two reasons to check in with how your child's behavior makes you feel. The first is that you can pretty much tell what your child is after by how you respond. The second reason is to think, maybe later, about your own anger, frustration, and hurt, and to examine better ways of addressing those feelings in yourself.

Once you determine what your child is after, you can turn the tables on the behavior. You can meet the child's needs directly and positively. You can break the cycle of misbehavior that gets everyone bent out of shape and breathe a little more freely around the house.

It's useful to go back to square one when approaching behavior difficulties. For one thing, it helps to take a step back and view your child's behavior in the context of his growth—doing so can help you get yourself out of the heat of the moment. It can be useful to remember that your child is doing whatever he's doing to get a response from you. Watch a baby throw his banana over the side of a high chair. He doesn't watch the banana—he watches your face. So that primary attachment relationship is at work even when your child is misbehaving like mad. Children are in a constant state of self-definition, so behavior is going to be an ongoing challenge to one degree or another. As he reaches new developmental milestones, your child is going to check it out with you—see exactly where his new abilities get him and where they don't get him.

Children who are acting out do not know why they are doing it—they are not aware of the goals of their misbehavior. Remember that they are actually trying to get something they need, whether it is power or attention or comfort. They aren't doing this just to drive you mad. Your task is multiple. You need to:

1. Discourage the misbehavior.
2. Help your child get what he needs in a positive way.
3. Help your child connect with himself to better understand his own needs—by giving him better tools for self-expression. Part of this is encouraging your child to make an effort, not focusing on successful outcomes but on the ethic of trying and participating, accepting failures as part of a larger process of growth.
4. Show your child you accept him, even though you don't accept his behavior.

If your child is *disrespectful*, he is interrupting, not listening, not following-through on requests. (Sounds fairly low-key, doesn't it, but hasn't this kind of behavior made you blow your gasket?) You feel irritated. The goal of this behavior is attention and connection.

If your child is *defiant,* you say "don't," and he does it. You and your child are at loggerheads. Kids hit and kick. Defiant behavior makes you angry, and the goal is power.

If your child is hurting other people, he is *retaliating* for feeling hurt. He refuses to cooperate and gives you a lot of attitude. Retaliatory behavior makes you feel hurt, and your child is after a positive feeling of loving protection from you.

If your child acts like a *snail in a shell*, he's withdrawing. He won't fight or otherwise engage; he won't make eye contact. He is discouraged and feels like a failure. Your child needs encouragement.

When the Divorce Is Your Child's Excuse

SOME KIDS ARE rather brilliant at taking advantage of whatever situation they find themselves in. You may find yourself with a school-age child who, when confronted with a piece of bad behavior says, "Well, if you and Mom/Dad weren't getting a divorce I wouldn't do it!" This can really push your buttons, if you're feeling guilty. Remember, your child is testing a new situation. He or she is essentially asking, "Do I have this excuse?" You can answer, "We can talk about how the divorce makes you feel, but you can't act this way." Take this as a cue that you really do need to talk about the divorce. But in the moment, deal with the action at hand, and resist letting it become about anything else.

When Your Child Is Disrespectful to You

When your child is engaged in this kind of behavior, you feel he isn't listening to you. He is not understanding all you do for him and that your relationship is a two-way street: he needs to participate in a positive way, which he is not doing. If the child is pushing this behavior hard, you may feel he doesn't fully appreciate your authority. You are the boss and must be heeded.

Disrespectful behavior makes you feel: irritated. The goal of this behavior is: attention, connection, recognition.

Disrespect gets your attention pretty quickly. Your child employs it in the morning, when you're trying to get out the door—you ask your son to get dressed and brush his teeth, and nothing happens. The morning routine is a big occasion for this kind of behavior, partly because it's hard for most of us to get it together first thing! But your child also has you within his range for an hour or so before going off to his day, and he wants to maximize the opportunity to have you fully engage with him. By wheedling, cajoling, and so forth, you get his clothes on him. Is it over? Nah, why should it be over? You go through the whole rigamarole again over the teeth-brushing. Chances are you are snappish and brusque, but you are in more or less constant contact with your son. From his perspective, he got what he wanted.

By the time you get the kid on the curb bound for the school door, you're ready for a martini, or a nap.

What to Do

Let's just stay with the early morning example. Depending on the child's age, you can have a discussion with him at dinner, in which you say something like: "It's very hard for me in the morning when you don't do your part and get dressed. I feel like I'm always yelling at you while you're certainly big enough to get yourself ready. What should we do about it?" When you treat your child respectfully, you eventually get respect in return.

Sometimes talking isn't the answer at all, although it's worth a try or two. You may have to use logical consequences or natural consequences to get a child out of the habit of resorting to this behavior. If it's very persistent, you need to act and not talk. You can talk later.

An example of natural consequences in the morning might mean you actually hand the kid his clothes in the car and tell him he'll have to get dressed at school. You can also say, "If I have to ask you again, you also lose television privileges. If you freak out about that, you lose them for tomorrow." It's critical to follow through when you do this, and it works beautifully when you do. You have to be prepared to not have the television on when you are used to getting that break yourself, but a day or so of that kind of inconvenience will reap many rewards for you and your child.

If you're dealing with a child under about four years of age, obviously the long discussions don't work. Try to engage a preschooler in the task of getting ready by putting several choices of clothing out, maybe the night before, and telling him to go ahead and pick out what he wants to wear. If he doesn't do it, he loses the opportunity to choose—you do it. For the younger kids, the morning example isn't the best, because you are likely doing most of the getting ready for them.

Another way of looking at this type of behavior is to see it as attention-seeking. For a child under school age, that's a more accurate definition of what they're doing—"disrespect" is too large a concept. Your task is to discourage the pesky behavior in the moment, while acknowledging the child's need and giving it to him later in a way that shows him how to get your attention in a positive way for both of you. You want to teach your child that he deserves attention, but not on demand. So give it to him at unexpected times, and don't always respond when he is seeking it.

It's a pretty mature child (and there are plenty of those!) who will be able to examine his own behavior and tell you he wants some quality time with you in the morning. But you can suggest it yourself. If there is any margin of time for you in the morning, you could propose doing a little quiet reading together in bed. If there is no possibility of this, you could say, "You know, I think it's hard to get out of bed and get going in the morning and be gone all day without some time together. I'm sorry that it has to be this way. But why don't we make sure and plan to have some time together right when I come home from work? We could throw a ball for half an hour before you buckle down to homework and I get dinner. I can't do it everyday, but we could do it every other day." Or whatever might work.

Ways to Fit in Contact Time with Your Kid

1. Quiet reading first thing in the morning. Get yourself a cup o' joe and crawl into bed with your kids. You can do this half asleep and it's a great way to wake up. It's also a great way to read stories that are more complex—later in the day or before bed, most kids want something kind of simple.

2. Arrange your schedule so that you don't always have all the kids at the same time; in other words, let another parent do the carpooling for soccer for one child, and take the other child to the grocery store with you. If your schedule has no margin in it for a more child-centered activity, the time alone in the car and going down the aisles or doing some equivalent task will at least give you a moment to focus on this one child.

3. While in the midst of the daily rounds, give your child positive reinforcement about his contribution. Even if he's setting the table because that's how he earns his allowance, verbally acknowledge that he's helping you out and you appreciate that. A child acting out this way needs to know he is a valued participant in the family.

It bears mentioning that there are differing levels of acting out. Some kids have gotten into entrenched habits of behavior and are in danger of forming their self-concept around acting this way: I'm bad, the only way I fit in is by making people pay attention to me, I can only deal with people by trying to dominate them; and so forth. When the behavior is really going on and on, get some help. Your child's school is a great resource for counselors and others who are trained and may already know your child. The child's teacher may have valuable input.

All kids act out from time to time. Most will do so at times of transition, or in a kind of delayed reaction just after a transition. If your child is doing this disrespectful stuff and he doesn't usually do it, it's a sign that he's moving on developmentally to a new stage, and unsure of how it's all going to work out. Having a bit of context for the behavior can help you deal with it calmly. As kids get older more is expected of them at school, and they are repeatedly confronted with tasks they've never done before. Sometimes kids who learned to read easily and for whom early schooling was a breeze hit a roadblock when confronted with a dense conceptual challenge, like multiplication. The child who isn't used to having to try may feel like a failure just because he has to try now. You want to be a bit patient and let him know that trying is part of life, failing and trying again is part of life, and to be comfortable with that.

When Your Child Is Defiant

First things first with defiant behavior—make sure nobody's hurt. Don't let your child hit you, and don't hit your child. Younger kids doing this stuff on the playground have to be stopped. Older kids bullying at school or destroying property have to be stopped. Use logical consequences first—don't bother with talking. You hit me, you get a time-out. And so forth.

Defiant behavior makes you feel angry. That can be hard because anger is like a fireworks display that's hard to stop once it gets set off—and that goes for you as well as for your child. Spend some time thinking about what happens when you get angry. Do you yell and scream? Are all bets off? Your child is soaking in your response to anger and mimicking it. It's important that you make the effort to understand yourself in this situation because it will become a reflex for your child that will be very hard to unlearn.

The goal of defiance is power. All children need power—all people need power, and will do what they can to get it one way or another. It's very important that parents give children power in as many situations as they can without going to the other extreme and becoming permissive. Children who feel empowered won't use misbehavior in order to get power. The good news is, it's relatively easy to help kids feel independent and responsible. There are many, many opportunities for giving kids power in other situations.

If a child is employing defiance and it seems related exclusively to the divorce, rather than being one of the natural resorts of your child's temperament, it may very well be that your child is feeling helpless: helpless to stop the divorce, helpless to get his parents back together, helpless to have any influence at all over a radically changing lifestyle and reality. The truth is, your child *is* helpless in the divorce, and that's a bitter pill to swallow.

All kids need to be communicated with regularly about the divorce, but a defiant child is really struggling with it. As mentioned above, when your child is in the midst of this behavior, act, don't talk. But later, when things have cooled off and the venue has changed, make sure to bring up the subject. "You know the divorce is not your fault, right?" Try to be patient and let there be a space of no talking if your child doesn't have a response to this right away. Silence can be hard for all of us because, in fact, it is filled with sadness or confusion. Just letting those feelings come up is a big help to your child, who is trying unsuccessfully to squash them back down.

Even if you opposed the divorce, if it is happening you need to take responsibility for it. You are the adult. Be the container for the divorce so your child doesn't have to carry this too-heavy load. You can be honest: "I don't like getting a divorce. It wasn't my idea. But here it is so let's get through it together. You didn't make it happen. Your other parent and I made it happen."

A school-age child and a teenager are very likely to know what you want them to say, and they may respond, "Yeah, yeah, I know it's not my fault." Don't consider the case closed. It's very likely they *do* feel responsible for the divorce. It's very, very hard to reveal our deepest fears, even to our loved parents.

What to Do

Defiant children need to be empowered in positive ways. You may have a long road to travel before this style of acting out is completely turned around, but you can do it. Take a look at your child's life. Responsibility, which is empowering, needs to be built into the details of the day.

1. What's the homework situation—does he do it responsibly, on time, with at least a modicum of concentration?
2. What's his room like—do you ask him to make his bed and keep the room tidy, or is it a disaster area?
3. Does this child have responsibilities around the house—paid or otherwise? Setting the table, taking out the recycling, bringing dirty laundry to the washing machine twice a week—small, regular chores are a good way to teach responsibility. Actually, tying these to an allowance is not a bad idea, because it builds in a logical consequence. You don't do it, you don't get paid.

If you are sighing with misery because your child never does his homework, has a pigsty of a room, and doesn't care about getting an allowance, take a deep breath and pick a battle. One at a time. Let's say homework is the most important, because it's tied to other people's expectations as well as your own, having even more impact on your child's self-image.

Sit your child down and have a talk about the homework. Tell him you know he's a smart kid and that homework is one of his jobs in life right now and he needs to do it well. Ask him what would help him get it done. Suggest: a regular time each day or evening when it's homework time. If at all possible, plan on being in the room with your child during this time. It can be while you are making dinner or reading the paper (if you have that luxury!) or it can be later, before bed. You can help your child keep focused on the work and prevent feelings of loneliness and isolation, which may be part of the problem to begin with. Also, if at all possible, designate a homework spot, which is the same one each day. A place at the dining room table, with a shelf nearby for paper and pens to be stored. Set up the association with a particular place in the house: I do my homework here. If it's a desk in his room, try to be in there with him, doing whatever.

Once you've set up an orderly way to proceed around homework, ask your child about how he'd like to be rewarded or penalized for doing or not doing it well. Cut a deal. A month of solid homework and I buy you a book. Or a video game. Don't be afraid to be crass and commercial. What you're setting up here is a system that we all more or less live by—work hard, get rewarded.

Some parents, especially those with more than one child, set up a big calendar on the wall and devise a system for crediting good behavior and taking off for bad. The reward in one case was a trip to a nearby amusement park. When his older sister earned a demerit, a usually very rascally boy admonished her to be better. He really wanted to go. For a day in which either kid set the table or took the dog for a walk, they got a blue star. When one of them hit the other or disobeyed their father, whose idea this was, they got a red star on that day. When they reached a certain number of blue stars, they got to go to the amusement park. It worked beautifully.

These systems of rewards can sound pretty mechanical. You want your children to internalize good behavior, not act like Pavlov's dogs around petty enticements, don't you? But children are very concrete and they love specificity. They will in fact internalize this system. They will learn to stop before they act and think about the consequences, which is how we all operate to one degree or another. Then they can make a choice about how to be.

Underneath it all, kids want to be good. They want approval and love and a feeling of belonging. Always remember that and use it in your quest to get life into a pleasant shape. It's one of your more powerful resources.

If you are stuck at the moment with a child who is so defiant that it feels like all you're doing is logical consequences and nothing more, take heart. Try to fit in positive reinforcements. You've heard the phrase, "catch them doing good." Patiently try to teach your child to take himself seriously as a participant in whatever group he's in at the moment—family, peer, church, or other. Gently remind him that when he's angry he loses the priviledge of being around other people and that's not what he wants. Remind him that you want to hang out with him and his friends want to play with him. Not "You're ruining this for everyone," but more, "Hey, keep your cool and let's keep having a good time."

Of course your child may be too young to understand this. A toddler is doing defiance all over the place, and all you can really do about it is repeat

repeat repeat: no hitting, no throwing sand. It may be useful to remember the toddler's quest when you're dealing with an older child, because some of it remains constant. The child wants to do something and doesn't know how. He's frustrated and also discouraged. He wants power. Help him figure out how to succeed.

A defiant teenager is tricky because defiance is part of *being* a teenager. Parents with kids in their teens who find them "out of control" are often kind of frightened by the situation and can be tempted to wash their hands of the whole shebang. In some cases a bit of letting go is indeed called for. But, remember, it will help your teenager in the long haul if you require him to follow some basic family rules and those of basic etiquette. A teenager is looking for ways to assert his individuality, but he still needs to do this within a social context to be successful in life. The family is the primary social context. This is the critical practice field and after this, there is no more practice. It all becomes startlingly real and the consequences of behavior more serious.

Your teenager also needs to treat you with respect (and be treated by you with respect) because your relationship with him is the template from which he forms his other relationships. Now, you know this doesn't mean that every time you get a sullen look you should freak out and imagine your son or daughter isn't going to have successful relationships. With a teenager it may be very useful to make a list of boilerplate courtesies that must be obeyed in the house. When these are infracted upon, there will be logical consequences. Like, no car privileges, no television, and so forth.

Boilerplate Courtesies

1. No yelling or screaming. Conversational tone only.
2. No door-slamming.
3. You must let me know where you are at all times. If you change your plans, you must let me know.
4. I would like you to eat dinner with me at least four times a week. Dinner together means sitting at the table, sharing conversation and food, and being convivial for at least a half hour.

With teenagers, you probably don't want to set up any kind of system of reward because they will feel too old for such strategies. You don't want to give them any fuel for their basic sense of being insulted by everything you do. On the other hand, you can give them surprise or bonus rewards. If eating together is an issue in your house, and your teenager joins you pleasantly for a record number of days in a row, you might do something special for him. Be sure to say, "I love it when you have dinner with me, and I've really enjoyed your company." You can make a favorite food or take everybody out for a burger, or whatever else might be a bit special for your family within a reasonable range.

When Your Child Is Retaliatory

We can all understand it when a toddler wallops somebody who just took her shovel. But when a nine-year-old sets a trap for another kid on the playground and finds some novel way to humiliate him, we start to think about horror stories like *Rosemary's Baby* or *Carrie*. Where did this demon seed come from?

Or let's say your child is wounding *you*. Along with our anger buttons, children can very effectively push our vulnerability buttons. When we feel hurt, we become more focused on our own feelings, and less able to see the situation for what it is.

"My son would lie in bed at night and chant, 'I hate you, I hate you, I hate you,'" said the mother of her ten-year-old. "It was devastating. I felt like he wanted me to disappear."

She was wrong. He did not want her to disappear. Her son wanted her to comfort and accept him. He was picking the wrong time and the wrong way to express himself, so she wasn't able to see that. Luckily she consulted a therapist, who suggested that the next time he did it, she go into the boy's room and sit on his bed.

"The first time I sat next to him he started to really scream, and it scared me. I didn't know what to say. I started to cry and this enraged him all the more. I would say, 'What's wrong, why do you hate me?' And he would just get more furious."

By working patiently with the therapist the woman was able to get past her own feelings of rejection, which her son was fueling. "The therapist helped me see that I was looking to my son for reassurance, and that's what was making him so mad. It took me months to get down to the fact that this nighttime display was about *his* feelings, not mine!"

Hurt feelings can be among the hardest to address, since they tend to get traded back and forth until no one really knows where it all started, and everybody is waiting for an apology. Your children hurt your feelings because they've been hurt. This nine-year-old's mother had recently divorced; she was depressed. "I was caught up in how bad I felt," she said. "But to my son, I had simply withdrawn from him. He was needing me and I didn't even know it. He was feeling rejected by me, so he retaliated!"

It's common to forget that kids are reacting emotionally all the time. They are taking things personally, even more than we do.

When a child retaliates emotionally, you feel hurt. When you feel hurt by your child, take a deep breath. Your child is in pain. That's why he's inflicting it.

What to Do
1. Confirm your child's feelings. "You're frustrated." "You're angry." "You feel I don't pay enough attention to you anymore."
2. Reassure your child. "I have been distracted lately but my love for you will never change. Let's try to do something special together."
3. If your child has hit you or destroyed something of yours, and you've gotten to a peaceful conversation about it, forgive him. "I understand you were feeling hurt. I really liked that vase, and I wish you hadn't broken it, but I forgive you."
4. Give your child plenty of love and positive reinforcement. You're dealing with a bruised sense of self, which needs some tender loving care.

Never, never retaliate when your child tries to hurt you. If he or she hits a nerve, take a deep breath and move on from it. Your child is reacting and doesn't have the distance you do to understand that you hurt me because I hurt you—the child will take your hurtfulness very deep inside and it will be very difficult to heal it.

As with all behavior styles, revenge or retaliation can become a habit with a child, the first resort for how to deal with an uncomfortable situation. While you don't want to overreact and create even more heat around a kid's actions, it's very important to nip this one in the bud.

If you've noticed your child employing this behavior, try to get him straight back to his own feelings quickly. Not, "Why did you hit her?" But, "How are you feeling right now?" Get an answer. Depending on his age, you will want to then say something like, "OK, you're feeling hurt. Don't hurt someone else because of it." You'll have to use your judgment on this one, but when he's using revenge and it's more or less annoying rather than dangerous or damaging, try keeping the entire focus of the conversation on how *he* feels. Do this several times without attaching consequences to it. Some kids will get it: it's like a light bulb will go off and they will become able to observe themselves.

Other kids will now play this game with you where they think, great, I can throw a punch and my parent will ask me how I feel. Simply attach the consequences again. "OK, you hit your friend and now you get a time-out."

Strengthen your child's connection to his own feelings. Bring his attention to the fact that he feels hurt or frustrated or angry. Encourage him to think about his feelings before he acts.

When Your Child Acts like a Snail in a Shell

There's a difference between a seriously discouraged child and one who is temporarily or situationally shy or slightly withdrawn. A seriously discouraged child is apathetic, depressed, feels he can't succeed, so why try? He feels helpless and so do his parents.

Common situations where this behavior arises include high-conflict divorces, where the kids basically run for cover, trying to get away from the noise, the stress, the fear created by warring parents. Children who are treated as if they aren't really there at all will begin to act that way—that they don't count. If the household is full of strife, it may be very hard for this child to get some peace, and he may try to comfort himself by withdrawing into his own world.

Perfectionism can also create a lack of motivation in children. The pressure to do something special every time out is simply too much. Also, the child inwardly rebels against being valued based on performance. We all tend to be a bit perfectionistic and performance-oriented, so it pays to really be mindful of how we encourage kids to participate. When a child is doing a drawing, try to notice something in it or ask something about it rather than praise it as fabulous. It's hard not to be results-oriented in our world, but starting kids too young on that track can backfire. Children may decide that they can never get the results that seem to be called for, so they will avoid the whole stress of trying.

Parents who are constantly critical also help create children who feel like giving up. If every time a child does something you have a correction or an improvement to mention, the kid is going to feel that there's no way to do it right. Sometimes kids will figure out just how to do something the way you like it, but it can be at the expense of how *they* would like it. Overemphasis on doing things a certain way also totally discourages experimentation and spontaneity. If you want your child to be successful in life, he is going to have to know how to take chances, how to try things. How to think outside the box, as the saying goes.

What to Do
1. Encourage your child.
2. Ask your child's opinion and listen to it. Let the child have influence over something—what to have for dinner, what you do on a Saturday afternoon.
3. Respect your child's feelings. If you are having a verbal conflict with your parenting partner, do it out of earshot of your child. Better yet, do it in a mediator's office.
4. Focus on activities your child feels confident about and make sure to give him time to follow through—to finish a drawing, to play the whole ball game, whatever it is. Emphasize the process—"you feel like you don't play tennis well but you will get better and better the more you do it."

Insecurity: The Common Theme in All Behavior Styles

You'll notice when you really look at what's going on that whether a child is after connection, power, security, or needing to re-group, there's a common theme. It's insecurity. In some way or another, your child is feeling uncertain about his value, his ability to get what he wants and needs, his sense of himself among people he cares about. When a kid feels insecure, it can be helpful to remember a few things:

1. You are your child's primary attachment figure. You are home base. As such, your reassurance and guidance go a very long way. Make sure that along with boundaries and consequences you give your child healthy doses of connection, love, and positive reinforcement.

2. Your child is engaged in the process of developing a self. This is a complicated, lifelong business. We are all in the ongoing process of developing a self. Kids are going to go through phases where new bodily developments, new expectations at school, new social pressures, are going to cause them anxiety. You have a wonderful opportunity to give them tools now that they will use their whole life. These tools are:

   a. Boundaries.
   b. Self-reliance.
   c. Confidence that they are loved.
   d. Ability to observe their own feelings.
   e. Ability to "talk it out."

An Extra Word about Teenagers

Teenagers are on their way to becoming adults and have many adult qualities and capabilities. It can be harder to define consequences that matter to them, and it is certainly a lot harder to actually know what they are doing when not in your presence. Since the teenage years are about exploration, be aware that whatever limits you set, your teenager will test them. Therefore, set the limits hard. Let's say you have said to your child, "I do not want you to even experiment with marijuana. Whether or not pot is harmful is one question, but it is illegal. If you want to experiment with pot when you're over 18, that's up to you. But until then, you are forbidden from trying it." OK, you've been very strong, and then your daughter comes home from a party and smells like pot, or you find some in her room. Don't let it slide. Ground her (the teenage time-out) or enforce another consequence. The point is that you are setting a bar. Keep the bar very low, and although she will in all likelihood try pot, she will be much more inhibited about her experimentation if you are right there on it.

Relating to a teenager becomes much more of an adult affair of mutuality. Even if you have a teenager who is scraping with the law, try to establish a relationship with him where you appeal to his own good sense and responsibility. If your teenager destroys property or hurts someone else, you will have to enforce major consequences. But before you do that, appeal to your child's conscience. "What? You deflated your history teacher's tires? Oh man, after a long day of work and feeling tired and harassed your teacher gets to his car and the tires have been destroyed by the kids he teaches all day? I wonder how he felt? How do you think he felt?"

If you can say that and then walk away, leaving your child to turn over some pretty ugly feelings in his chest, you will go very far to driving the message home. In this case you could bring the subject up later, say at dinner. "By the way, you'll be paying for those tires, so let's work out a schedule of payment." The cooler you are and the more serious, the more your child will take responsibility for his own actions, which is what you are after.

Parenting Style and Behavior

For all behaviors it's relevant to do a little self-examination when figuring out the puzzle of your child. What happened in the house you grew up in when people got mad? In our contemporary generation, many of us had more authoritarian upbringings than we would dream of imposing on our children. Our parents were the undisputed authority figures, and talking back or not responding immediately had serious, quick consequences.

One of the reasons few of us are like that with our own children is that we recognize it as counterproductive. In our day and age, we value expressing feelings. We know that if you don't express them now, you can have trouble later with making relationships, finding personal satisfaction, fulfilling your total potential. To succeed in the workplace, you nowadays not only need an education and good work habits, you need to be creative, to innovate.

Things change fast in our world and the hierarchical model of authority just doesn't maintain.

Many of us have reacted against this authoritarian model and gone in the other direction. We've become permissive. Many of us indeed let our children make many decisions—from "I don't want to go to ballet today" to "I don't eat that for dinner." There are other influences on this permissive style as well.

Don't do for your kids what they can do for themselves—that's being a permissive parent. You're not doing them any favors. Children gain self-esteem from self-reliance. If you take over, they de facto ask themselves, "Why is this being done for me? It must be that I can't do it myself." There's a difference between doing a favor and being a crutch.

When you have limited time with your children, it can feel like all you ever do is struggle with them over discipline issues, and so you let it go. You want to have a positive experience with your kids, and if eating pizza in front of the television again is going to do it, then OK. Don't get me wrong. Sometimes pizza in front of the television again is just the thing to prevent (your) nervous breakdown and sometimes, indeed, whatever works works.

It's actually interesting that kids who don't see either parent all day do present power struggles the minute they get home. What this tells you is that your kids need to reestablish their relationship with you after an absence. The best thing you can do for them, and for you, is to muster the extra energy and do some positive disciplining.

Positive discipline may create a fuss in the short term. But even after a half hour or so things will be quieter and more settled. You will have shown your children that you are in charge. That they can breathe free and be children—everything isn't up to them; that there are parameters you observe and within these you have a pleasant, productive family time.

Positive discipline is setting limits and enforcing them. Say your child comes in the front door and throws her backpack on the stairs, and you say, "Please put that in your room," and she just keeps marching toward the television set. You are tempted to pick it up and put it in her room yourself, just because it seems easier. Instead, say, "I don't want to ask you again, and if I have to there will be a consequence." Say she brazenly disregards you. "OK, you lose your television privilege for the day," is your measured response. Bloody murder, screams your child. "Keep screaming and you lose it for tomorrow," you say, a model of reasonable firmness. Your daughter stops screaming and runs into her room, slamming the door. You go to the room, you open the door. "No slamming," you say. "I'd like an apology." Snarling, she apologizes. You leave her room.

You feel like lying down; drinking a cosmopolitan; going to the movies. Instead, you go into the kitchen and make dinner.

After awhile, the beast emerges. Turns out, she's hungry. How was her day? Well, let's have a bit of a talk about it....

Bearing through the unpleasantness of having to implement the consequences yields fruit for both of you. Firm boundaries make life easier for kids, they do. They want limits, they want to know you are in charge.

Looking at Temperament

All acting out behaviors are in a sense regressive—your child is falling back on a strategy to get what he wants. It's not from a spirit of maturity that he hits his best friend or tells you to "shut up." Children have many anxieties— and around a divorce they are worried about fundamentals, like, "Who will take care of me?" They are worried about the welfare of the noncustodial parent. They also pick up and express your anxiety. You can help your children by connecting with them and by reassuring them. Get your own anxieties expressed, but with your friends, family, and other support networks.

Most of the behaviors, whether on the one end of the spectrum defiant and on the other snail in a shell, have to do not only with their specific goal of power or expression of failure. They have to do with a sense of not knowing a better way to fit into the present situation comfortably. Your defiant child who has trouble with cooperating in after-school activities may get overstimulated. He may need to cultivate smaller, more low-key activities for a while before actually being ready for a soccer team. If he's high-strung and gets agitated easily, putting him in a situation in which there's pressure to succeed and a lot of stimulation may not be helpful. Since you want him to feel like he's a responsible, valued participant, maybe smaller play dates with more low-key kids is the better way to go for a while.

On the other hand, an exuberant child who really needs to get her ya-yas out every day may not succeed as well at the small play dates. She may be a bull in a china shop. Larger, group-oriented activities might be just the thing. Many of us follow the pack when it comes to what our kids lives look like. Everybody does soccer, everybody does ballet. These activities are age-appropriate and enjoyable for a broad range of kids. But maybe not yours, maybe not now.

Even with teenagers, it is useful to dig back down to your basic assessment of their personality to get at the roots of their behavior. Say you have a teenager who is acting recklessly in high school, getting busted for small stuff like tipping over wastepaper baskets or some other such nonsense. What was he like when he was younger? If he was socially insecure, his behavior may have to do with trying to fit in with a crowd, even a crowd of ruffians. If he was exuberant and had trouble sitting still, that same kind of kinetic imperative may be prompting him now. Figuring out where it's coming from can help you devise the best strategy for dealing with particular behaviors. He may need to reconnect with a secure base, to spend more time with you or more time alone. Or he may need to have more physical outlets during his week.

Other Styles of Behavior

• *I want this I want that*

Constant demands for stuff on you. You want your child to be happy, and even if it's for ten seconds, a new gimcrack makes him happy. You're tired and you don't feel like going through a power struggle in the store. You're thinking about other things. You don't know if your child has tried to get your parenting partner to buy this for him, and now he's trying you. One dad said, "I don't know what nine-year-old girls need. Does she need this to feel part of things, or is she using the divorce to get stuff out of me?" In the moment this can feel like a battle not worth embarking on.

When you are actually in the store and hearing the whining and the wheedling, you can use some consequences. "If you ask me one more time, you'll lose television privileges. If you throw a fit about *that*, you'll lose the privileges for tomorrow." If you can just remember, you're the grownup, this is your job, your child's job is to push your limits and he is not, in fact, doing this to drive you insane, then you can present this to your child in a clean, measured tone.

Sit down and think about the limits you would like to enforce, and the occasions on which you feel it would be fine to indulge your child. You will feel better about saying no to a fuzzy pencil holder at the checkout line in the supermarket if you know that later in the week, or in the month, you're going to take your child to the bookstore to get a paperback. Remember, if you are inconsistent about this one, your child will feel it is worth trying you every time. If you give in once at the supermarket, you're in for it.

- *Overcontrolling behavior from kids*

  Some kids approach stress by manipulating their own environments a bit too much. There's a fine line between having a child's input on how he spends his time, and letting the child run the whole show. School-age kids are testing out their social power and some may overstep the bounds. One mother was shocked to hear her seven-year-old on the phone talking with a friend about who was to be invited to her daughter's birthday party. "My daughter got off the phone and said, 'We can invite this one but not that one.' I said, 'Who is deciding this?' And it turned out her friend was deciding this. When I said, 'We can make our own invitation list,' my daughter seemed to become afraid of the fallout from this girl."

  It's normal for kids to try to control their world, and for girls their world is often social. The fact that adults are in charge is an important message to convey. When this mother mailed out the invitations, her daughter's friend took matters into her own hands by calling up the girl she hadn't wanted at the party and telling her not to come. "It was way out of line," said the mother. "It wasn't her party, it wasn't her choice!" Such behavior can get a child labeled manipulative, and other parents may want their kids to stay away from her. The truth is probably simple. The girl who wanted so much external control was having difficulty with her own feelings—what she couldn't manage inside, she would manage outside.

  "I called her mother, but I don't know how it was handled, ultimately. I do know I became very wary of this girl and began to limit the amount of time she spent with my daughter. I didn't want my girl to learn this kind of behavior. I didn't want her to feel overcontrolled by her friend, either."

At school age, it's possible to have an influence over who your children spend time with, but of course that becomes more problematic the older they get. Which is why it's important to impart values and self-confidence when they're young. And set some firm limits. Kids want power, they need power. It's important to give them power whenever you can. Then in the moments when you need to retain power, they don't have so much self-esteem at stake. They'll get another win, some other time.

When to Engage

SOMETIMES IGNORING BAD behavior sends the right message—that this isn't the way to get attention. As in all things, use your judgment. Are you in a good space to deal with the situation without losing your cool? Or should you wait til the next time (and there will, of course, be a next time). Is your child experimenting with something you can easily dissuade him from, or is the behavior more entrenched? If so, you may not be able to take the luxury of letting it go even once—the message has to get across that the behavior is not acceptable. Don't be afraid to get help if you are overwhelmed. Armies of people with Ph.D.s are out there, and they know a thing or two. Avail yourself.

An Encouraged Child	A Discouraged Child
Is more accepting.	Rebels with intense feelings against rules and regulations and against those viewed as authority figures.
Is motivated from a desire to be creative and expressive.	Is likely to feel inadequate and think of himself or herself as a failure—will be prone to undue competition and perfectionism.
Learns from failures and moves on.	Blames others for problems.
Is more willing to accept ideas from others.	Is likely to withdraw from social contact.
Is more willing to try for the sake of the effort and what's to be learned from it.	Will often resort to daydreaming or escapism to feel rewarded.

Will let go of defensiveness.	May hold on to bitterness too long, making it a habit.
Sets realistic goals.	Has difficulty setting goals.
Is more open to empathy and compassion, to sharing.	Tends to be selfish.
Has a sense of humor.	Can't let go of personal tension—isn't relaxed enough to have a sense of humor.

- *Temper tantrums, whining, and generally annoying behavior*

For many parents, it's not the large infractions that wear away one's patience and forbearance. It's the endless niggling, the embarrassing hissy fits in public, the endless negotiations about whatever the child has dreamed up now. Logical consequences are pretty effective for this kind of behavior. You've come to pick your daughter up from a friend's house. She doesn't want to go. You give her a five-minute warning that you'll be leaving soon. She decides to stage a meltdown. You are embarrassed and start to cajole her. She whines, she runs away, she holds on to her friend's bedpost.

"I am leaving in five minutes and you are coming with me. If I have to ask you again to get ready then you will not be able to play soccer tomorrow." It's a good idea to name a consequence that's very immediate. You could say, "You won't be able to play here again," but since that is a potential privilege in an unspecified future, it will be hard for your child to visualize it as a loss.

As always, it is important to encourage your child, to notice her efforts at improvement. If you go a week without any major whining, you might say, "Congratulations. I'm proud of you." "Why?" "Well you haven't whined for days now and I think you're really growing up!" Mentioning behavior when it is not occurring is a good way to bring your child's attention to her impulses. The more she can observe herself, the more control she will develop over her feelings.

The Next Step

One of the main challenges of being a parent is knowing when to let go. Part of your job is to instill self-reliance and independence in your child, so that in about twenty years (!) he is able to live productively on his own. From even the earliest months of an infant's life, a parent needs to provide opportunities for independence, for the child to explore and establish his boundaries, and to feel power and agency in the world. At the same time, young children need a great deal of protection. A two-year-old may feel pleasure at being able to put a lid on a jar, but he isn't going to understand this as something he has to do to keep his room clean and play his part in the family. By the time he's five, he may understand that.

Accordingly, behavior issues are sometimes up to the parent to take care of, and sometimes it is better left to the child to deal with it. Toddlers are going to need a great deal of adult intervention—we've all taken sticks and shovels out of hot little hands, or stopped a slug mid-swing. Preschoolers are getting to where words like "stop" and "don't" will do the trick. But from six years old and up, there is more gray area about what should be done in the event of conflict.

School-age children are repeatedly exhorted to "talk it out" on the playground. When so and so hurts so and so's feelings, the grownup on duty doesn't solve the problem by saying "Hey, that was mean," but contributes to the growth of both children by encouraging them to tell each other how they feel and to keep talking until they come to some agreement.

We are important teachers of our children. Experience is an even greater teacher. Ask yourself, whose problem is this? If it is your child's problem, let your child deal with it.

The Kids' Turn Guide to Effective Parenting:

1. Establish a routine and follow it. This reduces anxiety and tension.
2. Encourage the child to be cooperative and have respect for the rights of others.

3. Resist the child's coercive demands: "I know you really want to stop at the store right now, but we will be late for school. So we'll stop when...."

4. Enforce the rules consistently. Never say: "If you do that one more time...."

5. Don't promise what you can't fulfill.

6. Follow through on what you say you'll do, whether it's a promise or discipline.

7. Give praise and encouragement for a task attempted or well done: "Good try!"

8. Stay actively involved by taking time to talk and play.

Stories

Molly on the Rampage

IT'S HARD TO imagine, looking at Molly Sands, that she is capable of bringing detention on her head almost daily at her elementary school. At nine, she's got a bright, freckled face and a ready smile. She's obviously smart—and indeed, scores very high in math and reading skills and does very well academically. "Her behavior went from rascally to insane," her mother says, sort of laughing. Then sighing, "I let her get away with everything for too long."

Molly's parents, Jack and Annette are in a bitter divorce. "We never got along smoothly," says Jack. "I'm fifteen years older than she is and we dated for maybe six months before we got married. We didn't tell our parents for a year—we kind of knew we shouldn't have done it."

Molly has an older brother, born with severe birth defects and currently in a home where he receives round-the-clock care. "We had a huge ethical dilemma about tubing him," Annette says, and starts to cry. "For the first five years he was home with me. Then people started using this word, 'placement.' You become part of another world when you have a kid like Molly's brother. There was me before he was born, and there's me after."

When Molly came along, Annette and Jack were overjoyed. "She was so perfect. It was like she had her brain and her brother's brain," says Annette. "We had been so focused on a child with problems for so long, it was a miracle she had all her fingers, all her toes, and was also totally beautiful. Molly walks on water. Thank God for Molly," she says. Then, upon a moment's reflection, "I know that's not a good thing for Molly, but I can't help it."

Both Annette and Jack have high-level jobs in nonprofit organizations and devote themselves to doing good. They are clearly dedicated to parenting their disabled son in the best way they can. Molly felt like a reward, at long last, and her existence kept the marriage going for a number of years. "But we never really got along," says Annette. "We're very kind in our relationship to the outside world, but we're awful to each other. Let me tell you what I think of my ex-husband. I think he's a piece of dirt." It's almost remarkable, how this delicate, sweet-faced woman begins a sentence in a very reasonable tone and ends it with a bitter hiss.

"I wasn't good to her," Jack says. "I had affairs. I'm an alcoholic. We had big fights, the neighbors calling the police, everything. Molly slept in the same bed with Annette for years before I actually left. I slept on the couch."

Both Annette and Jack were highly distressed when they started to get calls from Molly's teachers and other adults in her life. "This incredibly bright and cooperative child started hitting people, like with sharp objects," says Annette. "She became totally impossible to be around. I'd be in a store with her and she'd want something, and I'd say no, and she'd lose it. Start screaming, throwing herself on the floor. This is at age seven, age eight. We're not talking toddler here."

During these years the marriage was officially ending. Jack had gone into AA and gotten sober; he'd also let Annette buy him out of the house they had purchased together. Although they can hardly speak to each other without screaming, Jack and Annette essentially agreed that they should divorce, and did it with a minimum of fuss. From the beginning, they split custody of Molly, and both of them have regular visitation times with Molly's brother.

Annette and Jack's parenting styles were certainly not the cause of Molly's distress and acting out, but bringing their attention to how they treated her differently helped each of them get a handle on becoming a better parent to her. "I have to admit it, he's better with the limits than I am," Annette says. "I just...she's brought me so much joy I want to give it back to her. She's all I have! But I see it now, how I was creating a monster." She sighs. "I love her so much I'll even listen to that S.O.B. about what's going on with her. He got me to let her take ballet and to have more time with her friends. He said, 'She needs a life even if I don't.' He insults me, but I see his point and I try to do the best for my daughter."

"Don't get me wrong," Jack says. "In many ways I'm a better parent, but my wife is a better person than me. Annette spoiled her, totally, but the love is there," Jack says. "I'm the disciplinarian. When Molly pulls her stuff with me I say no and she listens. It's a hundred percent easier now we're actually divorced, now that we're not together. Because if Annette was there, she'd give in, every single time. Annette didn't respect me so Molly didn't. Now it's different. Molly and I have our own relationship, and it doesn't have to do with her mother."

Living separate lives for several years now, things have calmed down with Molly. She still has behavior issues in school, but there are far fewer incidents, and of a milder variety, than there used to be. Her parents are high-conflict people, and as they struggle with themselves their daughter struggles with herself.

Sharing
Parenting

THIS BOOK HAS referred to that person from whom you are now separated or divorced as your "co-parent." In many cases, this term will feel like it is much too nice, too benign, to describe this person, and if you are really angry it may raise your hackles to think of having to "co-" anything with him or her. Fair enough.

The emotions between you and this other person in a divorce are large and messy. You may be hugely angry; feel deeply betrayed; you may feel frightened and lonely. Even though you and your former spouse have decided to split, or one of you has, there are many intimate ties still binding you. If nothing else, you know how to push each other's buttons.

"My wife can just learn to live with it," one aggrieved man said. "She decided to cheat on me, she decided to leave me. Well, she's going to hear about it. She's going to just have to listen to how awful I feel. She doesn't understand what she did to me and I'm going to make her understand."

Yes, revenge has its attractions. Making the sucker pay—sometimes that little piece of power is the only consolation on the horizon. The trouble is, your anger at your former spouse hurts your children. Anger and fighting are crippling to your children's self-esteem, to their ability to feel OK with the world. And your children are more important than your anger or your fear.

Co-Parenting in a High-Conflict Situation

IF YOU ARE in a high-conflict situation with your co-parent, make some adjustments along the lines of what follows in this chapter. Your first priority is to shield your children from your conflict, so schedule drop-offs and pick-ups on neutral ground, with a third party present if possible. Do not enter each other's houses even when your co-parent is not there. Give yourself time and space away from this person until you can approach co-parenting with some level of calm. Mediation is something to seriously consider. You can find a mediator through your attorney. In some states (California is one), the state provides mediation; others actually require it in every case of litigation. The mediator can help you with the nuts and bolts of your schedules, so that both of you feel heard.

Establishing New Boundaries

Even two splitting adults with the best of intentions can get pretty messed up when trying to deal with each other post-marriage. Bridget, a lively woman of thirty-two, had her former husband paint her house. She felt she could handle it—they didn't fight, they both agreed on the divorce, he was a housepainter and she needed the work done. "Then he came to me and wanted me to pay him for it!" she said. "I couldn't believe it. The house was half his, half mine—we never bought each other out. I said, well, pay yourself! He said he lost time he would have spent making money."

Bridget's story highlights just how hard it can be to reestablish a working relationship with someone to whom you have been married. You used to share costs, you used to do things for each other freely—and now there's an issue around all that. Your task is to move from one type of parenting arrangement—marriage—to another.

To get on firm ground with healthy boundaries may take some cautious, deliberate steps. Some of what is proposed in this chapter will feel too labored for you—take from it what you will. Be advised that actually going through some of the formalities here is likely to help you in the long-term. This chapter contains:

1. A renewed focus on what it means to be a parent: the parenting project.
2. Separating your parenting from your marriage—some general guidelines for revising your relationship with your former spouse.
3. How to see your co-parenting project as a business relationship.
4. A word on fathers.
5. Tips for making smooth transitions for the kids and staying in touch with them when they are with your co-parent.
6. Several "parenting plans."

The Parenting Project

On some level, no matter what the circumstances, divorce feels like a loss. At the very least a marriage is ending. So is family life as you have known it. People often get stuck in this feeling of loss—they feel that they are not quite right, not quite whole without being part of the traditional man, woman, children setup. Many people who aren't legally married have children together, and they feel the loss of the unit just as keenly. People can lose the sense that they still fit the description of "parent." Parent implies something whole, active, and supported, and you may not feel that way right now.

Part of your task is to move on from this characterization. Perhaps you need to mourn, and everything in its time. But at a certain point it's important for you and your children that you understand yourself as a whole parent with a whole child or children. You are not a "broken" home—you are a home.

While your ability to be an effective parent is definitely going to go through some challenges and readjustment, the fact is, you are still a parent. You are still a *good* parent.

What does it take to be a good parent?

1. You love and appreciate your children and you tell them so.
2. You hug, kiss, and cuddle with them.
3. You discipline your children in a balanced way that is neither too strict nor too permissive (and it's OK if you're working on this).
4. You respect yourself and you respect your children.
5. You face challenges and you help your children face challenges not based on external measures of success but on an ethic of trying and participating. You move on from your mistakes, providing redress where it's called for, and you encourage your children to do the same.
6. You help your children adjust to the social world at large by getting them to school and to other engagements on time. Homework is an important priority. Peer relationships are another priority.
7. When you are overwhelmed and can't meet some of these ideals, you get help.

It may help to view the definition of a family from the anthropological perspective: a family is a kinship unit that raises offspring. The members of a kinship unit cooperate with each other to function within its larger social definition—for us human beings, that means making sure the kids are clothed, fed, and schooled. It means teaching the kids how to adapt to the adult world. In our millennial democracy, we might add that the social definition of a family includes nurturing self-esteem and promoting individual potential.

A Word about Stepfamilies

REMARRIAGE AND ITS impact on kids is a book unto itself, but for our purposes several points are worth making. One is that when a parent makes a healthy, successful relationship with a "new" wife or husband, that is good for the kids, because a healthy, successful remarriage is going to create a container that is stabilizing and comfortable for the children. Additionally, if the kids have learned some negative lessons about intimacy from their parents' inability to get along, a new, peaceable relationship has the chance of reeducating them about the possibility of lasting ties.

If the kids feel welcomed by the new spouse, they are going to be able to relax, to feel safe and secure, and to explore their creativity and pursue other goals. If, on the other hand, the kids are not accepted by the new spouse, it's going to be very problematic for them. They won't feel welcome in this home, and they won't relax. It will endanger their relationship with this remarried parent, who is put in the position of having to choose between the new spouse and the children.

If a new love is the source and cause of the divorce, it is important to gradually and gently introduce this person to the kids. Because you have strong intimate feelings for this person does not mean your kids instantly will. They have to warm up to this person slowly, to put this person in a place in their minds that works for them and doesn't seem to knock out the relevance of the mother or father whose role they are replacing in your life.

Separate Parenting from Your Marriage

After you have refocused your inner commitment to your role as a parent, take a moment to think of the areas in which you clearly shared parenting responsibilities with your former spouse, and areas in which you feel you always were on your own. Many mothers have a similar story to tell—that part of what tanked the marriage was that their husbands were de facto absentee parents, working all the time, not participating in the feeding, clothing, and chauffeuring that are the nitty-gritty of parenting. Many of these women don't have difficulty at all with separating their parenting from their marriage—part of the problem is that these two areas were separate all along. It is also common to hear from both men and women that after the divorce, the father who suddenly does have responsibility for brushing teeth and applying sunblock at least part of the week feels much more connected to his kids than he did before the divorce.

But as has been mentioned before, anger at the co-parent leads many people into overt and sometimes covert manipulation of the kids' lives—the kids remain a common ground between people who have otherwise deleted their connection. If you find yourself struggling with your co-parent over the details of your children's lives, it may be that you are investing those details with residual feelings about your former spouse.

Some Strategies

Set up a regular time to have a "conference call" with your ex. This is when you go over the next week's calendar, birthday parties, soccer practices, and so forth. Try to have both parties agree to get out datebooks, palm pilots, whatever, and get the stuff down on paper. If your spouse isn't there at the appointed time, leave a detailed message.

Say you have a phone appointment and your ex isn't where he or she is supposed to be at that time. You leave a detailed message, but it has several really important points to it, points that affect your child. For example, maybe your spouse picks your kids up from school on Fridays, and the next Friday is a half-day. Do you call again to make sure the message was heard? While you run the danger of "enabling" your spouse to be irresponsible, you may have to make the extra effort to make sure your child gets picked up from school. The child is the priority.

Sometimes it will feel as though your ex is deliberately manipulating you to get your negative attention. Angry people do indeed do this sort of a thing. Your best response is to keep your cool. Don't gratify the other person with your rage; it will reinforce the behavior you are responding to.

You might say, "Gee, I know you care about our kids and want them to have a good life, and it seemed like a once-a-week phone conversation was a way we could both help them out. But you haven't been available at the time we selected. Is another time better for you?"

Are you going to get fed up and want to scream? Yes. Scream into your pillow when no one's around. Go to a support group. Call a friend. Pat yourself on the back and encourage your good intentions.

Work on your mind-set. "Ralph" or "Trixie" may conjure a world of experience and elicit an immediate visceral reaction in you—so try to refer to your former spouse as "the children's father," or "the children's mother." Even just doing this will help keep your focus on the parenting project rather than on your slimy ex. When you speak to your kids about this person, also refer to "your father," or "your mother."

Be businesslike, but leave the power struggles at the office. Many separating and divorcing people use their kids to get at their ex. Is that news? No. Are you doing it? Maybe. A mother who says, "Well you can see them if you pick them up at soccer practice at 4:12 on Thursdays" is making it very hard on the father. A father who doesn't show up to pick the kids up or "forgets" that it was his night to take them is making it impossible for the mother and for himself to have a good relationship with the kids.

E-mail Ettiquette

ONE OF THE blessings and banes of modern existence, e-mail both simplifies communication and bollixes it up. As we all know, it is very, very easy to dash off an e-mail without thinking much about how or why we are saying something. What's worse, even carefully considered e-mails often backfire. The recipient reads an unintended tone into a communication, and the fireworks start. Jeanne Ames offers these guidelines for using e-mail to communicate with your parenting parnter:

1. Gather your thoughts before sending or responding to an e-mail.
2. Problems often arise when the sender of an e-mail assumes the communication has been received—due to the vagaries of various software and telecommunication issues, e-mails are sometimes not in fact received. When you receive an e-mail, promptly acknowledge it. If you send an e-mail with vital information in it, back it up with a telephone call.
3. E-mails should be factual, confined only to issues regarding the children. Check your information to make sure it is accurate.

4   E-mails, when acknowledged, should provide a time-line for when a reply will be made, if possible.

5.   Read over your messages before you send them to make sure they adequately reflect your intention. In the heat of a reply it is easy to type "I agree" when you meant to type "I disagree."

6.   Strictly control the number of e-mails you send. More than several e-mails a day can subvert productive communication.

7.   If you do not get a response to an e-mail, do not assume that any terms or suggestions in the e-mail have been agreed to. Silence does not mean consent. It may mean the e-mail was not received.

8.   It is a good idea to save an e-mail as a draft, re-read it later, and then send it.

9.   Be careful of the "reply" feature. You may be sending your response to more people than you are aware of or intend.

Keep Yourself Clean as a Whistle

Honor your custody decisions. Don't find ways to subvert them. Be honest in all your dealings. "Oh, I thought you would understand if I made a play date for Alyssa on your weekend. She really wanted to play with her friend Sandy and there didn't seem to be another day." In a similar situation, give Sandy's parent your co-parent's phone number. Don't insert yourself where you don't belong.

Be careful in the way you communicate. Are you being direct or indirect? Are you saying what you mean? And discipline yourself about believing everything you hear—consider the source. How direct is it? Friends and in-laws will naturally want to further consolidate their allegiance to you by finding evil in your co-parent. Send a message to them that you don't want to wallow, you don't want to interpret things in the worst possible light. Teachers, after-school instructors, doctors—all the myriad people in and out of your life—are capable of saying off-the-cuff stuff that sets your teeth on edge. But remember, they don't know the full picture, aren't sensitive to the situation. Save your reactions for when you really need them.

Figure out what really sets you off and gird yourself for the next time it happens. Say your co-parent never gets it right—shows up an hour early or an hour late. Say you have a telephone call and set a time for the kids to go from one parent to the other. Follow it up with a memo! This is time-consuming but amazingly effective—because you have proof of your agreement. Prepare yourself to (calmly) hammer out a general etiquette between the two of you. Say your co-parent doesn't honor the memo. In your next appointed phone call, you say, "It's really hard for me when you don't show up when you say you will, even when we agree on the time and confirm it in writing." Say he or she then says, "You don't trust me! You give me this insulting memo!" You very calmly say, "It sounds like you feel disrespected. But the memos help me organize my schedule. Is there a better way to make sure we're on the same page?"

It may take months of frustration on your part before your co-parent comes into line about this kind of thing. If you are firm and cool, it will give him or her a chance to adjust to the new level of behavior being required, without losing face. If he or she is absolutely recalcitrant, make back-up arrangements. "I really need to leave the house at 2 P.M. this Saturday. So if you haven't come by to pick the kids up by 1:30, I'm going to bring them to (a friend's) house."

OK, OK, so some slime buckets will even push the envelope on this one, taking the opportunity to pick the kids up whenever from the friend's house. The friend, understandably, is wronged in this situation. "It doesn't work for (my friend) for you to pick the kids up whenever you get to it. I feel like I've tried everything to get this worked out and yet it is always frustrating. We're going to have to reconsider our custody agreement. I'll bring copies of all my memos to the mediator."

Even if you have to struggle like this for a year, don't be tempted to tell your co-parent anything like, "Your actions are hurting your kids." As discussed in the chapter on communication, you can help empower your kids so that they can talk to the co-parent themselves, but don't even think about that. Just keep the lines of communication open between your kids and yourself. Be strong and steady for them, and let the chips fall where they may with their other parent. It may really hurt you to see your kids hurt by their other parent, but remember: it's not your business.

How to See Your Co-Parenting Project as a Business Relationship

Sometimes placing a different mental framework around a situation provides just the guidance one needs to operate effectively. In that spirit, try approaching your co-parent as you would a business client. This business client represents a really important account you need to keep—your kids' health and well-being. When the client gets difficult, you keep yourself in a professional mode, no emotions, no personal details. You don't get into the whys, the you-saids, the you-betrayed-me's. You take a deep breath and work around them in some way. How do you work things out with co-workers when you disagree? You develop civility.

The children are the prize you are preserving, but they shouldn't be treated as part of the management team. Never use your children as a source of information; never make them deliver messages.

One big feature of the business model is that it respects boundaries. Somehow all of us know and follow customary boundaries when dealing with our work. We don't get in people's faces (unless we're football coaches), but we communicate using faxes, letters, e-mail. Relegating your former spouse to a business model will help contain your feelings and it will help your kids too. We expect a certain amount of conflict in business and understand that what we're doing is looking for mutually advantageous ground between at least two different parties. In order to get to this mutually advantageous ground, we contain conflict—you might cuss and kick when a client frustrates you, but you do it behind closed doors. In all likelihood, you go to great pains to make sure your client doesn't know how you really feel.

Divorce is an event, but it is also a process. There will be times when you slip back into one form of intimacy or another with your former spouse. Screaming rages are one way of staying intimate; because you would never show all those feelings of yours to someone you didn't know well—they could have you locked up. Some people end up sleeping together again on their way to an eventual break up. Divorce is confusing. Try to stick to some guidelines even while your feelings for this other person waver.

It is regularly said that parenting is the most important job you will ever do, and right here is where to take those words literally. Keep your focus on the parenting role: that's your job. Take pride in your work and bring all your resources to the task at hand: raising healthy, happy kids.

The New Orbit of Your World

Your relationships form a kind of constellation, if you will, in which the people in your life occupy certain orbits. When you were married your spouse formed a kind of twin planet to your own central one. Now you have to reconfigure your relationship constellation. There's you, and there are your children. There is your extended family, there are your friends, there are people you know from the various activities that make up your life (including the work you do for a living). Your former spouse no longer sits beside you in the center of this constellation, but occupies a very important tangential place near your children (all the way on the other side of the map, if that makes it easier).

Many people unconsciously or otherwise evict their former mates from the close position of intimacy in this constellation through anger and conflict. Many of us know people who have been divorced for ten, twenty years, and they still foam at the mouth when talking about their former spouse. Why should this be? It's a kind of negative intimacy, an ejector seat that yet keeps the person attached to you with a spring—your anger. The business model can help you avoid this trap. Put your former spouse somewhere else in the constellation, somewhere that has nothing to do with intimacy and everything to do with a working relationship. Resign yourself to the fact that you must work with this person, that their place in your space is not going to completely go away because you have children together.

Go over the points of behavior you routinely give to coworkers and clients. You probably:

1. Give them the benefit of the doubt. Even if you deeply suspect the integrity of a crucial client, you always listen respectfully to their point of view and try to accommodate it.
2. Respect their space and their time. You don't barge into their office and expect them to stop what they're doing to deal with you. You

call to arrange meetings at mutually advantageous times and places. You don't act like you have a special dispensation with them.

3. Value what they have to offer. In fact, in this case, you NEED what they have to offer, because their relationship with your children is part of what helps create happy, healthy kids. You let them know you appreciate their input.

4. Thank them for their time and effort.

5. Go all out to cross your *t*'s and dot your *i*'s when fulfilling your end of the deal.

6. Don't take them for granted. You don't take it for granted that they know what you're thinking. You provide detailed information about who, what, when, and where. You give advance notice when you plan a vacation.

7. Do not make assumptions about what the other person feels or wants from a situation.

8. Do treat your interactions formally. Meet in a restaurant, or in a public space like the library. Keep the ground extremely neutral. Do this for several years at least—don't think, "Hey, I can handle this. She can come over here and that's OK." The turf of the other person has too many personal associations built into it.

9. Don't talk about your personal life. This is tricky, but stick to it. Despite your own prurient interest, don't encourage your former spouse to tell you about his or her personal life. You may feel all rational and disinterested at the outset of a conversation about dating, but when you start to hear the details you will be prey to some bad reactions.

10. Keep the emotions low, or nonexistent. Treat your former spouse as you would a new doctor you are consulting—someone you essentially don't know and don't need to know.

11. Don't expect emotional gratification from this arrangement. You are no longer working with intimacy as the ground between you. Your good efforts at working things out need to be reward enough—don't expect to be congratulated by your former spouse.

12. Compromise all the time, so that when you really want to hold your ground, you have built up some positive goodwill on the subject.

13. Empower your former spouse. Listen to his or her suggestions honestly and try to accommodate them.

14. Don't judge your former spouse's parenting style (unless it could endanger your children). Stick to your knitting—your own parenting style.

A Word on Fathers

The deadbeat dad is a cultural byword. For good reason: one study put the number of children between eleven and sixteen who had no contact with a divorced father for a year at 50 percent. Why do fathers fall out of the picture after a divorce? It's really not that they don't care, and it's really not that they don't love their kids.

"I couldn't deal with my wife," said one man. "She got control of the kids just like she wanted. She told me when I could come and when I could go. And she was always wanting more money." Underlying the man's complaint was a sense of powerlessness in the situation. It never occurred to him to get a mediator involved, and the mother of his children indeed wanted him out of the picture. When he "gave up" trying to see his kids, she was vindicated in her judgment of him as a lousy father in addition to being a lousy husband. Unless a parent is abusive, however, it is much better for everyone when both stay in the picture.

Often, divorcing adults are so angry and aggrieved that they try to gain power over each other whatever way they can. For men, who usually have more of it, power is often money. They can give it and they can withhold it. For women, power is often located in the kids themselves, and they can give the kids or they can withhold them. Needless to say, the behavior on both sides is totally destructive to the health of the children.

Children who grow up without a father after a divorce suffer. Their developing identity suffers; a part of them is missing. These kids feel abandoned, like there is something wrong with them.

Many men "leave" their families in response to the divorce itself. These men feel like rootless, incompetent failures. There may be a mythos of the footloose and fancy-free man in our society, but manhood is still very much predicated upon being the head of a household. The pain of these men is deep, their sadness often masked by anger and aggression. Often they leave as a way to avoid the shame they feel at the whole event. "The sight of my pretty daughter's face just reminded me of how I had failed her," said another man. "It was easier for me to try to forget about it." But his daughter didn't forget about it.

Some women respond to the divorce by totally retrenching, pulling up the troops, like Old Mother Hubbard sweeping the brood under her skirt. Sometimes women feel that not only the marriage has been betrayed, but so has the family. The man therefore should have no right to enjoy the family he treated so badly. There may be ample reason for feeling this way, but women in this position need to do a lot of soul-searching. You don't want to facilitate wounding your children. And they need a father. All the negative stuff you feel about him needs to be processed within your support system. Logistically, you need to put a good face on things for the kids. You need to present their father in a positive light and help, not hinder, his relationship with them.

On the other end of it, men can become disenfranchised from the family during and after a divorce. We still look at men who maintain a very involved role in their kids' lives after divorce and say, "Wow, what a great guy." We take it as some mark of an extra effort on the man's part, not as a natural impulse to be expected—as we expect from the children's mothers. There's almost an expectation that men will abandon their families. That's an expectation to work against.

Even when you are being pushed away from your kids by their mother, men need to make the effort to stay involved. It might be useful to remember that many women who do this are feeling powerless, like they've been hurt and can retaliate no other way—their kids are all they have left. Remember that the period of intense anger and acting out will not last forever—but patterns of custody and visitation that get laid down during this period may persist.

The children themselves might appear to take sides during this time of struggle, but they are very likely confused. "The kids are just like her," says one man. "She's turned them against me." Children who are nervous about being abandoned altogether—and pretty much all children will feel this to one degree or another—may side with the parent they feel most secure about at the time. But they have a natural and persistent need and desire to stay connected to both parents. It is fundamental to their overall development and fulfillment of their potential.

Divorce for women in society often means falling several rungs lower on the social scale, worsening finances, and a sense of being "used up"—no longer relevant in the mating and dating game, yet single. But men have their own social hurdles—like many emotional issues with men, they are perhaps harder to see, because despite popular discussion of the issue, we still allow women more room to express their feelings. Difficult feelings of shame and failure, a deep sense of a loss that cannot be redressed and, therefore, should be forgotten are some of these feelings for men. Whether or not you can successfully suppress them forever, your children are going to suffer if they don't see you.

For both mother and father, try to gain some distance. Look at the divorce as bad, don't look at your former spouse as bad. If you do believe your former spouse is bad, try not to think about him or her as a shabby, no-good, incompetent nincompoop, but try to think about him or her in their long-term role as your child's other parent.

Take your decision to end the marriage as a starting point. It's the starting point of a shared-parenting project. Sure, there's plenty of deconstructing to do before, during, and after a divorce. Why and how it happened, what the emotional history of both people are, what precipitated the event, how to rebuild. Spend plenty of time with your friends discussing these issues blow-by-blow, or if you can, a therapist or support group. But as far as your kids are concerned, the divorce is a done deal. Move on to parenting in a new environment.

Tips for Making Smooth Transitions for the Kids and Staying in Touch with Them When They Are with Your Co-Parent

When kids are moving back and forth between two residences, they are likely to need some time to find "terra firma" again when they arrive. Give some thought to when you schedule pick-ups and drop-offs. Does it work best to have the kids come in the door and sit straight down to a meal together? Or do they need time to kick around the house and refeel its parameters again? Try to say "the kids are home" instead of "with my ex" whether they are at your house or your co-parent's, so they don't feel like perpetual visitors.

You may have to reeducate your own parents and your own friends about this. There's a natural learning curve to this new life and everyone around you will eventually adjust.

Going back and forth between two houses—with the toothbrushes and the clothes, the beanie babies, and the piano music—it can be a logistic nightmare. The best solution is to have two complete sets of everything.

Again, keep your kids out of your conflicts. One woman came up with a good solution to a common situation: "I would come home and play the answering machine, and my kids were in the kitchen with me. So a friend would have called, and said something about my husband and it was clear there was a conflict going on, and my children would hear it. I didn't want to wait until the kids were asleep before I played the messages, so I changed to voice mail. I check the messages, and only I hear them."

Kids will often need a transitional object or two to carry back and forth between houses. This can be a problem if the child goes to school between staying at either house. The stuffed animal can get lost. The school may have a pretty strict policy about bringing toys. You may have to talk this one over with the teacher. And also with your child—have her choose a small toy to carry in her backpack, where it has to stay during the day, so that it doesn't get lost and doesn't become an object of dispute among her friends.

Tips for Making It Work

- Start new traditions.
- Let little stuff go.
- Thank your co-parent for something he or she did and mean it.
- Rise above your feelings and do your best for your kids.

If the idea of moving the child between two houses seems foreign, think of it this way. If your own parents lived nearby and given that you have a positive relationship with them, wouldn't you consider it an added bonus to your child to spend a great deal of regular time with her grandparents, even having her own room at their house? It is thus with the noncustodial parent. Look at it as an enriching of your child's world, exposing her to different environments. You can feel good that your child is learning to be flexible and adaptable and understands from the get-go that there is more than one way to live a life.

As the child gets older, it becomes more possible for the noncustodial parent to retain a connection without his or her physical presence. At three to four years of age, a child can recognize and appreciate photographs of the noncustodial parent. You can also send tapes—verbal letters in which you chat about whatever, repeating the child's name, perhaps telling favorite bedtime stories or singing favorite songs. The mail is a great way to keep up a connection—postcards, souvenirs of your day, like a bookmark or a special stone, can remind the child of your existence and let her know you're thinking about her.

Ways to keep in touch: the telephone. Kids under the age of about six aren't too great at talking on the phone, so don't expect a chatty time. Still, it's helpful for your child to hear your voice and know you are thinking about her. Keep yourself up to date on what's going on in the child's life—talk with the custodial parent about details, if you can do so amicably, or connect with the child's day-care provider or preschool teacher. If you can find out from an adult about field trips and events in the child's life, you can ask specific questions about them that the child may be able to answer.

Mail is great. You can send pictures, drawings, mementos of your day and any places you've been. Tell the child about what you're doing and how you're thinking about her a lot. Tapes are great too. Read stories, sing songs, tell about your day. As the child gets to be about six, she'll be into e-mail and faxes. Share fun Web site information. Most children are interested in animals and nature—send pictures of these with comments. Tell them stories about animals in your life.

It gets easier to connect with kids from another location once they reach school age. When they're reading they will love to get letters, faxes, and e-mails, which give them an opportunity to use their skills. Keep the language easy to read as age-appropriate. Foster a mutual discussion of an interest your child has gotten into. One dad totally dove into the Pokémon craze with his son. This was a terrific venue, since the cartoon character had baseball cards associated with it that were easy (and not too expensive) to send; the dad also familiarized himself with the whole hierarchy of Pokémon and would e-mail little made-up vignettes about the creatures.

Popular culture may make you gnash your teeth, but kids do tend to gravitate toward it—pick your poison, some trends are worse than others. Harry Potter is a good one by most people's standards, though not all. The American Girl series offers books, dolls, Web site activities, and so forth and also has some cultural content to it (heaven forfend!). Unfortunately, it's the very commercial nature of these phenomena that make them easy to use as conversation-connectors with your kids, since they offer many avenues of accessibility. Connecting with your child is more important than keeping them culturally pure, so unless these things really offend you, consider using them. Of course if they really do feel wrong to you, it would be a mistake to pretend otherwise.

School-age kids love puzzles, mazes, wordplay, magic tricks. E-mail them a joke-a-day. You can read the same magazine (age-appropriate!) and compare notes about the content. As the child gets older, some article topics may lead to bigger discussions about important issues. Stay abreast of your child's school curriculum. If they are studying snails, find out something interesting about snails and send that along. Have your child read to you over the phone, using a headset so the whole thing doesn't become too burdensome.

Add a special patch to your child's backpack, or make a tradition of finding fun key rings to add to your child's collection. Whatever you are good at, share with your child. One dad, a chef, simply sent his kids something homemade every week—cookies, bread, pizza. The idea is to show your children that you are consistently thinking about them, that they are a part of your life even though you are physically separated much of the time.

There are some real advantages to connecting with teenagers, and some unique hurdles. Remember that even a sullen teenager does want to connect with you, and if they don't seem too responsive on the phone, don't let that discourage you from calling. On the other hand, if they ask you not to call, you should ask why, but then respect their wish. Ask this age child what would work best for him or her in terms of keeping in regular touch with you, but remember you are the adult and you make the rules. Teenagers don't want to be making the boundaries, they want to be breaking them.

You Are Only Responsible for Your Parenting

It's pretty hard sometimes to think calmly about your former spouse and his or her parenting style. Many of us are stuck with a parenting partner who is inconsistent, incompetent, or even mean. It's very frustrating! Even when you are justified in being angry it's very important to rise above it. Don't let it go if your ex physically endangers your child through neglect or by aggression. If the issue is not inadequate parenting, but safety, involve a judge, social services, or the police in the problem. If the situation is less urgent but far from good, you should definitely try to involve a therapist or a mediator. Bring the issue up at tactful intervals if you meet with resistance. Keep the focus on yourself: "I could really use some help in working out our parenting situation. I'd really appreciate it if you would join me with a therapist/mediator."

Pick your battles. Focus on what you need to have happen and don't niggle over who's responsible for it—you are. "I just decided I would rather do my children's laundry than browbeat my husband endlessly about sending them to school in dirty clothes. So I gave the kids these laundry bags, and I had them just bring me everything after they'd spent a weekend with their dad. More work, but I got what I wanted, which was kids in clean clothes."

Be honest and don't "trap" the other person through false pretenses—your co-parent will sense this a mile away and it will erode any goodwill between you. Remember how the brother felt in the very fine film *You Can Count On Me* when his sister invited a priest to their home—whatever good the priest could do was severely undermined by the brother's sense that his sister had betrayed him.

The Permeable Family

Often the way people really live doesn't bear all that much resemblance to the mom-dad-children model we use to denote "family." Mainstream American culture operates with the implicit assumption that every individual grows up to be independent, virtually free of obligation to anyone but themselves, husband, wife, or child. When parents divorce, in the American model, the child is expected (optimally) to be the equal responsibility of one woman, his mother, and one man, his father. Yet many, many people in the United States have worked out other arrangements.

Part of how people really live today reflects community values maintained from various immigrant countries of origin. Asian and Latin immigrants, in particular, are collectivist as opposed to individualistic. Traditional "family values" like religion and marriage are paramount, but additional responsibilities are understood, including taking care of parents into old age, and helping siblings and cousins when they need it. Many African American communities include children in extended family networks, in which the various responsibilities associated with child-rearing are dispersed among several adults. Not only does this provide a broader economic net for children's welfare, it also provides an emotional bumper for children when their parents split. Since other adults with an important role in the child's life may remain constant through the divorce, the child has an important piece of emotional continuity.

Although these groupings don't get much official recognition by the courts, they can be very productive for the health of children, particularly when parents divorce. What children really need through their childhood in general and divorce in particular isn't confined to a cultural model of man-woman-child, but is based on consistency, predictability, and love. These can be provided by any number of people.

While the collectivist view of how to raise children and support each other has much to recommend it, other traditional values can bring a special sting to the experience of divorce. People from very Catholic countries, for example, may feel a divorce is an irreparable break with a community that places tremendous value on marriage in the church. Asian cultures that emphasize keeping family trouble behind closed doors can create a barrier to individuals seeking outside help with their conflicts.

Amelia

"None of my family back in Mexico had white weddings," Amelia says. "But my mother still won't tell them about the divorce." Amelia shrugs. She and her former husband came to the U.S. separately six years ago, quickly got married, and had a son. The strain of having a child and getting established was more than their marriage could bear. "My mother doesn't want them to know. It's a failure. She thinks everyone will talk about it all the time."

Amelia speaks in a soft torrent of Spanish; her words are translated by Cynthia Yannacone, the family planning coordinator for Good Samaritan Family Resource, a support agency located in the heart of San Francisco's Mission district. Yannacone explains that on the West Coast, most Latin immigrants are from Mexico or Central America, and as such are very Catholic. "Being married and a mother is the goal of women," she explains. "It's what you want."

Amelia has embraced much of what is on offer in the U.S. She works in a travel office and makes a decent living. She's justly proud of her independence, and her ability to support her son. "I love the support groups," she says of Good Samaritan. "It is so powerful to know you are not alone, you are not wrong, even when you hear whispers from the past that say you have failed." Amelia and her son are currently living with her mother, though she is looking forward to getting their own place soon. "My mother really helps out and my son loves her," she says, "but it's nice to have some space." Bridging cultures can sometimes mean taking the best of what each has to offer.

Same-Sex Parenting

Ethnic families are often more elastic than the mainstream American model, and thus provide more resources, rather than less, for children. Home life often includes grandparents, cousins, aunts, and uncles. Numerous adults feel a sense of responsibility to the children in their midst, even when they are not their own progeny. While traditional ethnic structures can sometimes hamper an individual's ability to cope with the change divorce brings (by stigmatizing it), they yet provide tremendous resources that can really ease the transition for everyone.

Although also outside the mainstream, same-sex parents are on the opposite end of the spectrum. Gay couples can have a very difficult time creating a child-centered world. It often has to be done very deliberately. One lesbian mother with a 12-year-old girl shares custody with the gay man who fathered the child. "I have two friends who pick Lisa up after school once a week. They have spent this time with her since she was born," Dede says. "These friends are family. Lisa's father and I share the week with her, basically 50-50. He and I are friends, and we are family, because of Lisa. It's just

a different way of looking at what family is. I don't have a romantic relationship with her father, but he's my kin." Lisa is a lucky girl, and Dede is
also really lucky to have such cooperative, supportive friends.

"A gay couple is trying to set up home rituals," says Jeanne Ames, who
has a booked-solid mediation practice in San Francisco. "But their families
often disapprove of their union. Their support systems are different." Often
a group of like-minded friends will chip in with child-care, as in Lisa's case,
and help create and attend the rituals of family life that are so fundamental to a child's sense of belonging. Lisa's parents were never romantically
involved, but both are equally committed to parenting her well. But gay parents who split in the same way as a heterosexual couple can have an even
harder time providing consistency to their children. "When a gay couple
splits, the through-lines are often very unclear," says Ames. "The child can
really lose everything."

Gay parents may not get the social approval heterosexual couples get, and
they often have to bear approbation on top of everything else. But children
care much more about having regular contact and a continued relationship
with both caregivers than they do about the particular sexual orientation of
their parents. Ames reiterates that no matter what the relationship among
the parents, children need the same things. They need: consistency, stability, acceptance, predictability, and love. No matter who her clients are, she
asks them to commit themselves to providing these things for their children.

Never-Married Parents

Single motherhood has taken on a new dimension of meaning in our current culture, in which economically independent women can decide for
themselves whether to have a baby or not, with our without a partner. Obviously there are many permutations to the story of a woman getting pregnant
and deciding to raise the child on her own. Many women don't have the luxury of turning away the support of their child's father. Many of them don't
know the father at all, or have been abandoned by these men. But in the
case of women who are independent and making a deliberate choice, it is
still important to remember that "father" is not just a biological role but an
emotional one, for the child, too. It is best for a child who grows up without

a father that she have other adult male figures in her life. It is best for the child if the absent father can be spoken of, if not positively, then at least neutrally. If you are angry at being abandoned (and who wouldn't be), put a shield up between your feelings and your child. "She should know her father's a worm," is not productive for the child, who has an internal sense of even a father she has never met, and identifies part of her own self with that internalization.

Adults who know they want to be parents, but don't know how much they want to make a life with a potential partner, can build a reasonable framework for rearing a child together, even if they live apart. The goal is the same for any couple: set up safe, nourishing environments for your child, and stick to a plan together. The challenge for people who don't know each other well is that there has been no time to agree on shared values. Going to a mediator can help hammer out the basics.

Jeanne Ames offers these guidelines for adults who have a child together and have never been married:

Tips for Good Parenting:
1. Children should never be used as messengers between parents. Parents should communicate directly before involving the children, either by phone, e-mail, fax, or regular mail. Putting children in the middle causes unnecessary stress, anxiety, and confusion for them.
2. Joint legal custody requires both parents to be involved in all major decisions including:
   Medical
   Educational
   Religious
   General Welfare
   Significant commitments of a child's time to an extra-curricular activity.
3. Parents, absent a restraining order, are both able to attend children's school and extra-curricular events, regardless of whose time of responsibility it falls under.
4. Children should be informed by both parents that, at all reasonable times, they are free to call the parent in whose home they are not presently residing.

5. Parents, during a time of responsibility, may delegate the care of the child/children to another responsible person as long as it does not violate an agreement regarding the Right of First Caregiver (exceptions would be made for vacation periods away from his/her regular residence).

6. Children should be informed that each parent encourages them to express their love and respect for the other parent. Children should have permission from both parents to express this in either home.

7. When children enroll in an activity (i.e., teams, lessons, etc.) they are to be encouraged to honor their commitments until both parents decide otherwise.

8. Parents should never refer to the other parent in the children's presence in a negative or derogatory manner. This has great implications for the child/children's sense of self-esteem and worth.

9. Parents, in spite of anger, disappointment, and unrealized expectations, should, in the interest of the children's self-esteem, always treat the other parent with civility and respect when with the children.

10. The children's community (i.e., school, teams, health providers, etc.) should not be exposed to the negative aspects of the parents' relationship or divorce.

Adam's Struggle

Adam will be the first person to tell you he is something of a lout, or used to be. "Hey," says this charming salesman, "I'm your classic type. I'm everybody's friend, and I would be everybody's lover, if there was time!" Adam found himself in a telephone relationship with the receptionist of a client he did a lot of work for. She worked in one city, and Adam was located in another. "We flirted on the phone, all the time," he says. "And then one day I was paying them a service call and she picked me up from the airport. She was pretty, and what can I say, I'm such a hunk!" Adam has the disarming shrug of a born narcissist on a downward trend. The receptionist and he went to dinner and back to his hotel room. He later returned home, where he resumed his bachelor's life of so many women, so little time. He kept up his flirtation with the receptionist over the phone. But as she pressed him for more commitment, he balked. "She found out she was pregnant at just about the same time she figured out I wasn't exactly her prince charming.

She was, to say the least, angry and betrayed. She told me I'd never see our child." Adam has spent the past two years trying to get partial custody of his child, whom he has seen only a handful of times. "I'm rotten but not that rotten," he says. The woman will have nothing to do with him and fights him at every turn. "She thinks she owns the child," he said, and a flicker of anger tenses his affable face. "She matches my kind of immaturity with her own kind of immaturity. It's the kid who will suffer." For all his blather, Adam is obviously suffering too.

Parenting Plan Outline

It's amazing what can fall through the cracks when responsibility divides along with a marriage. The following outline is provided to help you keep track of the many details critical to your child's well-being. If you are on good terms with the child's other parent, it would be ideal to sit down and agree on these together. If you are not willing or able to do that yet, still take the time to jot down your assumptions about who does what and what fundamental plans are. This can help you identify areas you need to discuss or resolve one way or the other.

Decision-making plan

Identify major decisions, e.g., educational, medical, general welfare, religion, extra curricular activities.

Identify who is responsible for what decisions.

Identify how decisions are to be made cooperatively—on the phone, through e-mail or fax, in a mutually agreed-upon meeting.

Information sharing

Who possesses the relevant information about the following, and how should this information be shared? For example, do you make a folder with all the relevant information and copy it for the other person? Do you agree to update the other person's files as needed?

1. School.
2. Medical, dental, therapy.
3. Social (birthday parties, etc.).
4. Cultural (religious holiday observances).
5. Any other relevant activities.

Medical emergencies

One suggestion is to make a "telephone tree" of relevant phone numbers. Agree between you which person should be notified first by school and other authorities. Put the other person's number down next, if desired, followed by other relatives, friends, and so forth.

School participation

Many parents want to contribute to their children's school activities. This may necessitate dividing up volunteer opportunities, like lunch/playground or after school projects and so forth. Parents working outside the home may need to fine-tune the scheduling of weekend and evening school activities.

Travel plans

Itineraries, emergency numbers, and so forth. Agree to provide each other with this information as relevant.

Mutual commitment to the kids

This includes a specific designated time to talk about issues and plans that come up regarding the children. Decide how best to have this meeting—over the phone or in person. Agree on a good time, i.e., Wednesday mornings at 9:00. This also includes the agreement to refrain from making negative remarks about each other in front of the kids, and pledging not to use the kids as messengers.

Right of first caregiver

This refers to giving your co-parent the first right of refusal when you are going away and would need to hire a babysitter or have someone else care for the kids. This gives your co-parent the opportunity to take the kids during that time—the thinking is that both parents should have the opportunity to care for their kids before a third party is brought in to the picture.

Continuity of experience for children

Determine the activities and schedules the children are accustomed to and make every effort not to interrupt them. For example, ballet class on Tuesday afternoons, soccer practice on Saturdays.

Basic time-sharing plan

This of course is "custody and visitation." Probably the major point of your parenting plan.

Summer plan

Discuss it—you probably have made assumptions that the child's other parent at least needs to hear about.

Holidays, special days, vacations, sick time

Here are two hot spots: where the kids spend the holidays (and how), and who takes care of them when they're not in school. If both parents work outside the home, who deals with the sick child—is it always the parent who has custody on that particular day? Discuss visitation when the child is too sick to be moved, how and when that judgment call will be made, and how the other parent might still have contact with the sick child.

Mediation in future at request of either parent (prior to court action)

Ideally, you have agreed to use a mediator when things get sticky between you. You agree to use a mediator to help you:

1. Resolve controversies in this agreement.

2. Accommodate changes in life circumstances (one parent is moving, or remarrying).

3. Reflect the developmental changes of your children as they grow up, and as their own needs and schedules change.

Sample Parenting Plan #1

1. The parents agreed at the _____, 20__ meeting that they were committed to trying to develop a better plan than had existed in the past. They agreed to discuss educational, medical, developmental, and counseling issues with the goal of more shared decision-making.

2. They plan to communicate on a regular basis regarding the needs and welfare of their children _____, so that he/she/they are not messengers and therefore do not feel responsible for any misunderstanding that may arise.

3. They agreed to accept and not interfere with the differences that exist in each home.

4. All schools, health-care providers, and counselors shall be selected by the parents jointly.

5. Each parent is empowered to obtain emergency health care for their child/children without the consent of the other. Each parent shall notify the other parent as soon as possible if an illness or injury requires a physician's care. All matters for surgery or major medical or dental work shall be discussed and resolved before the work is started.

6. Should either parent need to be absent from the home overnight while _____ is/are in his/her custody, the other parent should be advised and given the opportunity to care for her/him/them before other arrangements are made.

7. If the opportunity is taken advantage of, the other parent agrees to an equal exchange at his/her convenience within ___ months of the arrangement.

8. Each parent will provide the other with the address and telephone number of _____'s residence while with him/her. Reasonable notice will be provided for any anticipated travel, and itineraries will be provided.

9. Each parent shall be entitled to reasonable telephone communication with _____. Each parent will respect their child's/children's right to privacy during such telephone conversations.

10. The parents will share custody of their child/children according to the following physical custody plan:

A. Holidays and special Days

Day	Even Years	Odd Years
Memorial Day		
July 4th Weekend		
Labor Day		
Thanksgiving Vacation		
Father's Day Weekend		
Mother's Day Weekend		
Christmas Vacation (50/50)		
Winter Vacation (50/50)		
Spring Vacation (50/50)		

B. Three-day weekends

It is our intent that each year's three-day weekends be spent equally in each home. We will meet in _____ to review the year's balance, and adjust in the final three months if an imbalance exits.

C. Summer school vacation

Same as basic schedule except for family vacation trips on an exchange basis and agreed upon by _____. Mother's preference in _____. Father's preference in _____.

D. Basic schedule

Child's name _____ Days _____

Child's name _____ Days _____

Child's name _____ Days _____

Whenever a school or legal holiday falls upon the Friday preceding or the Monday following a weekend, the parent who has physical custody for the weekend shall also have physical custody on the holiday.

E. The parents will communicate on a regular basis as follows:

a. Blocks of time to be resolved by 30 days prior to the start of each calendar year quarter.

b. Other communication to be written and mailed and, if necessary, the matters to be discussed over the phone.

11. Each parent shall be responsible for keeping himself/herself advised of all school, athletic, or social events in which _____ participate(s). Each parent will be responsible for arranging for *joint* meetings with their child's/children's individual teachers, whether requested by the parent or the teacher. Major school activities and all matters with school/parent communications should be shared.

12. Except as otherwise agreed between the parents, each parent shall pick up the child/children at the beginning of each of his or her physical custody periods.

13. In the event that a decision cannot be made jointly by us, we propose to submit the differences to: _____ for mediation services.

14. Each parent will at all times exert every effort to maintain free acess and unhampered contact between _____ and his/her/their other parent and agree to foster a feeling of affection between his/her/their other parent. Neither parent will do anything to estrange _____ from the other parent or which would distort his/her/their opinion of their father or mother or would impair his/her/their *love* and *respect* for each of them.

15. Our intention in order to promote optimal continuity and stability for _____ is to remain within (a geographical area or school district) _____.

Dated: _____

Signed: _____

Dated: _____

Signed: _____

Sample Parenting Plan #2

We, _____ and _____, the mother and father of _____, born _____, have developed the following plan in order to insure _____'s optimal development. We wish to set forth what we can reasonably expect of the other parent. We wish to provide continuity, stability, and predictability for _____, while insuring that she will have frequent and continuing contact with each of her parents.

I. Joint Decision-Making

We agree to jointly make all major decisions regarding _____'s education, health, and general welfare. We agree that all day-to-day decisions will be made individually.

II. Information Exchange

We agree to exchange information regarding all of _____'s activities, including but not limited to health, education, general welfare, and activities. We are in agreement that this should be done in a manner that is not intrusive on the other parent's personal life.

III. Medical Emergencies

We agree that if _____ requires emergency medical or dental care, the parent she is with will secure the necessary services and inform the other parent as soon as possible.

IV. Basic Schedule

We agree to the following basic schedule:

Monday—Wednesday—Mother

Tuesday—Thursday—Father

Friday—alternate between parents

Weekends—Split

When a parent cannot be with _____ during his/her time of responsibility, adequate notice will be given of that fact. Adequate notice is considered _____.

V. Holidays, Special Days, Holy Days, Three-day Weekends, Christmas, Easter

We agree that _____ will be with her _____ for _____ days during Christmas. For Easter, we agree that _____ will be with her _____ for _____ days.

We agree that _____ will be with her mother for the first two nights of Passover, the first night of Chanukah, the first night and first day of Yom Kippur, and two days of Rosh Hashana.

We agree to alternate the following three-day weekends: Martin Luther King, Jr. Day; Presidents' Day; Memorial Day; Fourth of July; Labor Day.

We agree to alternate Thanksgiving. Odd years _____. Even
    years _____.

We agree that each parent is entitled to vacation with _____. Noti-
    fication of intended dates of vacation will be forwarded in a
    timely fashion and mutually agreeable dates determined. No
    unilateral decisions will be made.

During the summer, the basic schedule will prevail unless vacation
    plans have been made.

Special days include: Mother's Day; Father's Day; Mother's Birth-
    day; Father's Birthday; _____'s Birthday; and the relevant par-
    ent will have _____ on these days. _____'s birthday will be
    handled by:_____.

VI. Communication

We agree to set aside time after _____ has gone to bed to discuss
    matters concerning her. (Or) We agree to speak on the tele-
    phone every Wednesday morning at 9 A.M. while _____ is in
    school to discuss matters concerning her. The conversations
    will be confined to parent/child issues.

VII.   Enhancing Behaviors

We agree to be civil and courteous to each other in front of
    _____ at all times.

VIII.   Right of First Caregiver

We agree that if we cannot care for _____ during a period of des-
    ignated responsibility, the other parent will be given the oppor-
    tunity to care for her prior to making other arrangements. The
    time frame for this will be twelve hours/twenty-four hours/forty-
    eight hours. (circle one)

IX. Make-Up Time

We agree that when one parent must be away and not see _____
    for a period of more than four days, the away parent will have
    the opportunity to make up for that time by _____.

X. Mediation

We agree that at the request of either parent, we will return to
    mediation with a mediator mutually acceptable if a disagree-
    ment arises out of this agreement, life circumstances change,
    or _____'s personal development indicates. The mediation
    process will be utilized prior to taking any parental matter
    involving _____ to court.

Signed: _____

Other Useful Forms

Child/Children Information Memo

Dated:

1. Our Children:
2. Emergency Information:
3. Dr.'s Appointments:
4. Dentist's Appointments:
5. Medicine and Dosage:
6. Plans/Friend/Parties/Gifts

    Date:

    Time:

    Invitation Has Been Forwarded to You:

    Invitation Has Been Responded to:
7. School Trip – Date/Time/Where:
8. The Following Dates Need to Be Noted:

    Special Occasion:

    Need to Adjust Schedule:
9. I Need From You:
10. I Have a Concern/Request:
11. The Children Have a Concern/Request:
12. In Response to Your Request:
13. Homework/School Projects – Date Due/Subject, etc.:

Permission Form

To Whom It May Concern:

I, _____ mother/father of _____, born _____, give my permission for him/her to travel to _____ for the period of _____ through _____.

Signed:

Dated:

Medical Action Plan

In case of _____'s outbreak of allergies/asthma or in order to treat _____'s juvenile arthritis/juvenile diabetes, the following procedure will be followed by both parents:

1. Treatment, consisting of _____, shall be administered.
2. Doctor _____ at _____ shall be contacted.
3. Other parent shall be contacted.

If hospitalization is necessary, child shall go to _____ hospital at _____.

Signed: _____

Dated: _____

Continuity Between Households

1. Bedtimes, school nights:
2. Bedtimes, non-school nights:
3. Get up on school mornings:
4. Limitations on television and video viewing:
5. Boundary setting:
6. Personal hygiene routines (tooth-brushing, bathing, shampoos):
7. School preparation:
8. Scheduling extra-curricular activities:
9. Other:

Itinerary

This information to be provided two weeks prior to departure unless otherwise agreed.

Date of departure:

Method of travel:

Flight Number(s):

Time:

Leaving From:

Destination:

Date of return:

Method of travel:

Flight number(s):

Time:

Leaving From:

Destination:

Principal residence while away:

Emergency phone numbers:

Times for parent/children communication:

Stories

Aaron Agrees His Parents Disagree ℘

JAKE IS AN affable man in his late forties. He teaches fifth grade in a city school, is happily remarried, and enjoys the "blended" life made up of his second wife's two girls and Aaron, his ten-year-old son from his marriage to Linda. "Oh man, we put a lot of effort into our divorce, but it still wasn't easy! Things have gone up and down and now we have what I consider some equilibrium—but life with kids is always topsy-turvy!"

Jake and Linda were married for seven years and Aaron was five when they decided to get a divorce. "Linda is the most competent woman in the world," he says, giving his former wife her due but rolling his eyes a little while he does it. "She's a very successful oral surgeon. The house was basically hers. Aaron had learning disabilities stemming from some trauma to his eyes at birth, and she never felt sorry for herself in having to deal with the operations, the physical therapy. She does everything like a trooper."

Jake and Linda had gotten married during a time when her father was seriously ill; several years later they both agreed they had predicated their relationship on Jake giving Linda emotional support. When she didn't need emotional support so much anymore, they realized they had two very different views about how life should be lived. "Linda wants the suburban split level, she drives a Beemer. More power to her, she earned it. But I'm a granola-head. I don't show well at the dentistry conventions!" They went to the bookstore and got several volumes on do-it-yourself divorce. They were both always committed to Aaron. Everything seemed free and clear.

And then the trouble began. "We had a bad time. It was Linda's idea to get a divorce, and once she decided that, I started seeing someone who lives about forty-five miles away. It was definitely a rebound relationship, but I spent a lot of time at that country house. Aaron hated going there—it was a long drive. This woman had dogs and horses, but Aaron was severely limited in his ability to play with them, because one eye was bandaged for about two years. We were also hyper-vigilant about him not getting injured. Linda was cranky about me going out there with Aaron, and we started to fight about it."

Obstacles in this life do seem to cluster, and at about this time Jake lost his job. "I'm a school teacher. It's not like I had all the savings in the world to just keep living on. I moved to the country with my girlfriend." Linda was angry about this turn of events, and she declared that Aaron didn't have to visit his father at this stranger's house. "I wasn't feeling too good about myself," says Jake. "I said fine, keep your little son."

When his relationship with this woman broke up, Linda allowed him to move back into the house they had previously shared. Jake laughs about that now. "You can imagine, that was the utter low point. I had been half of what made up that house. Now it was hers. I didn't sleep in the master bedroom anymore—I slept on a cot in the attic. Aaron was totally confused and upset. Linda and I couldn't share a pot of coffee without her letting me know it was her coffee and she was doing me, a total loser, a huge favor by sharing it. Aaron stopped speaking for a while and we had to do some heavy-duty therapy for him."

This went on for only about a month—Jake soon found another job and another apartment. With his second wife, he recently bought a small house. "My wife is good with Aaron. He's ten now—three years older than her oldest girl. He's cute with his little sisters, and really loves them." Linda and Jake have reestablished workable terms. "There was never any question we both would stay totally involved with Aaron," says Jake. "We've had our difficulties about that. She takes him to R-rated movies!" He shakes his head. "Aaron says, 'get over it, Dad, you agreed to disagree with Mom.' And you know, that's just what makes it all work."

8

The Emotionally
Healthy Divorce

W E'RE GETTING A divorce." "We got divorced last year." "We're separating." These are seemingly simple statements, like "I brushed my
teeth this morning." And yet what a world of experience is
described. Maybe the worst experience of your life. Certainly one that takes
some time to get through. In fact, give yourself two to three years to fully process
the dissolution of your marriage and the reestablishment of your life.

The purpose of this chapter is to briefly touch base with what happens
emotionally to you, the parent, in a divorce. Of course there is a wide range
across different types of people in different life situations—so take from this
only what is useful. I hope this chapter will give you a sense of the emotional
trajectory of divorce, so that you can see yourself as going through a normal
process which, yes, will come to a natural place of closure.

Your Marriage: Now You See It, Now You Don't

The time leading up to separation and divorce can be amorphous and ill-defined. Some people can look back to their wedding day and see the seeds of their future unhappiness; others are completely sideswiped by a partner's declaration that they want a divorce. Most people who get married spend at least some time building a life around this union and at the very least the end of it means a loss of balance.

In general, the process by which a marriage erodes takes time. There's a loss of trust, of communication. Maybe your sex life goes first—maybe it's the last to go. A great many people report that their marriages were bad far earlier than they admitted to themselves. And of course there are levels of stress before a marriage reaches its breaking point. There are moments when it is possible, perhaps with the help of a therapist, to heal the marriage. If the momentum keeps going downward, however, it is very unpleasant. There is anxiety, depression, disappointment. Depending on the relative individual health of each person, there can be outright despair. People can start to behave in desperate ways.

When an actual separation occurs, it can be a relief. Escalating hostilities find a peaceful ground, even if it's temporary. For some people, the worst is truly over. They've done the emotional work, perhaps over a number of years. Now they can approach dissolving the union in a logistical manner, and look forward to building a new life. For probably most others, however, the hard times have just hit harder.

The realities of divorce start to set in. Everything changes: where and how you live and work, how and when you see your children. Add to these the grief that comes from an ending. On both sides there are resentments about money and control. One former partner has a new squeeze and the other doesn't, and feels deprived, left out in the cold, even hoodwinked. Emotions can run pretty strong. They can get out of control.

Wild Horses

Even relatively mild-mannered people can start getting carried away by their feelings, saying and doing things they would never have dreamt of before.

Part of this is due to the disruption of a previous stability. Most of us manage our emotions pretty well within the context of everyday life, but this involves some measure of control, of repression, even in the healthiest people. Not too many of us give our feelings the room we really need for them—there isn't enough time in the day. Now those feelings are not hemmed in by the protocols of the usual social reality. It's common to feel completely abandoned, to feel shamed and alone at the outset of a divorce. These feelings can be so very unpleasant that we try to master them through other emotions, like revenge. Much of the anger which gets tossed around during a divorce has a lot to do with sadness and fear, which in many ways are harder to live with than rage.

Getting Back Together

For many couples there can follow a bargaining period in which reconciliation seems possible and maybe desirable. At the very least, it's natural to want to go back to the way things were. When it is one person doing the leaving, in contrast to a mutual decision to part, the person left may hold on to the dream of reuniting for years. It's pretty hard to reconceptualize a new life for yourself after you've poured years of effort into the one that you're now losing. It can seem a lot easier to hope against hope than to get out there and make a new life.

Often people hold on not to each other but to the idea of the marriage itself. It's painful to let this fundamental part of your life go. If you haven't already, this is a good time to try couples' counseling. At the very least, the idea to separate and/or divorce is a commentary that the terms on which you base your relationship are no longer satisfactory to both of you. It is possible that you can renegotiate terms with each other that don't involve divorce. Sometimes, indeed, damaging and negative behavior patterns between people can derail a relationship all on their own. A counselor or therapist can help you differentiate between core issues that might not find any other resolution than divorce, and more surface issues of how you relate to each other. A therapist can help uncover your real desires in the conflict. If you and your partner are at eternal odds, the therapist can help you negotiate your separation in a way that mitigates damage both to you and your children.

Bad Mojo Rising

When a marriage goes kaput, more than wedding rings get thrown out the window. So do many of the basic elements of goodwill that went into the marriage in the first place: trust, respect, healthy boundaries, shared dreams. You have probably noticed that some individuals remain rankled and enraged at their former spouse for many years, sometimes for a longer period of time than the marriage itself. Ask yourself, "Do I want to become one of those people?" Part of this is a reverse intimacy process. The positive energy and faith you invested in placing your hopes in a marriage are now being withdrawn, with heavy interest. Paradoxically, this negative intimacy can keep you attached to the very person you wish to detach from. To be Californian about it, when you are feeling outrage at your former partner you are holding that person in your energy field. What would happen if you actually stopped thinking about that person?

I know, I know. You can't stop thinking about that person because he or she is busy manipulating you in new and even more torturous ways. It's very hard to separate emotionally from a partner when they are not making the same effort. Try to separate what your former partner does, his or her actions, from the person. Try to deal with just the actions.

It's possible that if you didn't have the other person to be angry with, you would feel blank and lonely. It's very human to mask sadness and grief with anger. Anger is easier to deal with because it feels active. But it will never resolve the harder feelings underneath.

Define what kind of person you want to be, what kind of parent. Do you want to be angry, bitter, an emotional wreck? You don't have to be. You can:

1. Get emotionally healthy.
2. Get physically healthy.
3. Keep a sense of humor.
4. Improve yourself on the job or in your social world by taking risks and trying new things.
5. Be positive.

Changing Self-Image

OK, you were married and now you're not. You were in a "long-term" relationship and now you're single. You were used to participating in social routines and school functions in one way, and now that way is gone. Maybe you have to go to your child's school auction alone, and your former spouse is there with some young hottie. One woman's former husband asked her to please drop their daughters off at his company's annual summer picnic. It was a big request because she had felt humiliated by him—and his partners and their spouses and children would all be there in their undivorced splendor. She mustered her goodwill on behalf of her children and took them. When she got to the picnic, her former spouse was not there, but she was greeted by the woman he'd left her for. "I didn't know what to do," she said. "All I wanted was to cry. I couldn't possibly leave my girls with this woman." Finally, she took a deep breath and walked over to another mother with whom she'd been friendly, and asked her to look after the girls until their father arrived. "I got in the car, I got out of there, and I sobbed for an hour."

The story is a bad one—bad for the girls, especially. Their father put them in the position of being party to hurting their mother. This woman had felt like she wanted to heal the marriage, to get back together. "After I got a little distance from my own humiliation, I thought, what a jerk. He put his daughters in a terrible place. It made me not want to be with such a person at all."

It's possible her former spouse, consciously or not, was actually trying to behave very badly in order to get this woman to really despise him. He may have even felt ambivalent about leaving his wife and wanted to make the choice to separate come from her as well. Or, he may have been indulging his floozie! People act in perverse ways around the breakup of a marriage.

"I had wanted the marriage to work, especially for the girls. But I realized that I had to take care of the girls myself, not within the context of my husband's bizarre and awful behavior. I could be humiliated by him, but I could not let them be humiliated by him."

Now, the hard part comes after this event, when she still has to stay in contact with her former husband to arrange visitation with their daughters. After some time, the situation cooled down. "We went to a mediator and in addition to hammering out vacations and holiday schedules, I made sure we had a written agreement about any of his company events." In some relationships there is simply no avoiding a somewhat arduous, step-by-step process to extricate yourselves from each other and to renegotiate the new terms on which you will deal with each other.

What You Need along the Way

Divorce hits you where you live: your identity as a man or a woman; your social place; your sense of purpose. You have to address this head-on, which means: grieve the loss. Take care of yourself. Get help. You need to connect to others. A divorce support group is an excellent resource. Ask at your child's school. Ask at your church. Even a local parenting center is likely to be able to put you in touch with other parents in your situation.

Time to Mediate

Even when a couple decides mutually to divorce, and neither one of them is stuck with horrid feelings of being worthless and rejected, people can still use anger to help them move apart from each other. Often, this is when they pull in the big guns, the lawyers. The law seems like a fabulous way to work out disappointment, to make an emotional reality into a concrete one.

If you approach the system with a productive attitude, family law does provide the opportunity to deal with mediators. Adversarial litigation should be avoided—it is a good way to lose money, create enmity, and hurt your kids. The adversarial position is polarizing: one side is right, the other wrong. You, of course, feel that you are right. Your former partner, however, feels that he or she is right. Primal feelings of appropriation and survival come up in even the most reasonable of folks. "I couldn't believe it but he wanted to fight me over the piano!" one woman said. "It was my mother's piano—I would never part from it!" Without being conscious of motivation, people can try to salvage some part of what they had with the other person through material possessions. Maybe this man wanted to retain some connection with his ex-wife's family, wanted physical proof he had once been intimately bonded with them. Or maybe he was just being greedy.

Although a divorce is a legal proceeding and most people use attorneys at some point in the process, it's better for all involved, including you, to use lawyers as little as possible when you are separating and divorcing. It isn't a good time in your life to lay down permanent legal decisions. Instead, use a mediator. Mediators are trained in conflict resolution and have been around the block on marital discord. They work to make peaceable results for both parties. Your attorney can recommend a mediator, or you can consult the courts for a listing.

Adversarial litigation can't help but create good guy–bad guy polarities. This is exactly what is bad for your kids. Your children need to have healthy, open relationships with both of you during and after the divorce. Yes, you need to work out the arrangements with a third party. You need support for your best interests. Hammer these things out with a mediator. Mediators are pursuing mutuality, not a "winner."

Litigation is also very expensive. One man said, "We were going to get divorced, no matter what. But my wife had to sue me. The result was, we got a divorce and paid a lot of money to attorneys. Both of us could use that money now."

If you find yourself gorging on rage at your former spouse, get help. It's likely that you are getting stuck on an emotional tsunami and need help getting off of it without crashing into emptiness and despair. Some people have a kind of pride around not going to a therapist—put your pride elsewhere. Put your pride in your self-concept as someone who does what needs to be done to live a healthy, productive life. Divorce is a major crisis and everyone needs help going through it.

Look at your divorce as a learning process. It has a beginning, a middle, and an end. You will be a deeper, wiser person when you get through. At the very least, you will know a lot more about yourself. And that will help you make future choices.

The first two to three years around a divorce are spent in something of a crisis mode. You are living by the seat of your pants. You didn't expect to be in this position—or, if the divorce was your idea, you didn't know it would feel this way. You hold on tight to your children or you don't see them as much and that feels awful. Elements of the way you live your life fall away and at times it feels like you are hanging in midair, wondering if you're going to make a safe landing anywhere, anytime soon.

After two to three years, you can expect yourself and the way you live to stabilize. You come out of the jungle, as it were. Your personal circumstances settle down. If you've had to move, you've done it. If you've had to get a new job, you've done it. Take a deep breath.

Of course there can be many new challenges related to the divorce, even three years out. Maybe your former spouse has remarried, or even had another child with a new mate. Maybe there have been changes in custody or support agreements.

Ideally, you will be able to observe and recognize your own behavior and your own feelings, so that you can separate yourself in this regard from your children. You will be able to see that some of what is natural for you to experience can still be very harmful to your children unless you handle it consciously. One example is sexual behavior—it is pretty common to go through a kind of sexual renaissance at some point during separation and divorce. It's as though you got sprung back in time to when you were single, before you had kids, and the world is your oyster. You may find yourself experimenting with partners like you did in college (or if you never experimented, you may be really on a tear now)! While this is normal, it can be very upsetting to your children and can confuse them further about relationships.

Keeping in Touch with Your Kids

As the divorce becomes real and you head out into an often bewildering new life, it can be very common to lose touch with your child's needs. You may be saying, "No, that's not me—I'm all about my kids." The fact is, even if it seems *to you* that you are all about your kids, it may not actually feel that way to them.

When one man left his wife, he said, "I would have left the state, certainly the town, if it weren't for the kids. My whole life is determined by them, seeing them every week, keeping their life as normal as possible." But in his acrimonious separation, there was a lot going on. His wife was devastated by his actions. "She should have seen it coming. I tried to get her to work on our marriage for years. She just wouldn't. To tell you the truth, her crying and sobbing about being abandoned makes me mad. It didn't have to be this way."

A great deal of fighting, bickering, manipulating, and withholding of the children went on between these two people for a good two years. Even though he felt his life was all about the kids, in fact this man hardly had an inch of emotional reserve left with which to look them in the eye and ask how they were doing.

Keeping connected with your kids is the theme of this book. There are deeper discussions of how and why to do it in the chapters on development, communication, and expression (chapters 3–5). Suffice it say here, again, that no matter how brave or indifferent your kids might seem, how amenable to the changes going on for them, they absolutely need to talk about how they feel. At the very least you need to ask them how they feel about the divorce, and listen to them.

The Threat to Parenthood

When there is little community or family support for divorcing parents, mothers and fathers both can feel suddenly like their claims on being parents at all are diminished. Just the way the words "broken home," "ex-wife," "ex-husband" are bandied about cause the people identified with those terms to feel less than whole. The effect can be devastating for children.

Kids need "home" to be a container for their growth. The wholeness of their selves is related to the mirroring, or feedback, they get primarily by their parents at home. The persons they are in the outside world is first determined by this primary identification. It's important to recreate home right now. If at all possible, try creating two homes and refer to them that way. So it's not that your kids are over "at their father's," but they are "at home with their father." Look at your own residence not as a compromised, lessened place, but as new material for a new conception of home.

It definitely takes time to recapture the feeling of being a family, which is temporarily lost at the time of separation or divorce. Some people are getting a divorce because in fact they never learned how to have a pleasant family experience to begin with. Let learning and creating a positive way to be a family be one of your primary goals right now. It will help heal your wounds. You will be engaged in a productive activity that greatly benefits both you and your kids.

And now's your chance. "I have this thing about ice cream," said one woman. "I like to have it for dinner sometimes. My children's father is a health nut and believe me, he never in a million years would let me serve ice cream to the kids for dinner. So one night I thought, hey, why not? He isn't around anymore. The kids thought it was a wild treat. We had a great time. Of course we all ate shredded wheat after the ice cream because sweets really don't make a meal." A bit of fun is a great tonic.

A healthy serving of self-worth is needed all around. Be cognizant of the fact that your kids are going to feel weakened by events and do what you can to keep their schedules the same as they ever were, so they don't miss out on school and other social functions and so feel even less a part of things. Take the opportunity to do things they love to do, give them a choice of what they want for breakfast on the weekend—little preferences that will send them the message that their needs and desires are valid and that you are available to meet them.

The self-worth equation includes you. Do you feel humiliated because you were left? Do you feel widely misunderstood and demonized by former friends because you left someone? These are common fallouts from divorce. "Common" doesn't make your pain and difficulty any less—it just means that you are in the same boat as many others who have felt the same way. It is something for you to confront and deal with. It's important to remember that while you are feeling off-balance now, a new equilibrium is possible for you and time will help you attain it.

Back to the Future

A divorce is often the result of having made an unconscious choice of mate, a choice that amplified your childhood issues rather than satisfied them. Now is the time to do the work, to take the responsibility for the choices you've made, keeping the focus on yourself in the process and resisting the urge to blame. Unless you are from a specific tradition and your marriage was arranged, you weren't forced into your marriage. A bad marriage is often a sort of repeat of the less than healthy situation you grew up in. So you get a divorce and do the excavation work of why you made that kind of choice so you don't do it again. The whole thing is a learning experience, and you learn to make better choices about how to be a parent as well as how to be a mate. Keep the focus on how *you* made the choice of this person, not to beat up on yourself, but to understand and take ownership of your part of the baggage. And to keep clear on what part of it isn't yours, but belongs to your co-parent. At the same time, don't play armchair shrink. Let your co-parent deal with himself or herself—you have enough on your plate. It feels good in the moment to say, "Well Laura was always treated as a princess by her parents and she expected me to do it too." It's much harder and much more productive to say: "I chose a woman who wanted me to treat her like a princess because my self-esteem was low and I thought the only way someone would marry me would be if I served her every whim. I need to work on my self-esteem."

The way we were parented had something to do with how we are proceeding with the divorce—whether we are dealing pretty well with the very steep challenges of divorce or whether we are involved in stonewalling our former partner, or igniting conflicts into firestorms. Breaking up a relationship touches on the primitive places where fear and anger reside, and some pretty raw stuff comes up. Trying not to act on it but to observe it, get help, use the opportunity to heal yourself. Be aware that you want to incorporate some of your hard-won knowledge into being a better parent. Being a better, more conscious parent will help you heal yourself also.

The New You

Many people experience renewed personal growth upon getting a divorce. Women who never participated in the work world find a new sense of power and participation by taking a job. Dreams that were on the back burner suddenly feel possible. That's fantastic—that's great. Just make sure that while you pursue your bliss, you are attending very closely to the emotional needs of your children as well. They love you, not what you are in the world.

Often this time is one in which a much younger, practically teenage self arises from the past and makes its immature, exuberant self known again. It can be very fun, very enlivening, to feel this resurgence. Maybe you feel like hanging out with younger people, people who don't have kids and party a lot. Maybe you suddenly need to wear red leather. New energy is important to your new life and should be welcomed. But again, remember that you are not actually a teenager.

Maybe you even have a teenager in the house. One woman said, "Oh, my daughter and I have really connected since the divorce. We go shopping for outfits at the mall together and she goes out with her friends and I go out with mine. Then we dish about it the next day." Chances are, this woman's daughter would actually like her mother to be more of a fuddy-duddy, so she could do the experimenting in the family.

Killjoy

Is this sounding awful, like you better sit home and stare into your children's muddy little faces and rub their feet all day long? That's not it, either. As with most of life, it's all about balance. Understand that right now you need some primal reassurance yourself, to gather up reserves of self-respect and belonging during a stressful time of challenge. And simply try to address those needs in a way that doesn't go overboard. Allow yourself a little Jekyll and Hyde. Be a red-leather wearing teenager and a mature, concerned parent at the same time.

Life's Little Moments

In addition to going though a sexual renaissance, in which you might go out and sleep with new partners, reactivating an adolescent-style experimentation, it is also quite common for people to fall back into the sack with each other at some stage of their separation or even after a divorce. Chances are you know someone who's even gotten married to the same person more than once. This is not really part of a new sexual reality for you—it is more of a sort of review process, where you both try to see if something has changed and you like each other again. Getting divorced can be very lonely, too, and you can be tempted back into a physical intimacy with this person it feels easy with. Sleeping with your former marriage partner can be part of the process of leaving each other. But it's a pretty sticky situation for your kids.

If it happens, try to have it happen offstage. It's not a great idea for your kids to wake up Saturday morning and find Mommy and Daddy in bed together again. It is simply confusing and sets up false expectations. Even if you go through a renewed kind of honeymoon with your former partner, if there is any chance that in fact you will remain separated, don't let your kids in on the ambivalence.

One woman with two teenage sons spent literally three years getting back together again with her former husband. The rub was, she wanted him back. Every time he came back she took him, hoping each time that he would stay. This was brutal on the kids. "Are you my father, or not?" said one of the boys one day. "His father was really taken aback. He said of course he was his father, but not my husband. It was like the distinction between husband and father was too much for my son." Her son was not a dummy, but the tentative relationship between his parents made him feel his relationship with his father was tentative too.

So what do you do if you are this woman or a man in the same position? Go get some therapy. This particular person couldn't let herself move on from the marriage and she allowed her former partner to walk all over her. That's simply not being realistic about the situation.

"My former wife always wants me to come to her parents at Christmas, Thanksgiving, holidays. She left me for the life of a high-powered, single career woman. But when those days come around, she wants to belong." Many people do share holidays even after a divorce, and that can be nice for the kids, as long as both parties feel agreeable about it.

Negative Intimacy

If you thought you were going to barf just thinking about sleeping with your former partner, it may be that you have got yourself into a "negative intimacy" mode. This is the therapist's term for how enemies are actually highly attached to each other. Again, it's a common development between people who are getting a divorce.

Like every other emotional state, intimacy has a range. If you were ever happily married, you once experienced a connection based on highly pleasurable feelings. This "positive intimacy" involves mutual support, deep affection, trust, confidence, and ease.

When you are moving or have moved into divorce territory, you move to the other end of the intimacy spectrum. Positive feelings of love and support are now hideous feelings of betrayal and insecurity. Respect has become disrespect. The comfort of love has become the discomfort of enmity.

Understand that these feelings are natural and temporary. Moving through the negative side of the spectrum of intimacy can help you fully process the relationship and let it go.

An emotional separation is necessary, an emotional divorce in which you honor and respect the good feelings you once shared or hoped to share with this person. You don't trash the past. You acknowledge your emotional investment in each other. One woman's kids asked her if she hated their father. "I told them, your father gave me the three most wonderful children in the world and he'll always have a special place in my life because of that." That comment is one of the healthiest, most affirmative things a person could say to her kids. You can bet her kids are doing pretty well with the divorce.

One thing to remember about being in a huge rage at your former partner is that it is very time and energy consuming and life is too short! It can take some serious effort to remove yourself from this kind of dynamic, but it is well worth it.

Sometimes this negative intimacy comes after a fairly amicable decision to separate. It's almost as if suddenly people had to get mad at each other. Sometimes, the unpleasant, destructive dissolution of the marriage has created these bad feelings over a longer period of time.

In both cases, it is best to view negative intimacy as a stage you are going through on your way to making the divorce true emotionally as well as legally. You may have to make an effort to disengage from your own tendency to remain negatively intimate. Your attitude might be: well, I'm fine, but she's horrible, impossible! That sentiment is going to get you precisely nowhere. If you find you are locked in very bad feelings even after a year of separation, it's time to get help.

A forewarning that just because you decide to end the negative intimacy, doesn't mean your former partner will immediately agree and cooperate. Yelling and screaming and manipulating are indeed points of contact, and when you remove those, your former spouse may feel a renewed sense of betrayal. He or she can experience your withdrawal all over again. Your removal from negative intimacy can really bring the divorce home to a former mate who is in some state of denial about it. He or she may have a latent feeling that if the stuff you fight about could be resolved, then so could the marriage. Continued fighting may be a wrong-headed but secret way to try to get back together again.

Respect and communication will go pretty far here. You may find the opportunity to acknowledge, "Hey, this is really sad. But since we are going to do this, we may as well do it in a productive way."

Separating Your Marriage from Your Job as a Parent

All along it's important to shield your children from these negative feelings you have toward their other parent. They need two things: the feeling of a whole home, not one broken by rage; and to have their own relationship with the other parent.

When people insist that their children take the same negative attitude toward the other parent that they themselves have, they are not separating their parental role from their previous role as a mate. It is important to examine your own tendency to influence your children in this regard—many of us do this kind of thing unconsciously. Whether you do it knowingly or not, the effect is just as bad for your kids.

This role confusion—parent, spouse—is pretty normal because if you functioned at all as a family these two roles were joined for some time. It's also normal to want to gather a fan base, as it were, to get others on your side against the other parent. Sometimes it can feel like a superhuman effort to resist "venting" about the other parent to your kids, your immediate family, teachers, friends, to whomever will listen. You're hurt, you're feeling aggrieved. You guessed it—go to a divorce support group and vent all you want. It'll feel great and you'll be helping yourself.

Enjoying the Freedom

For many, divorce is an impossible hardship. Money gets very scarce and time gets scarcer. It can be a total shock. A woman who was a stay-at-home mom suddenly had to go to work. Her young children had to be put in day care and after care. "In the morning I drive the car and park it near the bus stop at Allison's school. There's a zone for unlimited parking on that street. Then Toby and I drop Allison off, and get on the bus. We go ten blocks to his day-care center. Then I get on the bus in the other direction and go downtown to work. In the evening I reverse it—take the bus to Toby's, then down to Allison's, pick up the car and drive home."

Even the recitation of her day is exhausting, yet many people live this way.

"I really really miss quality time with the kids," she said. "But I'm hoping this will get better as they get older and go to the same school. I'm trying to get us all in the same neighborhood—school, work, home." She smiled. "And I do get Wednesday nights and Saturday nights free. It really helps to catch up on some sleep."

Many people report relief that their stress-inducing former spouse is finally out of the picture. "I was so worn out all the time from fighting, from being put down," said one man. "I'm loving this single parent thing. I feel closer to my kids than ever." It's amazing how many fathers report this—a renewed sense of parenthood after a divorce. Part of it is because if the father has any custody at all, he is often for the first time responsible for the daily routines on which closeness is built. Getting the kids dressed, ready for bed. Making sure homework is done. We have a changing society but in many households today it is the woman who does all that, whether she works or not.

"I have to give my ex-wife credit!" laughs another man. "Getting something hot on the table every night! Wow, what a concept! And then they turn up their noses at it! I'm surprised she didn't get totally fed up about that. She just kept trying new dishes and coaxing them to eat. Now I find myself doing the same thing."

Being a different parent to your kids can make you more, rather than less of one. Use the opportunity to set up your household totally in keeping with what you like. "My wife let the kids eat dinner in front of the television all the time," said one man. "When they came to my house, I said, 'We eat together at the table. We talk.'" He smiled. There was one less compromise he had to make.

Feel the Pain—Take the Time

Many people leave each other for another person. The temptation is to set up house immediately, to replace the "bad" partner with the good one. But families are not instant, just-add-water affairs. They develop slowly over time and many mutual transactions. Neither are relationships dissolved just like that. The best thing for you to do for yourself and your kids is: feel the pain, take the time. The whole situation is confusing, and you need to re-learn how to deal with the other parent in a new way.

Further Thoughts on Conflict

Conflict happens. There's a traffic jam, a scheduling misstep, a lay-off on the job, a downturn in the market. An unpleasant frisson of feeling disrupts our equanimity. Even in the best-adjusted homes, conflict is unavoidable. Dealing with conflict doesn't mean getting rid of it. But how conflict is handled in the home has far-reaching implications for children.

Hot households

Some people seem to thrive on conflict and habitually challenge other people to join them in the fray. "Marjorie would scream and yell at me, and it would really upset me. I would do anything to placate her, to get her to turn it down a notch. When she started in on something to me it was like a timer had gone off and if I didn't stop it, the whole relationship would go down the tubes." Stephen's parents had divorced when he was 12; although he saw his father after he left his mother, the contact was spotty, and the relationship felt precarious. "Expressing anger meant loss to me," Stephen, a corporate lawyer, explained. "I was always the guy who kept his cool, kept everyone on the same page. I have a decent marriage, but it's not because I solved Marjorie's problems for her. We went to couple's counseling and learned to become sensitive to what conflict means to each of us, and how to handle it better between us."

Marjorie, a diminutive dark-haired woman from New Jersey, was absolutely habituated to a "hot" household. Her parents fought constantly, and her father's gruff demeanor was complimented by her mother's screeching tirades. "I thought this was how you conducted yourself," Marjorie said. "I thought, if I don't scream and yell nobody will hear me. Well, nobody really hears the content when you express yourself through rage. Our therapist helped Stephen realize that he could be angry, I could be angry, and it wasn't a deal-breaker. And he helped me learn how to handle my own feelings without amplifying them all the time."

All of us grow up in households or situations where conflict is dealt with in a certain way—Stephen's mother had dealt with her own divorce by withdrawing, leaving him with the sense that the anger he had heard his parents direct at each other both made his father go away physically and his mother go away emotionally. Marjorie learned to be defensive pretty much all the time, shielding herself from the constant tirades batted back and forth between her parents in her contentious family of origin. When she wasn't cowering, she was giving as good as she got. "Basically it was exhausting," Marjorie said. "Such a waste of time and energy. I mean, we would have these giant conflicts over unloading the groceries, or doing the laundry. It was such a relief when I realized I could put down my weapons and deal rationally with my own needs and desires."

This couple did a good job of digging back into their families of origin for the beginnings of negative conflict styles. Essentially both Stephen and Marjorie had become habituated to certain pathways they had experienced over and over again—anger means loss, anger means you won't be heard. Marjorie's whole extended family is "hot," using loud voices and fists slammed on tables to go through even the most ordinary of quotidian events. This family has few divorces and most of the children seem pretty well adjusted. But there are hidden dangers to the "hot" style. Children never really "get used" to conflict. Instead, they become sensitized to it. Being sensitized doesn't mean that their response to hot conflict becomes less; on the contrary, research shows that children of parents who fight loud and often have quicker response times to the signs that a conflict is brewing. Adrenaline goes up and a variety of defense mechanisms kick in.

Stephen and Marjorie, like many of us, found themselves mimicking behavior patterns they picked up in childhood. Stephen employed his same-old defense mechanism against the conflict he was exposed to all through youth; Marjorie was completely unaware that she sounded as bad to others as her mother had to herself. Stephen and Marjorie were lucky enough to find a good therapist who helped them observe their own patterns, which is the first step towards changing them. If they hadn't, their conflict-style may well have led to their own divorce. The reason so many children of divorced parents get divorced themselves is that they repeat the bad habits of behavior they imbibed with their drinking water as children. Modeling better behavior and coping strategies is a major incentive for learning to do better ourselves, even if it is after the divorce.

"One of the reasons people stay in such contentious relationships with their former spouses is that they have never known how to resolve conflict together," says psychologist Sean O'Riordan. "This inability to resolve conflict probably contributed to the divorce. But two different styles of conflict resolution are very confusing for children, whether the parents are together under one roof or not. One person is intimidated, and the other person seems to be in control. And this is a pattern that develops and becomes entrenched over time. The passive person, the one who gives in, doesn't understand how they contribute to the problem. They put up and put up and then one day, they snap, they can't take it anymore. They'll say, 'help me, I can't say no to this person, she never listens to me, she always gets her way.' But by constantly acquiescing, the passive person has let the aggressor know her style is effective; on some level, the style has been agreed to."

When a couple like this parts, the problem continues and the children often become more victimized by it than ever before. "One woman came to me and said her former husband was violating a court order that he not step foot into her house. I asked her what happened, from the very beginning. Well, the first time the dad came to pick up the kids for a visit, she asked him to go get one of the kid's bicycles from the garage. The next time, he was in the house collecting their overnight bags. Essentially, she never abided the court order, either. Then one day she realized she has no control over her former husband's perceived freedom to come and go through the house. But she's created the situation as much as he has.

"One day, this mother stood at the back door and blocked her former husband's entrance to the kitchen. He was offended. He moved to step past her. She screamed that he was in violation of a court order and he disrespected her, and on and on. The children are standing there, and they don't know what on earth has happened, what it means. Their mother is saying their father is bad and mean— but where did this come from? The children become frightened and anxious and don't know what to do."

In high-conflict relationships, this sort of dance will occur with frequency. In the case of one angry parent who habitually escalates the conflict, everything may start out small and build gradually. O'Riordan says, "Sometimes it can help to view the really angry parent as the more vulnerable person. Anger is often a secondary emotion; it can feel more comfortable to be angry than to be sad. The angry parent may actually be very afraid of losing contact with his kids. He's in a defensive mode, trying to make sure he maintains his connection."

Tips for Talking

DR. RIORDAN gives these tips for conversing with a former spouse you have trouble communicating with:

1. Pay close attention to language before it gets out of control. Ask yourself, "What's in the language? Is the angry person saying something about himself, and would it help to acknowledge the content?"

2. Use active listening strategies. If your former husband says something hostile, like "You always get in the way of my seeing the kids," you may try not responding hotly yourself but saying something like, "I'm hearing you say you're frustrated about getting together with the kids."

3. Breathe deeply, and give yourself several passes at diffusing the situation. A really angry person may not let it go. It may be necessary to try again before anything productive gets accomplished. It always bears repeating that the reason for you to persist in efforts at tolerance and peace is that it's best for your children.

Under Construction: Emotional Security

Conflict that isn't handled well—that is, with balance and sensitivity, not with reactive aversion or rage—essentially threatens a child's sense of emotional security. As a child registers the signs of escalating tension between his parents, as his adrenaline starts to pump and his own defense mechanisms kick in, a panoply of further reactions occurs. "What am I going to do to survive?" is the main question asked by the child, consciously or unconsciously. Anger threatens the attachment he feels with his parents; maybe the child even perceives that one or both of the people he depends on is going to be hurt by the other—which means, by proxy, that he himself is going to get hurt. Children are helpless to interrupt an adult's rage—feeling this sense of helplessness over and over again lays down actual neurological pathways in child's brain, and over time, the child may feel helpless even when an actual incident of conflict is not present. Every child blames him or herself for the unpleasantness they are experiencing.

As discussed in Chapter 3, this is a developmental situation, a place where the child does not experience him or herself as separate from the world. Because the resulting feeling is a bad one, the child gets stuck with shame. Shame is the sense that there is something intrinsically wrong with the child's very self, something "bad" about him that he can't do anything about. Shame is one of the most debilitating of human emotional responses. Most of us feel so uncomfortable about our shame that we hide it even from ourselves.

It bears repeating throughout this book that many parents will tell you their children are fine, that the divorce is hardly affecting them—but this is patently untrue. Partly this is denial—no good parent wants to feel their actions are hurting their child; a parent may feel so much anger at their former partner that they cannot imagine even the child wanting or needing to spend time with that person. If you can possibly acknowledge the pain and loss your child is feeling—even if the child doesn't express it directly—you will go a very far way towards helping the child release feelings of shame.

Another aspect of what happens is that many kids won't want to discuss their feelings—they don't really know how to—and this is one of those cases where you need to wait and be alert for the "teachable moment." An educational concept, the "teachable moment" refers to that time, in the car, maybe, or on the aisle of the supermarket, when your child will unexpectedly bring up her feelings. If this moment happens when you absolutely can't address it, just tell your child that what they just said is important to you and you'll talk about it later—maybe before bed, which is often a good time to get down to real feelings.

Taking a New View of Life

"People create their own hopelessness," says Jeanne Ames. "I ask them, 'do you want to create hopelessness in your child?'" Ames asks what may seem like a question with an obvious answer, and yet many people are not aware that they are laying down those sorts of negative neurological tracks in their children discussed above. For many of us, it is very difficult to step aside from ingrained habits of mind, habits of emotional direction, that quite often take us down a dark path. "It's time for self-assessment and self-exploration," says Ames. "You don't want anger, confusion, and chaos as part of your child's experience. So when you are feeling those things yourself, stop a second. Ask: 'Am I reasonable? Or am I contributing to this situation?' People quite often don't recognize their own anger. They need to ask, 'How can I de-escalate this situation to make my child's life easier and more comfortable?'" And, incidentally, make their own lives easier and more comfortable as well.

First, Understand Yourself

A divorce is a very good time to take the opportunity to go into therapy. Figuring out why you made certain choices so you don't make them again, help handling stress and conflict, and support through the transition are the invaluable fruits to be harvested from this investment in yourself.

One particular inroad into understanding how we got to an untenable place and how to make a way out of it is to pay attention to our emotional weather. "It's about recognizing patterns," says Anabel Jenson, the founder and president of 6 Seconds, a non-profit "Emotional Intelligence Network" that provides various ways "to create positive and productive relationships in schools, homes, and organizations." As you might imagine, "6 seconds" describes the length of time it takes to have a reaction and for the emotions triggered to re-disperse.

Jensen, the former head of the Nueva School in California, bases much of the wisdom of her organization on the work of cognitive psychologists, most primarily Dr. Martin Seligman, the author of *Learned Optimism* and other highly-regarded books. Daniel Goleman, author of many books, including *Emotional Intelligence,* popularized the concept that there is more to succeeding in the world than sheer IQ. What he termed our "emotional intelligence" helps us forge meaningful relationships and to communicate important information effectively.

Part of what these writers and researchers stress is that feelings are not facts, and while they are very important to recognize and direct, they can indeed be changed. In other words, by sensitizing ourselves to our emotional weather, we can moderate the effects of our behavior, ultimately getting more of what we want out of life.

Habits of Brain

Two boys are playing in the grassy part of a suburban playground. As often happens, they forage for sticks, which they begin to wield in a "Star Wars" action play. The mother of one child jumps up from chatting on a park bench, yelling at her son even as her feet fly towards him and his stick. "Put it down, put it down! What the hell are you doing? You're going to poke your eye out or hurt your friend. We'll be on our way to the emergency room!" In less than five seconds, a child's private space of game-playing is invaded by an emotional tirade he won't soon forget. He may not consciously remember it, either, but this caregiver is laying down a hot highway in his brain.

Of course children do things that are dangerous and need our immediate intervention. Boys and sticks are one of the perennial challenges of their parents—many boys seem to gravitate towards weaponry with a primal instinct. Guiding a child's behavior in a game with potential negative consequences is very important. But flooding him with anger and fear isn't going to do the trick. Perhaps he'll associate initiative and experimentation with his mother's upset. If she keeps reacting so hotly all the time, he'll learn to inhibit his actions until he has her express pre-approval. This may make her happy in the short term, but she's helping raise a child who will feel help-lessness instead of pleasure at the prospect of new experience. This won't serve him well at all.

Mom number two agrees with her friend that sticks are problematic as toys. But she knows her son is drawn to them over and over again, and she doesn't want to disrupt the developmental path he's on with them. She gets up and walks calmly over to her son. "Low sticks," she says to him, repeat-ing a directive among hockey players. Gently she grasps the child's stick and points it downward. "You can play with the sticks but you have to be care-ful. Keep it low. It can't go up higher than your waist." In this way she allows him to stay in his make-believe world, with a directive that he can incor-porate into his game.

"But mommy, look at that kid, he has a sword!" (Of course, it seems that there are always children with advanced plastic weaponry at the playground, just to torment the other children and mostly, their caregivers.) "Different families have different rules," says Calm Mommy. "It's a rule in our house that sticks have to be kept low."

The child will likely comply, without getting anxious or upset about the event. The child may not agree with his mother—he may recognize a cer-tain dog-eat-dog spirit to the play and he wishes to "stay in the game." He may feel she has put him at a disadvantage by restraining his stick. But if she stays with him, not in an overbearing way but in a guiding way, he will be able to handle the game. As we've mentioned before in this book, invok-ing a fundamental connection to "our house" and the child's own sense of belonging will reassure him that there's a goodness to following his mother's instructions. He won't feel hung out to dry by having his weapon managed.

In a sense, this mother has taught her son to keep his mind open by not interfering with the child's emotional pathway. Additionally, she has boosted his sense of responsibility by entrusting him to play his game in a modified way that takes more account of consequences and the kids he's playing with. She hasn't added stress and strife to the situation. Stress and anger are like giant stop signs indicating to a child that there are only two options, obe-dience and disobedience. This is a very narrow pathway indeed. When you tack back and forth only between yes, obey; no, disobey, you automatically exclude a range of options including: responsibility, ability and willingness to modify according to situational requirements; consideration of others. You may notice that kids who are kept on a very tight leash by their parents often seem to lack compassion or sensitivity towards other kids. They haven't been allowed the room to develop those feelings.

It's likely that the stressed woman was parented in a similar, take-no-prisoners style. To her, life is an accident waiting to happen, a punishment waiting to befall her. Instead of feeling that life is intrinsically good, and that she is a competent participant in the world, she may feel she is ultimately defective or inferior, and only by the strictest of measures is she going to make it through. This extends to her parenting style.

Dr. Martin Seligman makes the staggering suggestion that life doesn't have to be one long litany of complaint. Learned optimism doesn't paint rosy pictures that would make most of us hurl the toast we had for breakfast. Learned optimism in many ways is a lever, a switch we can pull to interrupt a negative cycle of feeling from going around yet again. Here are some pointers to remember:

- Focus on the fact that however bad things are at the moment, it is only temporary; you are in an isolated situation, and you do have power. Sometimes it may feel like going too far to believe that much, but take it on faith.
- Stop yourself from making catastrophizing assumptions. Many of us go to the worst-case scenario and believe it's inevitable. In truth, the worst case is only one potential among many.
- Avoid making future-outcome predictions. Especially if you can only imagine negative outcomes, don't think that far ahead. It's that same old canard: live in the moment. Change the moment.

It's quite common to hear an echoing voice that says, "Great, now I'm divorced, and I will always be alone, always without enough money, excluded from every social group I might want to belong to." "It's a gigantic merry-go round," Anabel Jensen says. "You have one negative reaction, and it pushes the whole thought cycle around again."

Another psychologist, Dr. Susan C. Vaughan, makes it clear that what we perceive as external monsters, like conflict, exclusion, rejection, are essentially internalized beasts of feeling we have stored in ourselves since childhood.

"The problematic lessons of childhood . . . are the breeding grounds of pessimism," she writes, in *Half Empty, Half Full: Understanding the Psychological Roots of Optimism*. She uses Maurice Sendak's classic *Where the Wild Things Are* to illustrate. Max, our fearsome protagonist, is quite rude to his mother and gets sent to his room. In his own private space, Max encounters the "wild things," or his own threatening feelings of anxiety, anger, and sadness, and he becomes their king. Vaughan sees in this tale the ultimate happy ending: the negative feelings we have are managed without quashing the child's entire sense of power and utility. She posits that however we did or did not learn to manage our natural negative feelings of aggression and grief as children, is unconsciously guiding how we view our world in this very moment, as adults.

Essentially, positive psychology says that we see the past and the future through the lens of the present—not some objective present, but a present state of inner feelings. This present state of inner feelings was determined largely in our childhoods. The child whose mother screamed about the sticks is developing just the same sort of inner weather she has—dark and stressed. Like her, he will likely see the world as a dangerous place, and distrust his own ability to handle what comes his way. Whatever our inner emotional weather, it colors how we see things in the present moment. The "wild things" are still inside, still overwhelming many of us.

Optimism as defined by these psychologists is simply the ability to moderate our own wild things in the present. It doesn't mean not having negative feelings. It means experiencing them and letting them go, or redirecting your energy towards something neutral or even positive. Optimism in this definition is essentially an inner confidence; pessimism is insecurity. Confidence and insecurity are both related to a sense of control and comfort.

The Chemical Feedback Loop

All of this isn't a wishful thinking model, but one based on brain chemistry and neurology. In essence, the bodily effects of emotional states provide feedback to the brain—when you're afraid, neurotransmitters are released that profoundly affect what your brain then tells you to do. (Think about how effective the widespread use of antidepressants have proven to be—all those people on them are feeling better about essentially the same situations they were in before they started taking them. Many of them feel more positive about doing "talk therapy" and getting to the bottom of their feelings than they did before they took them.) And the chemical feedback loop starts in earliest infancy.

Essentially, the primary caregiver's first job (for economy's sake, we'll say "mother") is to act as a sort of trainer of brain reactions in the infant. Think about the rocking, soothing, positive cooing of a responsive mother—she's providing a comforting environment that allows her baby to feel at ease, free to address whatever's next on the developmental time line. The child's maturing brain gets a kind of go-ahead from the mother's positive care. Too much positive stimulation is of course just as destructive in its own way as negative inputs. A child who is over-stimulated can't handle any sort of input, even what we call positive, and shuts down in an attempt to re-organize herself.

Ideally, a mother and child are together creating a pleasure-circuit in the child's brain. The child sees her mom and kicks her little feet in joy; she knows this is going to be good. The child feels herself to be a good thing, because the sense she gets reflected back from her mother is pleasurable. As the child gets older, it becomes necessary for the mom to give some negative feedbacks. At first this is downright tragic and perplexing for the child. Why, just a few months ago, it was sort of funny when she dropped her oatmeal on the floor. But when the child is older, it is no longer acceptable for her to throw her cereal bowl. Mom's displeasure comes as a shock. Welcome, wild things. The child feels angry and alone, perhaps shamed. It is important for the mother to follow through on her displeasure—for example, take away the cereal without replacing it (this does not mean punishing with hunger)—and then after a suitable period of time, to make a repairing overture with the child, and give her positive feedback again. A suitable period of time is not too long—you want the child to associate the consequence of displeasure with the behavior you want to discourage—and not too short—you want her to get the message. It then becomes time perhaps to play with blocks together and praise the tower.

What the mom is doing here is allowing a negative emotion to be triggered in the child. Make no mistake, there is no avoiding negative emotions. Parents who never moderate their children's behavior, because they don't want their children to feel bad, are not helping their child learn to control themselves. We've all seen this phenomenon. What's cute in a three year old is damn ugly in a ten year old. But how would the ten year old learn to control her impulses if her parent never helps her do it? The key for the compassionate parent is to allow the displeasure, and then repair the rift in the relationship. This lets the child know that her negative feelings are temporary, and can be shifted.

It is of the utmost relevance that the feeling cycles we all experience are forged on the pathways of relationship. This is what therapy seeks to uncover—how were you parented, what were the pathways laid down by your parents, and how are these perhaps not serving you so well anymore. Referring back to the example at the beginning of this section, if you grew up in a "hot" household, you are likely to recreate that style of relationship in your intimate connections, including your children and your spouse.

When a divorce occurs, people often stay stuck in these behavioral grooves (of course, sometimes these grooves have caused the divorce, or at least contributed to it), continuing to antagonize one another long after there is really any material reason to do so. Part of the reason for this is that their emotions are so used to traveling down these neurological tracks towards conflict.

It is very difficult to sit with an unpleasant feeling. We can easily have the sense that if we don't act, if we don't do something to either discharge the feeling or to smother it, the negative feeling will stay with us forever. Yet this sense of hopelessness is based not on the present, but on past experience, and follows tracks laid down long ago. If you can attend for even six seconds to what your emotional state is at the moment, you have gone miles toward interrupting the merry-go-round of reaction.

Understanding your own relationship patterns can help you change them. Therapy can help you uncover what these are—some of our reactions go so far back into early childhood, they are hard for us to recognize unassisted. When you understand your own patterns, you will also see how you affect the people nearest to you. Emotional states are contagious.

The Flooding in a Negative Relationship

When two adults are in an adversarial relationship, such as is almost inevitable in a divorce, they often get in the habit of triggering each other's emotional responses, the bad trips down the highway to inflamed distress. While these adults did not create the highways in each other—this was done in each childhood by primary caregivers—each person's inner distress finds plenty of justification in the other person's behavior.

Psychologist John Gottman, something of a relationship guru, and the author of many highly regarded books, including *The Seven Principles for Making Marriage Work* and *Raising an Emotionally Intelligent Child,* describes what goes on between some couples as emotional "hijacking." This occurs when one person gets upset by something their partner does, and can't get out of it. Like Daniel Goleman, he posits emotional flooding as the source of the difficulty. So many bad feelings are triggered that the person is absolutely overwhelmed by them, and can't make clear, rational decisions for the moment. A person flooded with bad feelings reverts to a primitive reactive state that either means withdrawal, or aggression, neither of which are going to help the situation. The trouble with repeated bouts of this flooding is that the neural highway gets well-worn, and the unpleasant chemicals are released in greater quantity at greater speed. As emotions intensify, perceptions are clouded, narrowed by reactivity. It makes sense that at this point, emotional self-awareness is non-existent. One of the important things that goes out the window is the ability to soothe oneself, or the other person.

Some simple guidelines

Whether due to nature, nurture, or some combination of both, men and women tend to have different thresholds for emotional conflict. Women are often much less threatened by it, and in fact might relish a face-off as a sign of intimacy and communication. Women in general tolerate greater degrees of emotional intensity, without losing their sense of control. Men, on the other hand, are usually less able to stand the heat. Men can divert the conversation more quickly, pose a "rational" solution too quickly, and call it wisdom, when in fact, they are warding off feelings that threaten to overwhelm them. When a man stonewalls a woman, this can be infuriating, and set her off on an even hotter tear that will exacerbate the situation. The more inflamed she gets, the more he will shut down.

Even when a marriage is over, it is still worth trying to develop a better emotional habit between you and your former partner: for the sake of the children. Not only because you will come up with better strategies and solutions to the daily tasks, but because you will model healthy interactions to your children. They are absorbing every bit of what you do. The more emotionally healthy your divorce, the better your childrens' adjustment.

Steps for developing better emotional habits between you and your former spouse:

1. Be aware that tension is likely to develop during attempted communication. Your goal will be to keep this at a minimum, to take it down a notch whenever you can.

2. Keep your discussion on track. Listen to how quickly you want to take it off track when you get annoyed. Your former wife is throwing a wrench into your custody arrangement by saying she can't (or won't) drive your child to soccer practice on Wednesdays. You want your child to be able to follow through on his commitment to his soccer team, and to get all the benefits of participation. In your annoyance, you think: "She wants my son to fail, just as she's failed at everything she's done."

3. Don't go down the blaming thought-track. It is not your problem; it is not the task at hand. Maybe there is a carpooling solution. Maybe you need a mediation session to remind your former wife of her commitments.

Some people will definitely push as far as they can. The woman in the example above may come up with problem after problem until it seems that all she wants to do is keep you busy doing backbends for her. It's important to set boundaries, without anger. Instead of saying, "You're reniging on your custody agreements, I'm taking you to court," you could say, "I hear you're having trouble leaving work early on Wednesdays. I can certainly understand that." Suggest the carpooling, or another potential solution. If, at some point, you need to remind her that there are legal parameters around her custody agreements, you could put it this way: "We're having trouble meeting our obligations to our child. Do we need to go back into mediation to get some help with this?" Then you let the mediator be the heavy. You may have a former spouse who will go through this cycle over and over again, but eventually, if limits are calmly and firmly set, she will let it go, or at least your conflicts will get fewer and farther between As her own emotional responses are kept at a lower simmer, her fears will also be kept at bay.

It's important to soothe yourself during a bout like the above. Sometimes it is necessary to take a break from the discussion. Research shows that although you may feel ready to re-enter the discussion after a five minute hiatus, in fact it takes 20 minutes for negative emotions to be processed and released by the body. You want to give yourself that full 20 minutes, so you will have all your emotional sensitivity and rationality available to you. You won't revert so quickly to your own primitive defenses.

One of the most aggravating facts of divorce is that although on a daily basis you are now separated from a person you no longer want to be partners with, you still have to tolerate them to one degree or another. There is probably no greater gift to give to your child than emotional health. Emotional health is not only about feeling pretty good, but about making good decisions, about living a productive life, about having positive relationships. Yes, it's work. And well worth it.

Stories

The Bewildered Wife ॐ

SHORTLY AFTER THEIR second child was born, Elsie Small's husband David developed a distaste for his wife's company. "What did I know?" Elsie says. "He stopped speaking to me in a civil tone. He slept with his back towards me, as if he would be horrified by an accidental touch. David had been thrilled at the arrival of our daughter, Sarah—it was one of the most halcyon times we had together. But when the second child came along, he lost it. I thought he was worried about money, or ambivalent about having a son. I really had no idea at that time that what bothered him was me and that what he wanted was to end our marriage."

"One day I was in the kitchen making dinner. Sarah was sitting at her little table, drawing, and the baby was in his highchair. David and I had had a bad year. His hostility had grown, he had taken to not coming home about four nights out of seven, he refused counseling and in fact, he refused to tell me what was wrong. Except that he did tell me he found me disgusting. Again, I thought it was about childbirth and breast-feeding. I kept thinking, as soon as the baby is a toddler we'll be happy again." Elsie laughs. It's four years later now and she's in therapy; she's drawn some lines between her low self-esteem and her choice of David as a mate.

"That night in the kitchen, literally while bent over Sarah helping her draw something, David looked up at me and in a hideous whisper he said, 'You are a fat cow.' I ran sobbing from the room. Later, Sarah climbed into bed with me. David had gone out and clearly was not coming home; Sarah seemed to understand this better than I did. She said, 'Mommy, are you and Daddy getting a divorce?' She was five years old. She knew better than I did what was going on."

"Sarah and Jonathan were just merged with Elsie, there was not even one minute for me to speak with her as an adult," David says. "I took to whispering my thoughts because I wanted to protect the kids." Were his thoughts cruel? "Elsie can be pretty frustrating. I may have lost my temper."

When on the road to divorce or in the middle of one, people often act very, very badly. Does it mean they are horrible people? Well certainly there is something horrible in them. Divorce is the inverse of falling in love. It is like that magical state where anything could happen, where barriers collapse and lives are transformed, only backwards. People are reckless with word and deed—and their partner in this emotional car crash may well never forgive them, and indeed, doesn't really have to forgive them. What both people have to remember is: they have children.

"I can never forgive him/her." That's a pretty common statement when people are detonating their relationship. It's like the connection they have remains so strong, even when negative, they have to push themselves and each other to absolutes. All of this is part of the process of disentangling from one another. What's important is to keep the conflict to a minimum, and keep it out of the realm of the kids.

Conclusion

The End Is a New Beginning

I F YOU HAVE ever been up close and involved with a wedding in which the bride's parents or the groom's parents or both were divorced, you know that in many cases the old wounds of the split are all too ready to open up again. The bride's father is remarried, but her mother doesn't think the second wife should be in the wedding party. The groom's mother is the only single woman in the wedding party and she feels vulnerable and alone. Somebody cries, somebody refuses to pay. Is this about a new beginning for two people, or is this an occasion for everybody's hurt feelings to grab center stage?

In our society one of the most potent coming-of-age ceremonies remains the marriage. When our kids get married, we consider them grown, on their own, truly fledged. Who is your child at this point, what kind of an adult is he? Responsible, sensitive, adventurous? Is he embarking on his own marriage with an open heart and a sturdy attitude?

Every parent looks at their kid from time to time and just wonders: who will this person be? How much influence do I really have? And there is no doubt that people who grow up in stressed, even deprived conditions quite often succeed very well in life, in both personal and professional matters. And that others, who seem to have had everything from the get-go, can have a more difficult, often thwarted path. There is definitely an element of faith required in the tricky waters of child-rearing.

That element of faith is not a blind or a blank thing: it is instead a high ideal we have to hold in our hearts, an ideal of staying connected with our kids through thick and thin. This connection between parent and child is the roadway for growth. How you behave, what your intentions are, travel over this road and deeply influence how your children approach their own lives.

Sometimes parents complain that their children are inconsiderate or self-ish. A teenage son and daughter go on vacation with their mother every year but not with their father, who is remarried with a new family. He's hurt but doesn't say anything or invite them on vacation with him. Who's at fault? Are the kids insensitive or are the parents expecting the kids to solve their lone-liness, their own conflicts, which they are unable to solve themselves? Some kids do learn to behave better than their parents do—they seem to be more mature than the rest of us, from the very beginning. But most kids behave in the manner they have learned from you and your co-parent. It's ten, twenty years after your divorce and you still ask your daughter to call her father to tell him he owes you money. Just because your daughter is an adult and seems successful enough in her own life and is used to this stuff does-n't mean it's doing her any good. At some point the divided loyalty you keep provoking is going to become an impediment for her, perhaps in an impor-tant relationship.

Bringing up children often means bringing ourselves up all over again. Sometimes the job is a pure joy, and at other times it is bewildering, dis-couraging. There's no magic potion to parenting, just day in, day out effort. Yet, there are a few key points that do really matter when divorce is part of your parenting situation.

One of the most effective things Kids' Turn does to help ameliorate the potential negative consequences of divorce for children is simply focus everyone's attention on the fact that it is occurring or has occurred in the family. One of the best steps you can take to help your kids with your divorce is to face the fact of it head-on with them. Kids' Turn helps parents talk to their kids. It gives kids a safe forum for expressing their fears and sad-ness about the divorce. Kids' Turn and other programs like it normalize divorce for adults and children alike. This is not to say that divorce is made into some kind of an amusement ride. But divorce can make people feel iso-lated and different, and it really helps to become part of a group of peers experiencing the same thing you are.

To review some of the fundamentals of helping your kids with your divorce:

1. Kids need to be told directly and honestly about the divorce. Don't assume that because they are small they aren't noticing what is tantamount to a huge change in their lives. In many cases it will help your kids wrestle with the divorce if you give them a reason for it. This is a hard one, because "we don't want to live together anymore," will not quite cut it. Your child will wonder, "Why not?" and will invent reasons that negatively implicate himself. "We can't get along anymore," is better.

2. Kids blame themselves for the divorce and need to be reassured regularly that it is not their fault. Even years after a divorce it will help your kids if you address this with them.

3. Kids internalize both parents whether they see them or not; it is important for children to have contact with both parents unless it puts them in danger.

4. Don't bad-mouth your co-parent in front of your kids. Your kids identify with your co-parent and will experience themselves as the object of your scorn.

5. Kids have strong loyalty issues and feel torn apart by divorce. You can help them with this by not putting them in the middle.

6. High conflict is extremely detrimental to children's development. If you are in a high-conflict situation, make custody and visitation arrangements to minimize your exposure to your co-parent.

7. Children's needs for custody and visitation will change over time. Periodically reevaluate what's working and what isn't.

8. Use a mediator to help you set up a productive divorce.

9. Adults and kids alike will benefit from support groups or other divorce programs that put them in touch with others who share their experience.

In one sense, divorce is a process that takes an average of two years from start to finish. But it is one of those things that isn't ever really over. Accept this and work with it, and you'll help your kids.

The very good news is that by approaching your divorce with good intentions on the behalf of your children, you can help yourself get over it. By keeping your eye on the prize, you can keep your focus out of the muck. There's no way around some of the contacts you must have with your co-parent, perhaps for the rest of your life. That's a cross to bear in many cases. Yet, if you view it as a project you hope to get better at, and remember that the goal is the health of your children, you can bear this cross with some equanimity.

A yoga teacher once said, "There's the pain of doing yoga, and there's the pain of not doing yoga." Take the concept to heart. Yes, it takes effort to take the high road, to keep your focus, to find a better outlet for your pain and confusion and anger. You may feel like a failure as a result of your divorce. But you have an ongoing chance to become a huge success as a parent. Take the challenge. And good luck.

Acknowledgments

*The following acknowledgments are for the
Kids' Turn program,
by Judge Ina Levin Gyemant*

PUTTING TOGETHER A program the caliber of Kids' Turn did not come easily. I originally expressed my idea for a program designed for children of divorcing parents at a San Francisco Bar Association Family Law Section meeting in 1987, and immediately two attorneys, Jennifer Jackson and Ann Van Balen, approached me, stating that if I were serious about starting a program they would help. The rest is history. Kids' Turn was born through the tireless efforts and perseverance of numerous dedicated and caring professionals. The curriculum was the result of the hard work of John Sikorski, MD, the late Dorothy Huntington, PhD, and Jeanne Ames. The original policy decisions and workshop designs were hashed out by an ad hoc board comprised of Jeanne Ames, Ann Van Balen, Esq., Jennifer Jackson, Esq., Maureen Kammer, M.A., Carole Levine, Esq. Melanie Maier, Esq., Devora Parker, Esq., John Sikorski MD and myself. Christopher Emley, Esq., Geoffrey M. Dugan, Esq., Gil Guglielmi, Ana M. Horta, PhD, Jeffrey Mangini, CPA, Millicent Susens, Nancy Unobskey, LCSW, Bobbie L. Welling, Esq., and Anthony J. Zanze soon joined us. That group evolved into the board of Directors who took a very active role in running all aspects of the organization. We also benefited from the talented efforts of many people including public relations consultant Debra Levin, illustrator Molly McLeod, graphic artist Dennis McLeod, and

Administrative Assistant Jasmine Senyak. After two years of planning, the first workshop was held. Steve Zimmelman, LCSW, who made significant contributions to the curriculum, was the first program director, followed by Rosemary Bolen, LCSW, Diane Kaufman, MFT, and today Susanna Marshland, LCSW Millicent Susens became the first president and put into place the structure and stability upon which the Program flourished and through which it endures today. Ann Van Balen, Esq. was the second president and continued to solidify the structure and greatly expand the program. Each year the program has grown through the presidencies of Pamela Engel, W. Gregory Engel, Esq., and Susan Stephens Coats, Esq. In growing and expanding the location of the office, Kids' Turn was lucky originally to have the law firm of Landels, Ripley and Diamond as its benefactor. No single person or law firm, however, has been more generous in this respect than Suzie S. Thorn, Esq., who has housed the program in her office building since 1992. Julie Scribner was the first executive director, keeping the program on track and growing until it came under the direction of Claire Barnes, MA, who has guided it to new heights and in new directions with her energy and vision. Kids' Turn is the result of the vision and hard work of many individuals—many more than are mentioned here. Because of them it instantly became and has remained an enormous, unequivocal success at helping kids.

The following acknowledgments
are for this book,
by Mary Ellen Hannibal

IN ADDITION TO the Kids' Turn curriculum, the work of Rudolph Dreikurs is much in evidence behind these pages—he is responsible for the concept of "logical consequences" in disciplining children. Similarly, Michael Popkin's work called "Active Parenting" has been a big influence, and so has Dr. Ralph Gemelli's book *Normal Child and Adolescent Development*. As all parents know, guiding children through the shoals of their progress in this world is more art than science. Understanding what it feels like to be a child, and how to connect with a child on her own level, are improvisational feats that must be undertaken again and again. *The Emotional Life of the*

Toddler, by Dr. Alicia Lieberman, and *The Magic Years*, by Dr. Selma H. Fraiberg, are wonderful sources of inspiration for approaching children up to age six. T. Berry Brazelton, always large-spirited and a committed child advocate, also has a special book among his many: *Touchstones Three to Six*, written with Joshua D. Sparrow. Dr. Mike Riera's work, particularly in *Uncommon Advice for Parents with Teenagers*, is very helpful for understanding older kids.

There is a complete bibliography at end of this book, and many worthwhile sources of help and information beyond these pages. Of divorce books, my favorites are *Mom's House, Dad's House*, by Isolina Ricci, and *Helping Children Cope With Divorce*, by Edward Taybor. Both these works are very clear and full of useful information. Two divorce researchers who deserve special praise are Joan B. Kelly, whose work with Judith Wallerstein is well known, and Joan Johnstone. In her own work Ms. Kelly has gone far toward understanding what children of divorce need as they get older. Joan Johnstone's work on children who refuse visitation has offered some important insights into how kids act during divorce, and how they really feel.

Dr. Sikorski has vetted me every step of the way and my confidence in the solidity of precepts herein reflects my confidence in this generous man. Susanna Marshland has brought a critical and sensitive eye to key chapters, and I am grateful for her time, attention, and wisdom. Thanks to Jeff Cookston, PhD, and Emily Schneider for assistance with the second edition.

This book owes its very inception to the passion and vision of Jeanne Ames, who perhaps above all others has aided its progress and kept its focus. A former head of the Family Court in San Francisco, Ms. Ames has a deep, instinctive understanding of children and what they go through in divorce. In an integral way, this is her book, and the countless children helped by her ministrations join me in thanking her deeply.

Early funding for this project was generously provided by the Drown Foundation.

Bibliography

The American Academy of Child and Adolescent Psychiatry. "Prevention in Child and Adolescent Psychiatry: The Reduction of Risk for Mental Disorders," 1990.

The American Academy of Child Psychiatry and the Alcohol, Drug Abuse and Mental Health Administration. "Prevention of Mental Disorders, Alcohol and Other Drug Use in Children and Adolescents."

Ames, Jeanne and Dorothy Huntington. Child Custody Evaluation, Statewide Office of Family Court Services, Judicial Council of California, 1991.

Ames, Louise Bates and Carol Chase Haber. *Your Seven-Year-Old: Life in a Minor Key,* New York, NY: Dell, 1985.

Arbuthnot, Jack, David Segal, Donald A. Gordon, and Kelly Schneider. "Court-Sponsored Education Programs for Divorcing Parents," Juvenile and Family Court Journal, 1994.

Barker, Narvier Cathecut and Joseph Hill. "Restructuring African American Families in the 1990s." Journal of Black Studies, Vol. 27, No. 1. September 1996.

Baris, Mitchell A. and Carla B. Garrity. *Children of Divorce: A Developmental Approach to Residence and Visitation,* Asheville, NC: Psytec, Inc., 1988.

Bell, Diantha, Rosemarie Bolen, Michael Cogen, Holly Engs, Kristine Harleen, B.J.

Blake, Wayne M. and Carol Anderson Darling. "Quality of Life: Perceptions of African Americans." Journal of Black Studies, Vol. 30, No. 3. January 2000.

Herran, Elyse Jacobs, Maureen Kammer, Sharon Karp-Lewis, Diane Kaufman, Darlene Kelly, Lorie Kennedy, Nikki King, Lou Kohler, Melinda Martin-Clark, Janice Morgan, Christie Nichols, Lee Pollak, Debbie Salinger, Kathy Sinsheimer, and David Taheri. "The Kids' Turn Curriculum," 2002.

Bienenfeld, Florence. *Helping Your Child Succeed after Divorce*, Claremont, CA: Hunter House, Inc., 1987.

Bonkowski, Sara. *Kids Are Non-Divorceable*, Chicago, IL: Buckley Publications, 1987.

Bonnett Stein, Sara. *On Divorce*, New York, NY: Walker & Company, 1979.

Brazelton, T. Berry and Joshua D. Sparrow. *Touchpoints Three to Six*, Cambridge, MA: Perseus Publishing, 2001.

Brown, Laurene Krasny and Marc Brown. *Dinosaurs Divorce*, Boston, MA: Little Brown, 1986.

California Chapter Association of Family and Conciliaton Courts Institute for Training and Research. "Mediation of Child Custody and Visitation Disputes," 1981.

The California Child Abuse & Neglect Reporting Law. "Issues and Answers for Health Practitioners," State Department of Social Services Office of Child Abuse Prevention, 1997.

Carnegie Corporation of New York. Starting Points, Meeting the Needs of Our Youngest Children, 1994.

Cohen, Philip N. and Lynne M. Casper. "In Whose Home? Multigenerational Families in the United States, 1998-2000." Sociological Perspectives, Vol. 45, No. 1. 2002.

Crosbie-Burnett, Margaret, and Edith A. Lewis. "Use of African-American Family Structures and Functioning to Address the Challenges of European-American Postdivorce Families." Family Relations, Vol. 42, No. 3. July 1993.

Dancy, Rahima Baldwin. *You Are Your Child's First Teacher*, Berkeley, CA: Celestial Arts, 1989.

The David and Lucile Packard Foundation. *The Future of Children: Children and Divorce*. Vol. 4, No. 1, Los Angeles: 1994.

Dickson, Lynda. "The Future of Marriage and Family in Black America." Journal of Black Studies, Vol. 23, No. 4. June 1993.

DiLeo, Joseph H. *Child Development*, New York, NY: Brunner/Mazel, 1977.

Dinkmeyer, Don, Gary D. McKay, and James S. Dinkmeyer. *Parenting Young Children*, Circle Pines, MN: American Guidance Services, 1989.

Dreikurs, Rudolf. *Children: The Challenge*. New York, NY: Hawthorn/Dutton, 1964.

Drescher, Joan. *My Mother's Getting Married*, New York, NY: Dial Books for Young Readers, 1986.

Ehrensaft, Diane. "Discussion of Judith Wallerstein Paper: The Unexpected Legacy of Divorce: A 25-Year Landmark Study," 2001.

Erikson, Erik. *Childhood and Society.* New York, NY: Norton, 1963.

Faber, Adele and Elaine Mazlish. *How to Talk So Kids Will Listen & Listen So Kids Will Talk,* New York, NY: Avon, 1980.

Fitzimmons, Barbara. "Broken Families and Broken Dreams," and "An Emotional Tug Of War," Union-Tribune Publishing, San Diego, 1997.

Fraiberg, Selma H. *The Magic Years*, New York, NY: Fireside, 1959.

Fuligni, Andrew J., Vivian Tseng, and May Lam. "Attitudes Towards Family Obligations Among American Adolescents with Asian, Latin American, and European Backgrounds." Child Development, Vol. 70, No. 4. July-August 1999.

Furstenberg, Frank F. and Andrew J. Cherlin. *Divided Families*, Cambridge, MA: Harvard University Press, 1991.

Furth, Gregg M. *The Secret World of Drawings*, Boston, MA: Sigo Press, 1988.

Gardner, Richard A. *The Boys and Girls Book about Divorce*, New York, NY: Bantam Books, 1971.

Garfield, Patricia. *Your Child's Dreams*, New York, NY: Ballantine Books, 1984.

Gemelli, Ralph. *Normal Child and Adolescent Development,* Washington, DC: American Psychiatric Press, 1996.

Goldsheider, Frances. K. and Regina M. Bures. "The Racial Crossover in Family Complexity in the United States." Demography, Vol. 40, No. 3. August 2003.

Goleman, Daniel. *Emotional Intelligence.* New York, NY: Bantam Books, 1997.

Goodnow, Jacqueline. *Children Drawing,* Cambridge, MA: Harvard University Press, 1977.

Gray, Loretta J. "The Effect of a Divorce Intervention Program on Anxiety and Stress in Elementary School Children," (master's thesis) 1998.

Grych, John H., Michael Seid, and Frank Fincham. "Assessing Marital Conflict from the Child's Perspective: The Children's Perception of Interparental Conflict Scale." Child Development, Vol. 63, No. 3. June 1992

Hetherington, Mavis and John Kelly. *For Better or for Worse: Divorce Reconsidered,* New York, NY: W.W. Norton, 2002.

Hickey, Elizabeth and Elizabeth Dalton. *Healing Hearts,* Carson City, NV: Gold Leaf Press, 1994.

Huntington, Dorothy. "Enhancing Parenting Skills," California Alliance Concerned with School Age Parents, San Francisco, 1973.

Ives, Sally Blakeslee, David Fassler and Michele Lash. *The Divorce Workbook,* Burlington, VT: Waterfront Books, 1985.

Jacobs, Elyse. "Dream Theatre: Working from Children's Dreams," Dreamworks, 1982.

Jacobs, Elyse. "Puppet Play Explores Feelings and Emotions," Scholastic Pre-K Today, 1989.

Johnston, Janet R. "Children of Divorce Who Refuse Visitation," from *Nonresidential Parenting New Vistas in Family Living,* 1993.

Kabat-Zinn, Myla and Jon Kabat-Zinn. *Everyday Blessings: The Inner Work of Mindful Parenting.* New York, NY: Hyperion, 1997.

Kelly, Joan B. and Michael E. Lamb. "Using Child Development Research To Make Appropriate Child and Access Decisions for Young Children," Family and Conciliation Courts Review.

Kelly, Joan. "Longer-Term Adjustment in Children of Divorce: Converging Findings and Implications for Practice," Journal of Family Psychology, 1988.

Keyes, Margaret Frings. *Inward Journey,* La Salle, IL: Open Court Publishing, 1983.

Kindlon, Dan and Michael Thompson. *Raising Cain: Protecting the Emotional Life of Boys.* New York, NY: Ballantine, 1999.

Krementz, Jill. *How It Feels When Parents Divorce,* New York, NY: Knopf, 1984.

Krueger, Anne. "Unhappy Endings," Union-Tribune Publishing, San Diego, 1997.

Levine, Melvin, William Carey, Allen Crocker, and Ruth Gross. *Developmental-Behavioral Pediatrics,* Philadelphia, PA: W.B. Saunders Company, 1983.

Lichter, Daniel T. and Nancy S. Landale. "Parental Work, Family Structure, and Poverty among Latino Children." Journal of Marriage and the Family, Vol.57, No. 2. May 1995.

Lieberman, Alicia F. *The Emotional Life of the Toddler,* New York, NY: The Free Press, 1993.

Marshland, Susanna. Kids' Turn Questionnaires, 1989–1999.

McKinley, Cameron, ed. "The Diary Deck," The DiaryProject, 2001.

McLoyd, Vonnie C., Ava Mari Cauce, David Takeuchi, and Leon Wilson. "Marital Processes and Parental Socialization in Families of Color: A Decade Review of Research." Journal of Marriage and the Family, Vol. 62, No. 4. November 2000.

Mills, Joyce C. and Richard J. Crowley. *Therapeutic Metaphors for Children and the Child Within*, New York, NY: Brunner/Mazel, 1986.

Montessori, Maria. *The Absorbent Mind*, New York, NY: Henry Holt, 1967.

The National Council of Juvenile and Family Court Judges. "Child Development, A Judge's Reference Guide", 1993.

National Public Radio, "All Things Considered": Children and Divorce, June 11, 1997.

Neuman, M. Gary and Patricia Romanowski. *Helping Your Kids Cope with Divorce the Sandcastles Way*, New York, NY: Times Books, 1998.

Oropesa, R.S. "Normative Beliefs about Marriage and Cohabitation: A Comparison of Non-Latino Whites, Mexican Americans, and Puerto Ricans." Journal of Marriage and the Family, Vol. 58, No. 1. February 1996.

Pollack, William. *Real Boys: Rescuing Our Sons from the Myths of Boyhood*. New York, NY: Random House, 1998.

Popkin, Michael. *Active Parenting Today*, Marietta, GA: Active Parenting Publishers, 1993.

Ricci, Isolina. *Mom's House, Dad's House*, New York, NY: Collier Books, 1982.

Riera, Michael and Joseph Di Prisco. *Right from Wrong*, Cambridge, MA: Perseus Publishing, 2002.

Riera, Michael. *Uncommon Sense for Parents with Teenagers*, Berkeley, CA: Celestial Arts, 1993.

Rofes, Eric. *The Kids' Book of Divorce*, New York, NY: Vintage, 1982.

Russo, Francine. "Can the Government Prevent Divorce?" Atlantic Monthly, October 1998.

Shaw, Daniel S., Emily B. Winsolow, and Clare Flanagan. "A Prospective Study of the Effects of Marital Status and Family Relations on Young Children's Adjustment among African American and European American Families." Child Development, Vol. 70, No. 3, May-June 1999.

Steel, Danielle. *Martha's New Daddy*, New York, NY: Delacorte Press, 1989.

Sutton-Brown, Jane. "A Qualitative Study of Children's Perspectives of Their Parents' Divorce," (dissertation) 1998, p.198.

Teyber, Edward. *Helping Children Cope With Divorce*, New York, NY: Lexington Books, 1994.

Thompson, Sue. *The Source for Nonverbal Learning Disabilities*, Lingui Systems, 1997.

U.S. Bureau of the Census, 1991.

Van Horn, Patricia. "Kids' Turn: Early Years Program: the Dorothy S. Huntington, Ph.D. Memorial Curriculum," 2002.

Vaughan, Susan C. *Half Empty, Half Full: Understanding the Psychological Roots of Optimism*. New York, NY; Harcourt, 2000.

Wallerstein, Judith S. and Joan B. Kelly. *Surviving the Breakup*, New York, NY: Basic Books, 1979.

Wallerstein, Judith S. and Sandra Blakeslee. *Second Chances*, New York, NY:

Ticknor & Fields, 1989.

Watson, Jeffrey A., and Sally Koblinsky. "Strengths and Needs of African American and European American Grandmothers in the Working and Middle Classes." The Journal of Negro Education, Vol. 69, No. 3. Summer 2000.

Weninger, Brigitte and Alan Marks. Good-Bye, Daddy! New York, NY: North-South Books, 1995.

Whitehead, Barbara Dafoe. The Divorce Culture, New York, NY: Knopf, 1996.

Wickes, Frances. The Inner World of Childhood, New York, NY: Prentice Hall, 1966.

Winnicott, D.W. Home is Where We Start From, New York, NY: W.W. Norton, 1986.

Zigler, E.F., M. Stevenson, and B.M. Stern. "Supporting Children and Families in the Schools," American Journal of Orthopsychiatry, 1997.

Index

Index

Index

Index